MOMENTS OF BEING

VIRGINIA WOOLF

New Edition

Edited by Jeanne Schulkind

Introduced and revised by Hermione Lee

PIMLICO

Published by Pimlico 2002

10 9

Text © Quentin Bell and Angelica Garnett 1976, 1985
Editorial matter © Jeanne Schulkind 1976, 1985
Preface © Jeanne Schulkind 1985
Introduction © Hermione Lee 2002

First edition published in Great Britain by Sussex University Press 1976
Revised and enlarged edition published by The Hogarth Press 1985

Pimlico edition 2002

Pimlico
Random House, 20 Vauxhall Bridge Road,
London SW1V 2SA

Addresses for companies within the Random House Group Limited can be
found at: www.randomhouse.co.uk/offices.htm

The Random House Group Limited Reg. No. 954009
www.randomhouse.co.uk

A CIP catalogue record for this book is available from the British Library

ISBN 978-0-7126-4618-5

The Random House Group Limited supports The Forest
Stewardship Council (FSC), the leading international forest certification
organisation. All our titles that are printed on Greenpeace approved
FSC certified paper carry the FSC logo. Our paper procurement
policy can be found at www.rbooks.co.uk/environment

Printed and bound in Great Britain by
CPI Antony Rowe, Chippenham, Wiltshire

Contents

Introduction

"MOMENTS of Being" was not Virginia Woolf's title for this book, nor did she put together these five autobiographical essays, written over a thirty-three-year span, and none of them published in her lifetime. The phrase occurs in the last and longest of these autobiographical pieces, which Woolf called "Sketch of the Past". It's taken from the passage early on in the "Sketch" where she says that life seems to her to be divided between a great deal of ordinary, unimpressive, routine activity – what she calls 'cotton wool, or non-being' – and sudden violent shocks, 'exceptional moments', which function as a form of 'revelation'. That leads her on to her 'conception' of writing, and her rather mysterious philosophy of life, 'that behind the cotton wool is hidden a pattern' and that all human beings are part of this universal 'work of art', which specific artists – Shakespeare, or Beethoven – may give expression to, but to which we all contribute: 'We are the words; we are the music; we are the thing itself.'

Jeanne Schulkind, who first transcribed and edited these autobiographical pieces in 1976, chose the title to emphasise Woolf's alternation between two levels of being. Schulkind saw that as the link between the autobiography and the fiction, which she read as quests towards 'moments of being' when the physical, social self is transcended and 'the individual consciousness becomes an undifferentiated part of a greater whole'.* She drew a comparison between the "Sketch" and Woolf's essay on De Quincey, where Woolf says: 'To tell the whole story of a life the autobiographer must devise some means by which the two levels of existence can be recorded – the rapid passage of events and actions; the slow opening up of single and solemn moments of concentrated emotion.' (And Schulkind may also have been thinking of Woolf's 1928 essay on Hardy, where she borrows Hardy's title 'moments of vision' to describe the 'sudden quickening of power' in his novels when 'a single scene breaks off from the rest'.)†

The title "Moments of Being" sums up very well the intense emotions, the

* Jeanne Schulkind, "Introduction", *Moments of Being*, 1985, p. 18.
† "De Quincey's Autobiography", *The Second Common Reader*, The Hogarth Press, 1932; "Thomas Hardy's Novels", *The Essays of Virginia Woolf*, ed. A. McNeillie, The Hogarth Press, 1994, Vol. IV, p. 509.

shocks, the rushes of involuntary memory that "Sketch of the Past" is so much concerned with. But it feeds exclusively into the interiorised, sensitive, aesthetic, even mystical side of Woolf's posthumous reputation. There are many other aspects to this collection – social comedy, ruthless self-analysis, elegy, satire, family plot, caricature, autobiographical theory – which "Moments of Being" doesn't cover. The volume might have carried different associations if its title had been (to take some of the other phrases from these essays) "Am I a Snob?", "Writing my Memoirs", or "Good God! Here I am again!"

And the whole history of this volume has been an odd one. If five autobiographical essays by (say) Joyce, or Lawrence, or Eliot, unpublished in their lifetime, and containing sensational new material about their childhood and family life, had been posthumously published, a tremendous fuss would have been made of it. But Woolf's reputation in this country has always been extremely mixed. When *Moments of Being* first came out, published by a small university press, and again when it was reissued by The Hogarth Press in 1985, with a very significant seventy-page typescript version of the "Sketch" added in, no great stir was caused. And while the arguments over Woolf boiled on in the '80s and '90s – feminist heroine, child-abuse victim, Bloomsbury snob, modernist genius? – this volume fell quietly, and lamentably, out of print. Yet it is of the utmost importance for anyone interested in Woolf – or in autobiography, or in women's lives, or in late nineteenth- and early twentieth-century English society. It makes an absorbing, dramatic narrative, tragic, funny, historically rich, and profoundly revealing. It is an indispensable tool for her biographers and critics; it has changed the way her life story is read, and it throws a strong illuminating light on her fiction.

Alongside the developing interest in, and the professional editing of, Woolf's many different kinds of overlapping, genre-busting writings – essays, letters, diaries – these autobiographies have come to seem more and more central and important. And they are just the sort of writing she was most interested in herself. She loved reading – and writing – 'lives of the obscure'; she had a passion for marginal, undervalued literary forms like journals and memoirs. She was preoccupied, all through her writing life, with how a woman might write her own life story, when there were so few historical precedents and so little encouragement. How would a woman's writing of her life be different from a man's? Why were there no female autobiographers like Rousseau? Why were women, on the whole, inhibited and self-censoring? She was always writing to her women friends telling them to write their autobiographies. 'Very few women yet have written truthful autobiographies. It is my favourite form of reading.' 'There's never been a woman's autobiography. Nothing to compare with Rousseau.

Chastity and modesty I suppose have been the reason.'* In her feminist essays, *A Room of One's Own* and *Three Guineas*, she thinks hard, and painfully, about the representation of women's lives. Her fiction returned over and over again to the telling of a woman's life story, from Rachel Vinrace in her first novel *The Voyage Out*, trying to describe how she spent her days to the young novelist Terence Hewet, to the imagining of the secret interior lives of Mrs Dalloway and Mrs Ramsay, to the liberating fantasy-life of *Orlando*, and last to Isa's private unutterable thoughts, hidden in a notebook disguised as an account book, in *Between the Acts*, the novel Woolf was writing at the same time as her own unfinished autobiography.

Her own experiments in memoir writing are startlingly candid – up to a point. These essays give vivid, explicit accounts of some parts of Virginia Woolf's life. Here is the story of the Stephen family, its ancestry, its class, its social context, down to every tiny, telling detail of the fixtures and fittings – the biscuit tin shaped like a barrel in the dining room, the silver salver deep in visiting cards on the hall table, the stained pattern of leaves on her half-sister's writing table. She builds in, stroke by stroke and brick by brick, a whole architecture of houses, rooms, landscapes and habits, within which she places the personal stories. And though these stories overlap, recur and fragment, they can be itemised, like chapter headings or scenes in a play: The characters of her parents. The shocks and sensations of early childhood. The split between St Ives and Hyde Park Gate. The uncomfortable relations between the Stephen and the Duckworth children. The tragedy of Julia Stephen's early death and of Leslie Stephen's terrible grieving, which turned his children against him. His tyrannising over a succession of women – Julia, her daughter Stella, Vanessa, Virginia. The children's resistance. Stella's shocking early death. The claustrophobic lives of the teenage Vanessa and Virginia. The suffocating, aggressive, over-intimate demands of their half-brother George Duckworth. The characters of Thoby and Vanessa. Virginia's breakdown after her father's death. The move from Kensington to Bloomsbury. The growing intimacy with Thoby's young Cambridge male friends, which became 'Bloomsbury'. The change in decor, freedoms, behaviour, family relations, above all in conversation. And framing, or filtering into, these narratives of the past, there are passages about the present: the memoir club; her relations to high society; her life in wartime; her writing of these autobiographies.

These autobiographies – especially "Sketch of the Past" and "22 Hyde Park Gate" – have been made use of for very different – sometimes

* VW to Victoria Ocampo, 22 Dec 1934; VW to Ethel Smyth, 24 Dec 1940, *The Letters of Virginia Woolf*, ed. N. Nicolson and J. Trautmann, The Hogarth Press, 1975–80, Vol. V, p. 356, Vol. VI, p. 453.

competing – accounts of Virginia Woolf's life and writing. Her memories and stories of being touched and fondled by her half-brothers, told here in detail for the first time (though there are some comic, evasive references to George Duckworth's behaviour in her letters) provide crucial evidence for the version of her life which explains her as the victim of childhood sexual abuse. In particular, two pages of "Sketch" are repeatedly singled out for intensive analysis, where she is explaining her 'looking-glass shame' by drawing on a memory of Gerald Duckworth exploring her body, when she was very young, linked to a dream of a 'horrible face' looking over her shoulder in the glass. Psychoanalytical readings of these passages apply Freud's idea of the screening of unconscious memories, or Lacan's theory of the 'mirror-stage' of psychic development, when the child begins to structure an identity through awareness of division and separation. It's argued that Woolf is 'trying to tell the truth about the body' in these essays by 'tapping the unconscious mind for memories which the conscious mind has screened'.* Whether Woolf has been screening out, and is now trying to access, 'forced exposure, masturbation, and/or penetration of the female genitals', or 'the primal scene of parental sex', or the trauma of the mother's death, or the 'pre-Oedipal moments of oneness with her mother's body', psychoanalytical approaches all emphasise a process of repression and an experience of trauma.† But there is a division between readers who see these autobiographies as evidence of psychic disability, or as powerful expressions of political anger. Some read "Sketch", in particular, as a narrative of displacement and fragmentation, where representation is always under threat, the self is passive or absent, and the text is full of gaps and deferrals: as if the whole process of this writing was tending towards breakdown.‡ Other more realist readers see these memoirs as angrily 'showing the injustice of patriarchal domination', and 'the social construction of sexual difference within the bourgeois Victorian household'.§

* Sue Roe, *Writing and Gender: Virginia Woolf's Writing Practice*, Harvester, 1990, pp. 43, 45. See also François Defromont, "Mirrors and Fragments" in Rachel Bowlby, ed., *Virginia Woolf*, Longmans, 1992; Daniel Ferrer, *Virginia Woolf and the Madness of Language*, Routledge, 1990, trans. Geoffrey Bennington and Rachel Bowlby; Shari Benstock, "Authorizing the Autobiographical" in *The Private Self*, Routledge, 1988, for Lacanian/Freudian readings of *Moments of Being*.

† Barbara Claire Freeman, "Moments of Beating", *Diacritics*, 27: 3 (Fall 1997), p. 69; Ferrer, pp. 27, 46; Roe, p. 68.

‡ See Linda Anderson, *Women and Autobiography in the Twentieth Century*, Harvester, 1997, p. 74; Benstock, pp. 25–29; Roe, p. 57.

§ Kennedy Fraser, *Ornament and Silence*, 1996, p. 109; Sidonie Smith, "Identity's Body", in *Autobiography & PostModernism*, ed. Kathleen Ashley et al, University of Massachusetts, 1994, p. 277.

So Woolf's memoirs have become an arena for debate in feminist theory. But problems arise from treating *Moments of Being* as a whole, unified piece of evidence about Woolf's inner life, or as a continuous narrative to be mined for factual information and links to the novels. This is a peculiar, fragmentary book, whose five essays tell an overlapping story in different ways, with different motives, and over a long period of time. "Reminiscences", written in 1907 and 1908, is addressed to her sister Vanessa's first child, Julian Bell, and was begun before his birth. It sets itself in the long-running Stephen family tradition of memoirs written for the next generation – like Leslie Stephen's anguished memories of Julia, known by his children as the 'Mausoleum Book'.* It is written out of Virginia's equally intense feelings about Vanessa, who had married Clive Bell in 1907 – jealousy, competitiveness, bereavement, a sense of having been displaced. Its motive is to reclaim Vanessa as her own. It is a literary exercise (being written at the same time as her drafting and redrafting of her first novel), which mixes her emotions for her sister with the story of their parents, her own childhood, the deaths of Julia and Stella, and Vanessa's situation in the family after Stella's death. Though it reads formally and conventionally, almost as a pastiche of a family memoir, and though there are many things it can't or won't mention, it is also an experimental piece of writing, a mixture of autobiography, memoir and love letter.

Utterly different in tone are the three pieces written to be read to the 'Memoir Club', two from the early 1920s and one from 1936. The Memoir Club was founded by Molly MacCarthy in 1920 as a post-war regrouping of the network of friends which came out of Cambridge in the 1900s and became known as the Bloomsbury Group. The idea was for an auto-biographical paper to be read by one or two of the group at each meeting. In her Diary for 18 March 1920, Virginia Woolf expressed deep mortification at having 'laid her soul bare' to the Club, with a 'chapter' that was greeted at first with 'loud laughter' and then with 'uncomfortable boredom' from the male members of the audience. 'Oh but why did I read this egotistical sentimental trash!'† Whatever this 'chapter' was – and it doesn't survive – she had embarrassed herself by its candour and emotion. On 5 December 1920, however, she reports having been 'fearfully brilliant' at the Club, and a few months later on being congratulated by Maynard Keynes for her 'Memoir on George'. Clearly she had decided, after her earlier discomfiture, to give her memoirs of the family home, the doings of George and the

---

*See Christopher Dahl, "Virginia Woolf's *Moments of Being* and Autobiographical Tradition in the Stephen Family", *Journal of Modern Literature*, June 1983, Vol. 10, no. 2; pp. 175–96.

† *The Diary of Virginia Woolf*, ed. Anne Olivier Bell, Vol. II, p. 26.

beginnings of Bloomsbury, as entertainment rather than confession. There is plenty of dark material in these essays, but the tone is jaunty, comical and ruthless. In the first few paragraphs, we get a family idiot, a woman who has poisoned her husband by mistake, an old man who spouts tea and sultanas through his nostrils, and a son who has been eaten by a shark. Woolf was famous for her conversation and her letters, sparkling with caricature and anecdotes. These essays live up to her reputation: they make an ironic, colourful, conversational performance out of the difficult past. The naughty French farce she is taken to by mistake at eighteen lends its tone of high jinks and sexual bravado to these essays, which are full of ridiculous scenes – the bizarre vision of Holman Hunt, the gloomy first appearance of Thoby's young Cambridge friends, the backstage scenes of squalor and disarray at Lady Sibyl Colefax's once-grand house. This comic dramatising of her life allows for mixed motives to have play – part nostalgia ('Old Bloomsbury' called up the ghost of Thoby Stephen), part competitiveness (her private life is set against the fame of Maynard Keynes or Lytton Strachey), part revenge (her successful middle-aged audience are reminded of themselves as boring, self-absorbed young men), part self-criticism (she is quite as sharp about her own snobbery as any of her critics can be) and part self-defence.

To turn from the Memoir Club essays to the "Sketch of the Past" is like turning from her letters to her diaries – or her novels. "Sketch" begins what might have been a full-scale autobiography, had she lived. (She had begun to revise it and to type it up, as if working on a novel.) It was written in fits and starts, from April to July 1939 and then from June to November 1940. It was structured, not by chapters, but by dates, using the present 'as a platform' from which to view the past, moving between May 1895 and May 1939, or June 1940 and July 1897. The exercise was partly 'by way of a holiday from Roger': as an antidote to the 'drudgery' of writing her biography of Roger Fry, which she had begun, at the request of his widow, in 1938, and was revising through 1939, finding it a 'grind', frustrated by the need for discretion, the tyranny of chronology, and the clash between 'facts' and 'vision'. Many years of thinking about the limitations of biography – which had already produced *Orlando*, a dazzling biographical spoof – underlay this see-saw between her writing of an 'official' Life and a private life story.

She was reading Freud for the first time, whose ideas on regression, ambivalence and the unconscious disturbingly coloured this retelling of her childhood. The "Sketch" coincided, too, with the writing of *Between the Acts*, much concerned with the painful gaps between social masks and secret selves, and with a story called "The Searchlight", in which a woman in war-time London turns the searchlight or telescope of memory back onto a Victorian past. This woman is like Virginia Woolf, returning to St Ives in the 1880s as a consolatory, even therapeutic, escape from dark days: air raids, plans for suicide in case of invasion, the fall of France. "Sketch of the Past" is about how memory works and how autobiography – particularly a woman's autobiography – is written. And it makes a searching description of herself as a writer: her impulses, her 'conception', her materials (some of which is returned here from fictional to autobiographical use, like the puddle Rhoda couldn't cross in *The Waves*, or the marriage of the Ramsays in *To the Lighthouse*), her struggles and her satisfactions.

So *Moments of Being* is an evolving narrative about the process of 'life-writing'. She uses the term herself in a passage in "Sketch of the Past" on how impossible it is to isolate the individual 'subject of the memoir' from the surrounding forces of heredity, environment, society, family and relation-ships, that hold it like 'a fish in the stream'. "Reminiscences" and the Memoir Club essays display the subject in dramatic relation to such forces: family mourning as a constraint on natural behaviour, for instance, in "Reminiscences", or, in "Am I a Snob?", the effect of English class consciousness and class envy on a left-wing, upper-middle-class intellectual, with an appetite for coronets and a fascination for the landed aristocracy.* "Sketch of the Past" analyses how such forces, or 'invisible presences', are to be dealt with by the life-writer. How describe the stream as well as the fish? What should the entry-point be: first childhood memories, or the history of the ancestors? Should the structure of a life follow chronology (as in most biography), or the involuntary, arbitrary action of memory? How, if at all, can the writing 'I' access the 'I' in the story? And, given the inhibitions and anxieties of most women who write their autobiographies, how much gets left out?

Woolf speaks movingly in "Sketch of the Past" of her belief that the intense experiences of the past 'have an existence independent of our minds'. If we could only invent a way of tapping them, we would be able to 'listen in to the past': 'I feel that strong emotion must leave its trace; and it is only a question of discovering how we can get ourselves again attached to it, so that we shall be able to live our lives through from the start'. Her way of doing this is by the most vivid possible process of 'scene-making'. All these essays, not just "Sketch", are full of brilliantly dramatised scenes, which range in mood from sharp comedy to violent despair and grief: Lytton Strachey pointing at the stain on Vanessa's dress with the one word 'Semen?', thereby unleashing 'a flood of the sacred fluid' into hitherto repressed Bloomsbury conversation; Lady Sibyl Colefax hiding in the empty drawing room of Argyll House while her furniture is being auctioned; Julia Stephen clapping

* See Sonya Rudikoff, *Ancestral Houses: Virginia Woolf and the Aristocracy*, SPOSS, 1999.

her hands, with a little spring forward, when she comes to the place in the street where Little Holland House, enchanted house of her youth, once stood; Leslie Stephen thumping his fist and shouting at his daughters over the weekly bills; the sisters sitting in the hot grass in Kensington Gardens reading poetry, after their mother's death.

But this powerful scene-making is always doing battle against some resistance. That last scene, in which Virginia awkwardly tries to explain to her sister a sudden sense of intensified perception, and can't find words to do so, is a moment of failed communication in the past, matched by an inability to find the right words for it in the present: 'Nor does that give the feeling.' And that memory is of a time when none of them were able to speak out truthfully during the 'muffled dulness' after their mother's death: 'A finger seemed laid on one's lips.' A great deal of this eloquent book is about inhibition, evasion and silence. The story of the move from Kensington to Bloomsbury, from childhood to adulthood, is of moving from censorship and secrecy to candour and free speech. (It's also about the relief of substituting irony for sentiment, and sceptical intellectual discussion for lachrymose emotions.) She often remarks on how 'reserved' she and Thoby were, or how shy Vanessa was about herself, or how liable she herself is to embarrassment and shame. And she still finds it difficult to tell her story – snared, perhaps, by that embarrassment, and by that critical self-consciousness about sentiment. A great deal isn't spoken of, or is hardly mentioned, in these autobiographies – her breakdowns, her brother Adrian, the death of Thoby, her beginnings as a writer, her friendships with women – and they break off before we find out anything about Leonard or her married life.

"Reminiscences" starts with an inability to speak ('I can say nothing of that time'), and is full of negatives and refusals: the children refusing to answer Leslie's call, Julia never speaking about her first love, Leslie tortured by the thought that he never told Julia that he loved her, Julia not telling Stella she was ill, Stella hiding her grief in 'ordinary words', Vanessa's dumbness – 'she stood before him like a stone' – in the face of Leslie's bullying. And the narrative keeps shying away from its real subject, Vanessa, as if it's almost impossible to write her. The Memoir Club essays expose a history of censorship and silences with gleeful candour, yet, at the same time, with tantalising evasiveness (notably on sexual matters). And "Sketch" is as much about the challenge of writing autobiography as it is about the past. It begins, insistently, with 'difficulties', it digresses and deviates and keeps breaking off, it tries out all kinds of metaphors for the past, and it constantly tries to speak the unspeakable: 'I could spend hours trying to write that as it should be written' . . . 'I cannot describe that rapture' . . . 'I do not suppose that I have got at the truth' . . . 'The word is not the right one – but I cannot find one that is.' Characteristically, this is a daringly experimental new kind of life-writing, in which the process, with all its problems, becomes part of the story.

The problems tangle up most densely around the figure of Virginia Woolf's long-dead mother, whose character, influence and death have already been returned to over and over again in fiction and diary entries and letters, in an attempt to exorcise and lay to rest this powerful ghost. Every time Woolf describes Julia Stephen she says she can't do it, whether in the choked-up, formal rhetoric of "Reminiscences" – 'you will not find in what I say . . . any semblance of a woman whom you can love' – or in the complex investigation, in "Sketch", of 'why I find it now so curiously difficult to describe both my feeling for her, and her herself'. She can never come to a conclusion, as she so badly wanted to do in her novels: 'For there she was' (*Mrs Dalloway*); 'I have had my vision' (*To the Lighthouse*); 'That's done it' (*Between the Acts*). The death of the mother, that she found so hard to deal with in the novels – as a silent gap in *The Voyage Out*, in unbearable brackets in *To the Lighthouse*, coldly distanced in *The Years* – can never be settled. She describes it three times in her diaries, three times in these memoirs, always slightly differently.* The repetitive, inconclusive return to the mother's death is at the heart of this remarkable adventure in life-writing, where the past can never be solved or tidied away, the subject can never be finished with. As she said of her mother in "Reminiscences", in a haunting phrase that balanced the absence of the dead against the presence of memory and narrative: 'Where has she gone? What she said has never ceased.'

Hermione Lee
2002

---

* See Hermione Lee, *Virginia Woolf*, Chatto & Windus, 1996, 80, pp. 130–1.

Reminiscences

Chapter One

Y OUR mother was born in 1879, and as some six years at least must have
passed before I knew that she was my sister, I can say nothing of that
time.* A photograph is the best token there is of her appearance, and the face
in this instance shows also much of the character. You see the soft, dreamy
and almost melancholy expression of the eyes; and it may not be fanciful to
discover some kind of test and rejection in them as though, even then, she
considered the thing she saw, and did not always find what she needed in it.
But certainly it would be mere fancy to conceive that this was other than
unconscious at that age. For the rest, a mother who gazed in her face might
feel her heart leap at the endowment already promised her daughter, for she
was to have great beauty. And in this case the mother would also feel tender
joy within her, and some bright amusement too, for already her daughter
promised to be honest and loving; already, as I have heard, she was able to
care for the three little creatures who were younger than she was, teaching
Thoby his letters, and giving up to him her bottle. I can imagine that she
attached great importance to the way in which Thoby sat in his highchair,
and appealed to Nurse to have him properly fastened there before he was
allowed to eat his porridge. Her mother would smile silently at this.

Our life was ordered with great simplicity and regularity. It seems to
divide itself into two large spaces, not crowded with events, but in some way
more exquisitely natural than any that follow; for our duties were very plain
and our pleasures absolutely appropriate. Earth gave all the satisfaction we
asked. One space was spent indoors, in the drawing room and nursery, and
the other in Kensington Gardens. There were a number of little warfares, and
sometimes Nessa and Thoby fought with us and sometimes they were our
friends. I remember too the great extent and mystery of the dark land under
the nursery table, where a continuous romance seemed to go forward,
though the time spent there was really so short. Here I met your mother, in a

* 'Your mother' is Julian Bell's mother, Vanessa. 'The three little creatures'
whom she cares for are her younger brothers and sister – Thoby, Virginia and
Adrian Stephen.

gloom happily encircled by the firelight, and peopled with legs and skirts. We drifted together like ships in an immense ocean and she asked me whether black cats had tails. And I answered that they had not, after a pause in which her question seemed to drop echoing down vast abysses, hitherto silent. In future I suppose there was some consciousness between us that the other held possibilities. But though shot occasionally by stormy passions, when sympathies seemed to waken beyond the reach of circumstances, the great satisfaction was to be had from impersonal things. There were smells and flowers and dead leaves and chestnuts, by which you distinguished the seasons, and each had innumerable associations, and power to flood the brain in a second. There were long summer evenings, with white moths abroad; and bright winter evenings when the fire-wood could be cut into shape. "The others" were not brothers and sister,* but beings possessed of knives, or enviable gifts for running or carving; and your mother, partly because she did not seem to hold these views as completely as we did, was the first to disturb me from my contentment. Another influence was even then astir in her, the influence of an affection only to be gratified by people. No hole dug in the gardens however deep, so that it was possible to extract clay of a malleable quality from it, gave her all that she needed. Dolls did not satisfy her. At present, until she was fifteen indeed, she was outwardly sober and austere, the most trustworthy, and always the eldest; sometimes she would lament her "responsibilities". Other children had their stages, and sudden gifts and failings; she seemed to draw on steadily, as though with her eye on some far object, which attained, she might reveal herself. She was very silent, and the only peculiar tastes which she seemed encouraged to show were those that people called out; she cried when Thoby went to school, and she minded more than the rest when your grandmother declared with some passion and humour, as I think, that she could never trust a single one of us again; had we not gone hunting for a dead cat against her commands? But beneath the serious surface only legitimately broken by such affections, there burnt also the other passion, the passion for art. She drew indeed under the care of a Mr Cook, but talk of art, talk of her own gifts and loves, was unknown to her. What did she think then? For with her long fingers grouping, and her eye considering, she surely painted many pictures without a canvas. Once I saw her scrawl on a black door a great maze of lines, with white chalk. "When I am a famous painter—" she began, and then turned shy and rubbed it out in her capable way. And when she won the prize at her drawing school, she hardly knew, so shy was she, at the recognition of a secret, how to tell me, in order that I might repeat the news at home.

* 'The others' are George, Stella and Gerald Duckworth.

"They've given me the thing – I don't know why." "What thing?" "O they say I've won it – the book – the prize you know." She was awkward as a long-legged colt.

When I try to see her I see more distinctly how our lives are pieces in a pattern and to judge one truly you must consider how this side is squeezed and that indented and a third expanded and none are really isolated, and so I conceive that there were many reasons then to make your mother show herself a little other than she was. We lived in a state of anxious growth; school, reports, professions to be chosen, marriage for the elders, books coming out, bills, health – the future was always too near and too much of a question for any sedate self expression. All these activities, too, charged the air with personal emotions and urged even children, and certainly "the eldest", to develop one side prematurely. To help, to do something was desirable, not to obtrude diffident wishes, irrelevant and possibly expensive.

So your mother, whose sight seemed in some ways so clear, took it upon her to be what people call 'practical' though a generous talent for losing umbrellas and forgetting messages showed that nature sometimes delighted to laugh at the pretence. But the power which was not feigned and was probably recognized by those who trusted her, was what I call variously sagacity, and common sense, and more rightly perhaps, honesty of mind. She might not see all, but she would not see what was not there. Stories, shallow though they seem, and I cannot be sure that to other eyes they will show what they show to mine, float upon the surface and must be made to illustrate this flying narrative. One August night, very much later in date, when your grandmother was dead we walked in the garden at Ringwood.* Your grandfather sat indoors alone, and might at any moment call us in to play whist with him as usual; and the light and the cards and the shouting seemed to us that night too crude and close to be tolerable. So we walked in the shade, and when we heard him come to the window and call we stood silent. Then he came out on to the lawn, and peered round him and called us each by name. But still we persisted, and at length he went in and left us to walk alone. But as we knew from the first perhaps, such joy is not for mortals; we wandered without delight, and at last went in and found him impressive, consciously but truly impressive, old, solitary and deserted. "Did you hear me call?" he said, and I was silent, and so was Adrian; your mother hesitated, and then said "Yes".

But this shows her quality in a tragic light; exposed to the fiercest strain. In earlier years it was most often the characteristic laughable token by which we knew her; "Old Nessa's honesty" or "The Old Creature is so matter-of-fact"

* Julian's grandparents were Julia and Leslie Stephen.

or "She means well". For sometimes she clung to truth too tenaciously, too simply; and we, flippant or sometimes insolent, persecuted her with horrid titles, 'Saint', and so on; for children so soon as they have any wit to direct are apt to use it cruelly. But there were then days of pure enjoyment – I conceive them at St Ives most readily,* when your mother trotted about on various businesses, considering the characters and desires of dogs very gravely, skilfully contriving butterfly nets, under your Uncle Waller's tuition,† accepting his law as the divine law, painting in water-colours, and scratching a number of black little squares, after Ruskin's prescription.‡ She played cricket better for the same reasons, with her straight forward stroke, calculated to meet all emergencies; and began by means of such fidelity and outward simplicity to win respect for herself from those tyrants and demigods who ruled our world; George, Waller, and Madge Symonds.§ She was a happy creature! beginning to feel within her the spring of unsuspected gifts, that the sea was beautiful and might be painted some day, and perhaps once or twice she looked steadily in the glass when no one was by and saw a face that excited her strangely; her being began to have a definite shape, a place in the world – what was it like? But her natural development, in which the artistic gift, so sensitive and yet so vigorous, would have asserted itself, was checked; the effect of death upon those that live is always strange, and often terrible in the havoc it makes with innocent desires.

In this sense your grandmother's death was disastrous; for you must conceive that she was not only the most beautiful of women as her portraits will tell you, but also one of the most distinct. Her life had been so swift, it was to be so short, that experiences which in most have space to expand themselves and bear leisurely fruit, were all compressed in her; she had married, borne children, and mourned her husband by the time she was twenty-four. For eight years she pondered that active season, and as I guess, formulated then in great part the judgement of life which underlay her future. She had been happy as few people are happy, for she had passed like a princess in a pageant from her supremely beautiful youth to marriage and motherhood, without awakenment. If I read truly, indeed the atmosphere of her home flattered such dreams and cast over the figure of her bridegroom all

---

* St Ives, Cornwall, where the Stephen family spent summer holidays from 1882 to 1894.

† John (Jack) Waller Hills. See p. 19.

‡ John Ruskin, *The Elements of Drawing* (London, 1857).

§ Madge Symonds, a daughter of J. A. Symonds, married Virginia's cousin, William Wyamar Vaughan. Madge was the object of Virginia's first passion, the intensity of which is echoed in Mrs Dalloway's memories of Sally Seton. (See QB, I, pp. 60–1, and Lee, *Virginia Woolf*, 1996, pp. 162–3) the golden enchantments of Tennysonian sentiment. But it would need a clearer vision than mine to decide how far her husband, though now so obviously her inferior in all ways, was able then to satisfy noble and genuine passions in his wife. Perhaps she made satisfaction for herself, cloaking his deficiencies in her own superabundance. At any rate when he was dead she determined to consecrate those years as the golden ones; when as she phrased it perhaps, she had not known the sorrow and the crime of the world because she had lived with a man, stainless of his kind, exalted in a world of pure love and beauty. The effect of his death then was doubly tremendous, because it was a disillusionment as well as a tragic human loss. She had by nature a keen brain, remorseless of all insincerity and even too much inclined to insist that all feeling has an equivalent in action or is worthless. And now that she had none to worship she worshipped the memory, and looking on the world with clear eyes, was more scornful than was just of its tragedy and stupidity because she had lived in a dream and still cherished a dream. She flung aside her religion, and became, as I have heard, the most positive of disbelievers. She reversed those natural instincts which were so strong in her of happiness and joy in a generous and abundant life, and pressed the bitterest fruit only to her lips. She visited the poor, nursed the dying, and felt herself possessed of the true secret of life at last, which is still obscured from a few, though they too must come to know it, that sorrow is our lot, and at best we can but face it bravely. All these things certainly she would have learnt had her husband lived, but learnt them with wisdom and temperance, delighting, rejoicing in the exercise of her own gifts and in the enjoyment of blessings which, surely, were not singular. But it would be easy to exaggerate the significance of this attitude, for much of its crudeness came, not from native harshness, but from the mutilation which her natural growth had undergone. Slowly, as I believe, she came to exercise her mind, and sadly enough to determine that much of the interest of the world must come in future from the satisfaction of her intellect. She saw many clever people, and read with a desire to establish her own sad faith, the works of disbelievers who spelt God without a capital G. In particular she read some early articles by your grandfather and liked them better than she liked him.

Fate, who is thought by some to arrange human lives to her liking, chose that your grandfather, with his first wife, should live in the same street with your grandmother and further decreed that Minny was to die there, and that your grandmother thus should be thrown into contact with her learned and formidable friend under the conditions which she of all people felt most poignantly. Would any other arrangement of circumstances have so brought about the miracle? For she found one who had equal reasons with herself to believe in the sorrow of life and every incentive to adopt her own stoic philosophy; he also was of the giant breed, no light lover, no superficial optimist. She might go hand in hand with him through the shadows of the Valley – but, of a sudden, her companion became her guide, pointed on, urged her to follow, to hope, to strive once more. She could not so soon throw off what had come to be a habit of suffering almost, and yet his reason was the stronger, his need was the greater. At length with pain and remorse she, courageous as she was, more truly courageous perhaps than her husband, bade herself face the truth and realize in all its aspects the fact that joy was to be endured as well as sorrow. She rose to the heights, wide-eyed and nobly free from all illusion or sentiment, her second love shining pure as starlight; the rosy mists of the first rapture dispelled for ever. Indeed it is notable that she never spoke of her first love; and in treasuring it changed it perhaps to something far fairer than it could have been, had life allowed it to endure. The second marriage was the true though late fulfilment of all that she could be; and, but that it was rather late, rather crowded, and rather anxious, no match was more truly equal, or more ceaselessly valiant. Large words, perhaps, to use of fifteen years! with all their opportunity for smallness, failure, tolerance of mediocrity. But, although there were certain matters which seem to us now decided by her too much in a spirit of compromise, and exacted by him without strict regard for justice or magnanimity, still it is true whether you judge by their work or by themselves that it was a triumphant life, consistently aiming at high things.

These circumstances had taken their part in forming your grandmother's character; and by the time we, her children, knew her, she was the most prompt, practical and vivid of human beings. It was as though she had made up her mind definitely upon certain great matters and was never after troubled to consider herself at all; but every deed and word had the bright, inexorable, swift stamp of something struck clearly by a mass of hoarded experience. Four children were born to her; there were four others already, older, demanding other care;* she taught us, was their companion, and soothed, cheered, inspired, nursed, deceived your grandfather; and any one coming for help found her invincibly upright in her place, with time to give, earnest consideration, and the most practical sympathy. Her relations with people indeed were all through her life remarkable; and after her second marriage this decision, of which I speak, seemed to make her spend herself more freely than ever in the service of others. And as that phrase has a doubtful reputation, and might well lead you to imagine a different woman from the real one, I must explain that her conduct in this matter was

---

* The 'four others' were Julia's three children by her first husband, Herbert Duckworth, and Laura, the daughter of Leslie Stephen and his first wife, Minny.

singular, and by no means of a piece with the mischievous philanthropy which other women practise so complacently and often with such disastrous results.

Her view of the world had come to be very comprehensive; she seemed to watch, like some wise Fate, the birth, growth, flower and death of innumerable lives all round her, with a constant sense of the mystery that encircled them, not now so sceptical as of old, and [with] a perfectly definite idea of the help that was possible and of use. Her intellectual gifts had always been those that find their closest expression in action; she had great clearness of insight, sound judgement, humour, and a power of grasping very quickly the real nature of someone's circumstances, and so arranging that the matter, whatever it was, fell into its true proportions at once. Sometimes with her natural impetuosity, she took it on herself to despatch difficulties with a high hand, like some commanding Empress. But most often I think her service, when it was not purely practical, lay in simply helping people by the light of her judgement and experience, to see what they really meant or felt. But any sensible woman may have these qualities, and yet be none of the things that your grandmother was. All her gifts had something swift, decisive, witty even, in their nature; so that there could be no question of dulness or drudgery in her daily work, however lugubrious it seemed of itself. She was sensitive by temperament and impatient of stupidity; and while she was there the whole of that interminable and incongruous procession which is the life of a large family, went merrily; with exquisite humour in its incidents very often, or something grotesque or impressive in its arrangement, perpetually lit up by her keen attention, her amazing sense of the life that is in the weakest or most threadbare situations. She stamped people with characters at once; and at St Ives, or on Sunday afternoons at Hyde Park Gate, the scene was often fit for the stage; boldly acting on her conception she drew out from old General Beadle, or C. B. Clarke, or Jack Hills, or Sidney Lee, such sparks of character as they have never shown to anyone since. All lives directly she crossed them seemed to form themselves into a pattern and while she stayed each move was of the utmost importance. But she was no aesthetic spectator, collecting impressions for her own amusement.*

Life rather had taught her that facts, as she interpreted them, were by themselves of supreme importance; it was a matter of anxious moment to her that Lisa Stillman should like her brother-in-law, or that a workman wounded in an accident should find healthy employment. She kept herself marvellously alive to all the changes that went on around her, as though

---

* The ts (p. 14) is torn at mid-page. After 'amusement', instead of a full stop, there is a semi-colon and four deleted words. There is no doubt that the next page is meant to follow directly.

she heard perpetually the ticking of a vast clock and could never forget that some day it would cease for all of us. People of the most diverse kinds came to her when they had reason to rejoice or to weep; she seemed, if anything, a little indiscriminate in her choice of friends; but bores and fools have their moments. And it must be owned that living thus at high pressure she contrived to invest the whole scene with an inimitable bravery as though she saw it properly composed, of fools, clowns and splendid Queens, a vast procession on the march towards death. This intense preoccupation with the event of the moment arose partly no doubt because nature had fitted her to deal victoriously with such matters; but also because she had inborn in her and [had] acquired a deep sense of the futility of all effort, the mystery of life. You may see the two things in her face. 'Let us make the most of what we have, since we know nothing of the future' was the motive that urged her to toil so incessantly on behalf of happiness, right doing, love; and the melancholy echoes answered 'What does it matter? Perhaps there is no future.' Encompassed as she was by this solemn doubt her most trivial activities had something of grandeur about them; and her presence was large and austere, bringing with it not only joy and life, exquisite fleeting femininities, but the majesty of a nobly composed human being.

Written words of a person who is dead or still alive tend most unfortunately to drape themselves in smooth folds annulling all evidence of life. You will not find in what I say, or again in those sincere but conventional phrases in the life of your grandfather, or in the noble lamentations with which he fills the pages of his autobiography,* any semblance of a woman whom you can love. It has often occurred to me to regret that no one ever wrote down her sayings and vivid ways of speech since she had the gift of turning words in a manner peculiar to her, rubbing her hands swiftly, or raising them in gesticulation as she spoke.† I can see her, standing by the open door of a railway carriage which was taking Stella and some others to Cambridge, and striking out in a phrase or two pictures of all the people who came past her along the platform, and so she kept them laughing till the train went.

What would one not give to recapture a single phrase even! or the tone of the clear round voice, or the sight of the beautiful figure, so upright and so distinct, in its long shabby cloak, with the head held at a certain angle, a

---

* The 'Mausoleum Book', begun by Leslie Stephen in 1895 after the death of Julia. The last entry, dictated to Virginia, was made in 1903. It was published as *Leslie Stephen's Mausoleum Book*, ed. Alan Bell, Clarendon Press, 1977.

† Mrs Carlyle reminds me oddly of her, with her 'coterie' speech (VW).

little upwards, so that the eye looked straight out at you. "Come children," she would say directly she had waved her last fantastic farewell, and one would grasp her umbrella, and another her arm, and one no doubt would stand gaping, and she would call sharply, "Quick, quick". And so she would pass with her swift step, through the crowds, and into some dingy train or omnibus, where perhaps she would ask the conductor why the company did not give him straw to stand on – "Your feet must be cold" – and hear his story and make her comment, until we were home just in time for lunch. "Don't keep father waiting." And at lunch in answer to some languid question, "So those young people are gone? We . . . ll, I don't envy 'em", she would have her little story to tell, or perhaps her cryptic phrase which we could not interpret, but knew from the shrugs and "Perhaps" that it bore on one of those romances which they both loved to discuss. The relationship between your grandfather and mother was, as the saying is, perfect, nor would I for a moment dispute that, believing as I do that each of these much tried and by no means easy-going people found in the other the highest and most perfect harmony which their natures could respond to. Beautiful often, even to our eyes, were their gestures, their glances of pure and unutterable delight in each other. But, if I can convey my meaning by the metaphor, the high consonance, the flute voices of two birds in tune, was only reached by rich, rapid scales of discord, and incongruity. After all she was fifteen years the younger, and his age was made emphatic by the keen intellect, always voyaging, as she must have thought, alone in ice-bound seas. Her pride in it was like the pride of one in some lofty mountain peak, visited only by the light of the stars, and the rain of snow; it was enthusiastic, but very humble.

She delighted to transact all those trifling businesses which, as women feel instinctively, are somehow derogatory to the dignity which they like to discover in clever men; and she took it as proud testimony that he came to her ignorant of all depressions and elations but those that high philosophy bred in him. But she never belittled her own works, thinking them, if properly discharged, of equal, though other, importance with her husband's. Thus in those moments, breathing spaces in the incessant conflict, when each rested secure for a second in the other's embrace, she knew with just but always delighted pride, that he worshipped in her something as unchallengeably high as the lofty remote peak which she honoured in him. And each sprang rejoicing to do homage to qualities unlike their own – how sweet, released from the agony and loneliness of thought to recognize instantly the real presence of unquestionable human loveliness! as a seafarer wrapt for many days in mist on the fruitless waters lands at dawn upon a sunlit shore, where all nature enfolds him and breathes in his ear rest and assurance. She too whose days were spent in labours often trifling, and often vain, exulted as one clasped suddenly in strong arms and set above it all, silent, still and immortal. She was always the first to reinforce his own impulse towards the most remote and unprofitable tasks; it was on her assurance I think that he began his last long book, *The Utilitarians*,* which would yield no wealth and very little fame, for she undertook that all other matters would prosper meanwhile.

But these are the pinnacles of life, and as time drew on, the struggle grew sharper, and the buoyancy of youth diminished. His health was worn, and the kind of praise which would have encouraged him, delayed unduly, as he complained. And by this time she had expanded so far, into such remote recesses, alleys in St Ives, London slums, and many other more prosperous but no less exacting quarters, that retrenchment was beyond her power. Every day brought her, it seemed, a fresh sprung harvest that must be despatched and would flourish infallibly tomorrow. Each evening she sat at her table, after some laborious afternoon, her hand moving ceaselessly, at the last a little erratically, as she wrote answers, advice, jests, warning, sympathy, her wise brow and deep eyes presiding, so beautiful still, but now so worn, so profoundly experienced that you could hardly call them sad. When she was dead I found a desk shut when we left St Ives with all the letters received that morning freshly laid in it, to be answered perhaps when she got to London. There was a letter from a woman whose daughter had been betrayed and asked for help; a letter from George, from Aunt Mary,† from a nurse who was out of work, some bills, some begging letters, and many sheets from a girl who had quarrelled with her parents and must reveal her soul, earnestly, diffusely. "Ah, thank Heaven, there is no post tonight!" she would exclaim, half smiling and half sighing, on Saturday; and even your grandfather would look up from his book, press her hand, and vainly protest, "there must be an end of this, Julia!"

In addition to all her other labours she took it on herself to teach us our lessons, and thus established a very close and rather trying relationship, for she was of a quick temper, and least of all inclined to spare her children. "Your father is a great man." But in no other way could we have learnt, in the short time we had, so much of her true nature, obscured by none of those graceful figments which interpose themselves generally in the gulf which lies between a middle-aged woman and her children. It might have been better, as it certainly would have tired her less, had she allowed that some of those duties could be discharged for her. But she was

* *The English Utilitarians*, published in 1900; shorter works were to follow.
† Aunt Mary Fisher. See p. 110n.

impetuous, and also a little imperious; so conscious of her own burning will that she could scarcely believe that there was not something quicker and more effective in her action than in another's. Thus when your grandfather was ill she would never suffer a nurse to be with him, nor could she believe that a governess would teach us as well as she did. And apart from economy, which always weighed with her, she had come to attach a desperate importance to the saving of time, as though she saw heap themselves all round her, duties and desires, and time to embrace them slipped from her and left her with grasping fingers. She had constantly in mind that comprehensive view of the final proportions of things which I have noticed; for her words were never trivial; but as her strength lessened her respites were fewer; she sank, like an exhausted swimmer, deeper and deeper in the water, and could only at moments descry some restful shore on the horizon to be gained in old age when all this toil was over. But when we exclaim at the extravagant waste of such a life we are inclined no doubt to lose that view of the surrounding parts, the husband and child and home which if you see them as a whole surrounding her, completing her, robs the single life of its arrow-like speed, and its tragic departure. What is noticeable about her, as I am come to think, is not the waste and the futile gallantry, but the niceness, born of sure judgement, with which her effort matched her aim. There was scarcely any superfluity; and it is for this reason that, past as those years are, her mark on them is ineffaceable, as though branded by the naked steel, the sharp, the pure. Living voices in many parts of the world still speak of her as of someone who is actually a fact in life. Whether she came merry, wrathful or in impulsive sympathy, it does not matter; they speak of her as of a thing that happened, recalling, as though all round her grew significant, how she stood and turned and how the bird sang loudly, or a great cloud passed across the sky. Where has she gone? What she said has never ceased. She died when she was forty-eight, and your mother was a child of fifteen.* If what I have said of her has any meaning you will believe that her death was the greatest disaster that could happen; it was as though on some brilliant day of spring the racing clouds of a sudden stood still, grew dark, and massed themselves; the wind flagged, and all creatures on the earth moaned or wandered seeking aimlessly. But what figures or variety of figures will do justice to the shapes which since then she has taken in countless lives? The dead, so people say, are forgotten, or they should rather say, that life has for the most part little significance to

* Julia died at the age of forty-nine on 5 May 1895. Vanessa became sixteen on 30 May.

any of us. But now and again on more occasions than I can number, in bed at night, or in the street, or as I come into the room, there she is; beautiful, emphatic, with her familiar phrase and her laugh; closer than any of the living are, lighting our random lives as with a burning torch, infinitely noble and delightful to her children.

Chapter Two

HER death, on the 5th of May, 1895, began a period of Oriental gloom, for surely there was something in the darkened rooms, the groans, the passionate lamentations that passed the normal limits of sorrow, and hung about the genuine tragedy with folds of Eastern drapery. Your grandfather had in him much of the stuff of a Hebrew prophet; something of the amazing vigour of his youth remained to him, but he no longer spent his strength in climbing mountains or coaching crews; all his devotion for many years had concentrated itself upon his home. And now that against all his expectations, his wife had died before him, he was like one who, by the failure of some stay, reels staggering blindly about the world, and fills it with his woe. But no words of mine can convey what he felt, or even the energy of the visible expression of it, which took place in one scene after another all through that dreadful summer. One room it seemed was always shut, was always disturbed now and then, by some groan or outburst. He had constant interviews with sympathetic women, who went in to see him nervously enough, and came out flushed and tear-stained, confused as people are who have been swept away on the tide of someone else's emotion, to give their report to Stella. Indeed all her diplomacy was needed to keep him occupied in some way, when his morning's work was over; and there were dreadful meal-times when, unable to hear what we said, or disdaining its comfort, he gave himself up to the passion which seemed to burn within him, and groaned aloud or protested again and again his wish to die. I do not think that Stella lost consciousness for a single moment during all those months of his immediate need. She would always have some little device to offer him, observing him so closely that she would suddenly beg one of us to speak to him directly, or ask him to walk with us. Sometimes at night she spent a long time alone in his study with him, hearing again and again the bitter story of his loneliness, his love and his remorse. For exhausted and unstrung as he was he came to torment himself piteously with the idea that he had never told his wife how much he had loved her, that she had endured anxiety and suffering by his side in silence.

"I was not as bad as Carlyle, was I?"* I have heard him ask. Stella perhaps

* The exposure of Carlyle's marital behaviour in his *Reminiscences* and in J. A. Fronde's biography, shortly before Leslie began "The Mausoleum Book", was a major scandal. Carlyle became notorious for having been "ill to live with"; cf. p. 118.

knew little of Carlyle, but her assurance came over and over again, tired but persistent. There is, no doubt, a strange comfort in making the living hear your confession of wrong done to the dead; not only can they reassure you from their own observation, but they also represent, mysteriously, a power which can be appeased by your confession, and can grant you something approaching a final absolution. For these reasons, then, and also because it was his nature and habit to find ease in the expression of his feelings, he did not scruple to lay before her his sufferings and to demand perpetual attention, and whatever comfort she had to give. But what comfort could she give? From the nature of the case there was little to be done; all depended therefore upon what she was, for suddenly she was placed in the utmost intimacy with a man who as her stepfather and an elderly man of letters she had hitherto regarded only with respect and a formal affection. Stella's position, until this crisis, had been in some ways peculiar; indeed her character altogether, as one sees it now illuminated afresh by one's own equality of age, was remarkable; remarkable for what it was, and for its destiny; great issues hung upon her life; but the shortness and almost tremulous quality of the early years make it hard to tell the story with any decision.

She was not clever, she seldom read a book; and this fact had I think an immense influence upon her life, a disproportionate influence, indeed. She exaggerated her own deficiency, and, living in close companionship with her mother, was always contrasting their differences, and imputing to herself an inferiority which led her from the first to live in her mother's shade. Your grandmother too was, I have said, ruthless in her ways, and quite indifferent, if she saw good, to any amount of personal suffering. It was characteristic of her to feel that her daughter was, as she expressed it, part of herself, and as a slower and less efficient part she did not scruple to treat her with the severity with which she would have treated her own failings, or to offer her up as freely as she would have offered herself. Once before your grandparents' marriage, when your grandfather remarked to her upon the harshness with which she treated Stella in comparison with the other children who were both boys, she gave the answer I have written.*

As a child then, Stella was suppressed, and learned early to look upon her mother as a person of divine power and divine intelligence. But later as Stella grew older and developed her own beauty, her own singular charm and temperament, her mother ceased her harshness, if it were ever rightly called so, and showed only the true cause of it, a peculiar depth and intimacy of feeling. They always kept in the main the relationship which nature perhaps had ordained. Stella was always the beautiful attendant handmaid, feeding

* See p. 106.

her mother's vivid flame, rejoicing in the service, and making it the central duty of her life. But besides this she began very soon to enjoy the influence of her gifts on others; she was beautiful, more beautiful than her pictures show, for much of her phantom loveliness came from accidents of the moment – the pale luminous complexion, the changing light in the eyes, the movement and ripple of the whole. If your grandmother's was a head of the finest period of Greek art, Stella's was Greek too, but it was Greek of a later and more decadent age, making with its softer lines and more languid shape, a closer appeal. But in each case, their beauty was the expression of them. Stella was mutable, modest, but somehow with what is called charm or magic possessed of wonderful distinction, and the power of penetrating deeply into people's minds. It was not I suppose for what she said, for that was simple enough; but for her ripple of sweetness and laughter over a shape, dimly discerned, as of statuesque marble. She was so gay, so feminine, and at the same time had about her something of the large repose which in her mother, under stress of circumstance, had resolved itself into an enduring melancholy. Stella and her coming out, and her success and her lovers, excited many instincts long dormant in her mother; she liked young men, she enjoyed their confidences, she was intensely amused by the play and intrigue of the thing; only, as she complained, Stella would insist upon going home, long before the night was over, for fear lest she should be tired. That indeed was what, with desperate use of imagery, I have called her marble shape; for all her triumphs were mere frippery on the surface of this constant preoccupation with her mother. It was beautiful, it was almost excessive; for it had something of the morbid nature of an affection between two people too closely allied for the proper amount of reflection to take place between them; what her mother felt passed almost instantly through Stella's mind; there was no need for the brain to ponder and criticize what the soul knew. Your grandmother would no doubt have liked some brisker resistance, some intellectual opposition, calling out a different sort of care; she may well have felt that the tie was too close to be wholesome, and might hinder Stella from entertaining those natural feelings upon which she set so high a value. Even a short parting was unduly painful; Stella was white as a ghost for days before she went abroad, and broke once into a passion of tears. "What can it matter where we are", she said, "so long as we are all together?"

Her feeling during the last years became ever more anxious, as she detected signs of failing health in her mother, and could not contrive in any way to give her the rest which of all things she needed. Her silence with her stepfather almost gave way now and then to sharp and open remonstrance; for he never seemed to see, what was so plain to her eye, the innumerable things that his wife did, or how terribly she was worn. Then, in the spring of 1895 Stella was driven abroad, and half-way through the journey she became convinced by sign of handwriting or phrase, that her mother lay ill at home. She appealed to Vanessa, who could only send an answer dictated by her mother. Slight illness had indeed attacked her, but with the strange and ghastly fantasy of one who plays a part to the end, she would insist that the truth should not yet be told. Stella came home with a consciousness like that of some tormented dumb animal, that she had been deceived; and found her mother in bed, with the chill which was to end ten days later, in her death.

The shock to Stella was complete; she began, by sheer pure beauty of character, to do all that she could for everyone; but almost automatically. The future held nothing for her; the present was, I suppose, with a stepfather whom she barely knew, and four children who needed care and could as yet help her little, constantly painful. She was only just twenty-six, and in a moment she had to relinquish not only the chief source of all her life, but also the peculiar ways in which she best enjoyed her gifts. Indeed whoever she had been the position must have been painfully hard, but with her great distrust of her own powers, and her dread of books in particular, her task was terribly painful and almost bewildering. But still, had it not been for this desolation, laying her whole nature bare, and bidding it put forth its powers in entire loneliness, could she ever have shown herself as noble and as true as she was? All that she became in the future was firmly grounded, her own achievement; no one ever again was to serve her for prop; never again, perhaps, did she care for anyone as she had cared for her mother. That, whatever gain is to be set beside it, was the permanent loss.

Directly your grandmother was dead, Stella inherited all the duties that she had discharged; and like some creaking old waggon, pitifully rusted, and yet filled with stirring young creatures, our family once more toiled painfully along the way.

Chapter Three

YOUR grandmother's position in the family was such that her death not only removed the central figure from our eyes, but brought about such a shifting of relationships that life for a long time seemed incredibly strange. Your grandfather in his natural but surely unwise desire to do for us all that your grandmother had done, began to teach us our lessons; and gave up half his morning to us; a sacrifice indeed but that did not make his mood the easier. Then George, on the full tide of emotion, insisted upon a closer and more mature friendship with us; Gerald even became for the time serious and sentimental; and round this centre of profound emotion circled a number of friends, suddenly become conscious of a desire to take part in our lives, and of their right to have the depth of their own feelings recognized. Stella herself, almost stunned though she was at the moment, was never driven from her calm attitude of infinite consideration for others, of silence with respect to her own feelings; but this very calmness seemed to suffer, indifferently, a number of trials, and in particular to admit of quite unqualified self-surrender to your grandfather's needs. Any comfort, whatever its nature, that came to hand, she offered him to stay his anguish; all her day was at his service, she exerted herself as I have said, to find people to visit him, to help her in some of her innumerable minute plans for his welfare. It is easy to see now that where she failed for the time was in proper discrimination. Her own disbelief in herself, and her long season of dependence made her incapable of trusting her own clear instincts in the matter. Her stepfather was the charge bequeathed her by her mother. She gave indiscriminately, conscious that she had not the best of all to give; and your grandfather who would doubtless have understood a clear statement of the position, took all that she offered him failing this as his right. But one of the consequences was that for some time life seemed to us in a chronic state of confusion. We were quite naturally unhappy; feeling a definite need, unbearably keen at moments, which was never to be satisfied. But that was recognizable pain, and the sharp pang grew to be almost welcome in the midst of the sultry and opaque life which was not felt, had nothing real in it, and yet swam about us, and choked us and blinded us. All these tears and groans, reproaches and protestations of affection, high talk of duty and work and living for others, were doubtless what we should feel if we felt properly, and yet we had but a dull sense of gloom which could not honestly be referred to the dead; unfortunately it did not quicken our feeling for the living; but hideous as it was, obscured both living and dead; and for long did unpardonable mischief by substituting for the shape of a true and most vivid mother, nothing better than an unlovable phantom.

That summer, after some hot months in London, we spent in Freshwater; and the heat there in the low bay, brimming as it seemed with soft vapours, and luxuriant with lush plants, mixes, like smoke, with other memories of hot rooms and silence, and an atmosphere all choked with too luxuriant feelings, so that one had at times a physical need of ruthless barbarism and fresh air. Stella herself looked like the white flower of some teeming hot-house, for a change had come over her that seemed terribly symbolical. Never did anyone look so pale. And yet unexpected as it might seem, but still was most natural, the first impulse to set us free came from your grandfather; it came and went again. On a walk perhaps he would suddenly brush aside all our curiously conventional relationships, and show us for a minute an inspiriting vision of free life, bathed in an impersonal light. There were numbers of things to be learnt, books to be read, and success and happiness were to be attained there without disloyalty. Indeed it seemed possible at these moments, to continue the old life but in a more significant way, using as he told us, our sorrow to quicken the feeling that remained. But such exaltations doubtless depended for their endurance upon a closer relationship than age made possible. We were too young, and for sympathy that required less effort, he had to turn to others, whose difference of blood and temperament, made it harder for them to recognize as we did – by glimpses – his most urgent need. Beautiful was he at such moments; simple and eager as a child; and exquisitely alive to all affection; exquisitely tender. We would have helped him then if we could, given him all we had, and felt it little beside his need – but the moment passed.

It was exhilarating at times to peer above our immature world, and fancy that the actual conflict of recognized human beings had already begun for us. In truth the change which declared itself when we were once more settled in London and gone about our tasks, was partly invigorating; for we tried to prove ourselves equal companions for Stella and our lives were much quickened by the chivalrous devotion she roused in us. It was chivalrous because she was too remote for real companionship, so that there was always a kind of chance in one's offering; perhaps she would not perceive it; perhaps she would kindle rapture by a sudden recognition; her distance made such close moments exquisitely sweet. But alas, no such humble friendship however romantic, could give her the sense that we completely shared her thoughts; the nature of them made it hard for anyone to understand; and her sorrow was very lonely. Perhaps one would come into a room unexpectedly, and surprise her in tears, and, to one's miserable confusion, she would hide them instantly, and speak ordinary words, as though she did not imagine that one could understand her suffering.

And this, as I think, was the time when your mother first came somewhat tentatively upon the scene, her age being then almost seventeen. Her qualities of honesty and wisdom were precisely those that Stella was then most inclined to appreciate, both because she was often bewildered by the eccentric storms in which your grandfather indulged, ascribed by her too simply to the greatness of his intellect, and also because she found in Vanessa both in nature and in person something like a reflection of her mother. Vanessa too might be treated almost as a confidante, the single person who did not need any kind of sacrifice to be made for her. And Stella felt also, no doubt, that curiously intimate pride which a woman feels when she sees womanly virtues beautifully expressed by another, the torch still worthily carried; and the pride was very tender in this case and mixed with much of a maternal joy. I do not know how far I shall be guilty of over-ingenuity if I discover another, though an unspoken, cause for the growth of natural sympathy with Vanessa. For two or three years now the one suitor who stood out above other suitors and was greatly liked by your grandmother and tolerated by Stella herself was John Waller Hills. He was then a lean, rather threadbare young man, who seemed to force his way by sheer determination and solid integrity; suggesting the figure of some tenacious wire-haired terrier, in whose obstinacy and strength of jaw there seemed, at a time when all the fates were against him, something honourable, which appealed to one's half humorous sense of sport as even pathetic. He would come, Sunday after Sunday, and sit his hour out, worrying his speech as a terrier a bone; but sticking doggedly to the word, until at last he got it pronounced. His method was the same always. He knew what he wanted, and unless there occurred a sudden bursting of his stout skull and soft illimitable prospects opened on each side, which was incredible, there was little doubt that he would come by it – except indeed in this very instance. For, with so much that everyone could respect, and find admirable in his relations with others, there was yet very little that anyone seemed called on to love at first hand. It was natural to be indebted to him, for faithful services rendered over a score of years, and to requite him by a perpetual seat at the fireside, or a cover laid for him on Sundays, or the title of uncle to some one else's children. But to disregard all these oblique services, and meet him face to face, as one capable of the supreme gift of all, needed as Stella found, prolonged consideration and repeated rejection. He satisfied so many requirements, but the sum of all he gave did not need love to reward it. After her mother's death however, Stella became far less exacting, as indeed she lost interest in her fate, and had no contrast to oppose to it; Jack was persistent as ever, almost a natural if secondary part of oneself. No doubt he had a system plainly marked in front of him, arranged on paper in his little room in Ebury Street, and was simply following it out in detail. But that even had a kind of fascination for one so prone now to consider herself merely as the atmosphere that enclosed solid bodies. The long visits, when there were such long pauses, or spasmodic talk of indifferent matters, salmon fishing or Stevenson's novels, had yet an undeniable glow, a conviction of meaning lying at the base of them, which made them remarkable, and wore, like some dull heat, into her mind. It made her realize herself, turning solid much that floated vague as mist around her as she went about her daily life. But it threatened to be destructive of the compact which she had made with her stepfather, upon which by this time he had come to depend. It was natural then that she should turn instinctively to Vanessa, for many unformulated reasons, and for this obvious one, that Vanessa alone could justify her action if, as it sometimes seemed possible, she consented to marry Jack in the end. And also your mother was sympathetic without words; she had a great respect for Mr Hills, and her respect was warmed and at the same time sanctioned by the knowledge which was common to us all of his devotion. Insensibly, Stella grew to depend upon Jack's visits, for though she was sad to the point of despair, and physically tired, there was a pale flame in her which leapt at the prospect of an independent life, a life at least which depended upon one person only. For when some months had passed, and the first storm of distress was over, she found that she had completely pledged herself to her stepfather; he expected entire self-surrender on her part, and had decided apparently, and with sufficient reason, that she possessed one of those beautiful feminine natures which are quite without wishes of their own. She had to acquiesce, partly because it was easier to go on as she had begun, and partly because as she could not give him intellectual companionship she must give him the only thing she had. But Jack, with the shrewdness of a businessman who is in love, quickly saw how matters stood, and offered a very refreshing revolt. He considered Stella's wishes and Stella's health far more important than those of one whom he treated as an encyclopaedia who should be kept on the shelf, and must be humoured and tolerated in all his irrational desires if he chose to come downstairs. Stella would not have been human if she had not found this change of view a relief to her. Slowly then she admitted the thought of new life, and recognized that it was Jack and Jack only who inspired [it.]

But she had lapsed very far, into a kind of snowy numbness, nor could she waken at the first touch. He proposed to her in March (I think), almost a year after her mother's death, and she refused him. The thought of the break, the havoc played with delicate webs just beginning to spin themselves across the abyss, may well have deterred her; and, when she came face to face with her love, and tried to yield herself to his passion, his honesty, all his canine qualities glowing with their utmost expressiveness, did she still find something in her left cold and meditative, reflecting, when all should have been consenting? She remembered what she had felt before. But the summer wore on, and she looked with comfort at Vanessa, and there were not wanting authoritative voices who declared that such a sacrifice, for they gave it the definite name, was cowardly and short-sighted too. For in years to come, they argued, her stepfather would draw his best comfort from her home. Jack meanwhile, was persistent, and patient; and she had to confess that she had accumulated a reckoning with him that was serious however she looked at it; he meant a great deal in her life. The summer wore on, nor did anyone, unless it were your mother, suspect the change in Stella's mind; we depended on her as thoughtless men on some natural power; for it seemed to our judgement obvious enough that there must be someone always discharging the duties that Stella discharged. We had been lent a house at Hindhead, and one afternoon at the end of August, Jack came there, bicycling to some place in the neighbourhood. His visits were so often forced in this way that we suspected nothing more than the usual amount of restraint from his explosive ways, and much information about dogs and bicycles. His opinion on these matters stood very high with us. He stayed to dinner, and that also was characteristic of his method; but after dinner a strange lapse occurred in the usual etiquette. Stella left the room with him, to show him the garden or the moon, and decisively shut the door behind her. We had our business to attend to also, and followed them soon with a lantern, for we were then in the habit of catching moths after dinner. Once or twice we saw them, always hasting round a corner; once or twice we heard her skirts brushing, and once a sound of whispering. But the moon was very bright, and there were no moths; Stella and Jack had gone in, it seemed, and we returned to the drawing room. But father was alone, and he was unusually restless, turning his pages, crossing his legs, and looking again and again at the clock. Then he sent Adrian to bed; then me; then Nessa and Thoby; and still it was only ten, and still Stella and Jack stayed out! There was then a pause, and we sat together in Adrian's room, cold, melancholy and strangely uncomfortable. Your Uncle Thoby discovered a tramp in the garden, who begged for food and Thoby sent him away with great eloquence, and we felt a little frightened, for it was no ordinary night, and ominous things were happening. Your grandfather was tramping the terrace, up and down, up and down; we were all awake, all expectant, and still nothing happened. At length, someone looking from the window, exclaimed, "Stella and Mr Hills are coming up the path together!" Were their arms locked? Did we know immediately all that we had not dared to guess? At any rate we ran to our rooms, and in a few minutes Stella dame up herself, blushing the loveliest rose colour, and told us – how she was very happy.

The news was met, of course, by the usual outburst of clamorous voices which always threatens on such occasions to drown the single true utterance. Families at these moments touch their high, and perhaps also their low, watermarks. Your grandfather, I remember, spoke sharply to one whom he found in tears, for it should make us only happy, he said, that Stella should be happy; true words! But the moment after he was groaning to her that the blow was irreparable. Then George and Gerald, who lavished kisses and did their best to arrange that she and Jack should be left alone together, soon let her see that there would be difficulties if Jack came too much to the house. "It won't do; men are like that", she said once, without complaint; and Kitty Maxse,* who had the reputation with us of profound knowledge and exquisite sympathy, an irresistible combination, confirmed her no doubt in her sad estimate of mankind. "It won't do."

Their engagement then was at the mercy of many forces from the outset; still there were some walks at Hindhead, a week spent together at Corby,† and Jack found excuses for dining with us every night in London, and stayed on very late, till George came down and invoked the proprieties, or with some reason, insisted that Stella must rest. One thing seemed to survive all these vexations, and was miraculous to see; the exquisite tremor of life was once more alight in Stella; her eye shone, her pale cheeks glowed constantly with a faint rose. She laughed and had her tender jokes. Sometimes a fear came over her, possessed her; she had had her life; but then there was Jack to reason her out of her alarms, to kiss her, and show her a sane future, with many interests and much substance. She had come to stand by herself, with a painful footing upon real life, and her love now had as little of dependence in it as may be. He, it is true, had more wish to live than she had, but she took and gave with open eyes. It was beautiful; it was, once more, a flight of unfurled wings into the upper air.

But all these difficulties and jealousies resolved themselves shortly into one formidable question; where were they to live after their marriage? Your grandfather had taken it for granted that Stella would not leave him, since she had become indispensable; and in the first flush of their joy both Stella and Jack had agreed that it would be possible to live on at Hyde Park Gate. Then they began to consider rooms, and habits, conveniences and rights, and it soon became obvious that the plan was impossible. And if they started wrong disasters would accumulate. Stella was convinced, for she began to entertain a just idea of her independence as a wife; and George and Gerald agreed also. It is significant however of your grandfather's temper at the time that he

---

* Kitty Maxse (née Lushington) was a frequent visitor to Hyde Park Gate. See pp. 32, 105.
† Corby Castle, just east of Carlisle, was the home of the Hills.

continued to count upon their rash promise as though it were the natural and just arrangement, which did not need further consideration. His awakenment was bound to be painful, and there were many painful words to be said on his side; they had promised and they had deserted him. One night however Stella went up into his study alone, and explained what they felt. What she said, what he answered, I cannot tell; but for some time afterwards he could never hear the marriage spoken of without a profound groan, and the least encouragement would lead him to explain precisely how much he suffered, and how little cause there was for him to rejoice. But Stella was very patient, and just capable now under Jack's influence of seeing another side to her stepfather's remarks. There were signs that in years to come she would enjoy a lively and delightful companionship with him. They took a house at the end of the street, for that was the compromise, and in the beginning of April, 1897, they were married.

There had been so much talk of loss, loneliness and change that it was surprising to find that the house went on next day very much as usual. We went to Brighton, and letters began to come from Stella in Florence and from Jack giving promise, stirring as Spring, of happy new intimacies in the future. Indeed it was already a relief that there should be a separate house with a different basis from ours, untinged presumably with our gloom; under these influences that gloom itself seemed to lighten. For your grandfather, left alone with us, found doubtless much to try him in our crudeness and lack of sympathy but there was also great interest in our development, and we began to surprise him with voluntary remarks, bearing on matters of art and literature. Thoby was becoming, he said, 'a fine fellow'; he discovered that suddenly your mother was grown 'very handsome'; friendship with us, in short, was the great desire of his life, and Stella's marriage seemed to clear the way for it. We had our theory too, of the way to manage him, and it was not Stella's way, but promised well. Thus, when it was time to come back to London we were eager to see Stella again, and had many things to tell her, and much curiosity to see how she would live. But on the very morning of our return a letter came from George saying that Stella was in bed with a chill. When we got back home she was a little worse; almost immediately it seemed we were in the midst of serious illness, nurses, consultations, interviews and whispers. Like a nightmare it came upon us, waking terrible memories, confronting us with a possibility which we could not even believe, and then, like a nightmare, it was gone; Stella was said to be recovered. Indeed she went about a little, came in to tea and lunch with us, and walked out in Kensington Gardens. But she had a relapse, and then another; and the doctors ordered that for a certain time she should stay in her room. But she could see us; and it seemed that although the time was interrupted by terrible fears, to which we got accustomed however, and was never quite secure, our hopes were realized. She was certainly happy; she was less despondent, less modest than ever before, as though Jack had finally convinced her of her worth. That indeed was a service for which one might forgive much, and under the influence of her large presence and repose he lost many of his difficult ways, his emphatic insistence upon the commonplaces of life, and showed himself loyal and kind as he had always been, but more gentle, and far more sensitive of perception than he was of old. He only needed perhaps some such happiness to discard all his angularities, which were partly produced, no doubt, by the need he had been in for so many years of forcing his way through obstacles. All her arrangements prospered; she had her stepfather to tea with her regularly, and marvelled at his good spirits and health, and he was very tender to her when he heard that she was to be a mother. George and Gerald had their interviews alone. And your mother 'came out' that summer, and Stella had one of the purest pleasures of her life in gazing on her beauty and speculating on her success. She felt what a mother would have felt, and this was the sort of triumph that she could herself understand to the uttermost; she had attempted it. But once more she fell ill; again, almost in a moment, there was danger, and this time it did not pass away, but pressed on and on, till suddenly we knew that the worst had actually come to pass. Even now it seems incredible.

Chapter Four

IT generally happens in seasons of such bewilderment as that in which we
now found ourselves, that one person becomes immediately the central
figure, as it were the solid figure, and on this occasion it was your mother.
Many reasons combined to give her this prominence. She fulfilled the duties
which Stella had but lately fulfilled; she had much of the beauty and
something of the character which with but little stretch of the imagination we
could accept as worthy to carry on the tradition; for in our morbid state,
haunted by great ghosts, we insisted that to be like mother, or like Stella, was
to achieve the height of human perfection. Vanessa then at the age of
eighteen was exalted, in the most tragic way, to a strange position, full of
power and responsibility. Everyone turned to her, and she moved, like some
young Queen, all weighed down with the pomp of her ceremonial robes,
perplexed and mournful and uncertain of her way. The instant need was to
comfort, say rather, to be with, Jack. He had lost infinitely more than anyone
could calculate; his sorrow seemed to stretch over years to come, withering
them, and to cast a bitter light on his past. Never was there so cruel a loss, for
it was cruel in the harshest way, in that it somehow seemed to damage him.
Like some animal stunned by a blow on the head he went methodically about
his work, worn and grim enough to behold, taking an abrupt mechanical
interest in substantial facts, the make of a bicycle, or the number of men killed
at the battle of Waterloo. But in the evenings he would come and sit with
your mother, and loosen this tight tension and burst out what he could speak
of his sorrow. Poor inarticulate man! In his dumb way he had worshipped
beauty; it had been a long discipline; and he may well have doubted half
consciously, whether he could ever achieve such heights again. Stella had
been his pinnacle, all through his tenacious youth; he had loved her and her
mother with all that he had of love; they had been to him poetry and youth.
A very high nature perhaps might have preserved the echo; but Jack was
more inclined to set his eye upon the hardship of his loss, unflinchingly, as he
would have considered the harm done him by some unscrupulous human
enemy. His attitude was courageous indeed, in a dogged way; but there was
little of hope in it, and it threatened to cramp his future.

Your mother, as I have said, coming into this inheritance, with all its
complications, was bewildered; so many demands were made on her; it was,
in a sense, so easy to be what was expected, with such models before her, but

also it was so hard to be herself. She was but just eighteen, and when she should have been free and tentative, she was required to be definite and exact. It came to pass then that she acted at first as though she had her lesson by heart but did not attach much meaning to it; to George she would be devoted and submissive; to Gerald affectionate; to her father helpful; to us protective. She was more than anyone, I suppose, left desolate by Stella's death, bereft of happy intercourse, which had grown daily more intimate, and also she had much responsibility and there was no woman older than herself to share it with her. Strange was her position then; and an affectionate onlooker might well have asked himself anxiously what kind of nature she was able to oppose to it. One glance at her might have reassured him and yet served but to shift his anxiety. She looked so self-contained, and so mature that clearly she would never act foolishly; but also there was so much promise of thought and development in eye and brow, and passionate mouth, that it was certain she would not stay long quiescent. The calm of the moment was as an instinctive shield to cover her wounded senses; but soon they would collect themselves and fall to work upon all these difficult matters so lavishly heaped upon them – and with what result?

She was beautiful, but she had not lived for eighteen years without revealing that she was also strong of brain, agile and determined; she had revealed so much in the nursery, where she would meet Thoby in argument, and press on to the very centre of the matter, whether it were question of art or morality. She was also, on her secret side, sensitive to all beauty of colour and form; but she hid this, because her views did not agree with those current around her, and she feared to give pain. Again, she was as quick to detect insincerity of nature as fallacy of argument, and the one fared as ill with her as the other; for her standard was rigid. But then she was bound to certain people by a kind of instinctive fidelity, which admitted of no question; it was, if anything, too instinctive. Such was the feeling she had for Jack before his marriage, and it was the first thread in her devotion to her mother or to Thoby. If her mother had lived it is easy to imagine how Vanessa, questing about her, like some active dog, would have tried one experiment after another, arguing, painting, making friends, disproving fallacies, much to her mother's amusement; she would have delighted in her daughter's spirit and adventures, mourned her lack of practical wisdom, and laughed at her failures, and rejoiced in her sense. But that is one of the things, which though they must have happened, yet, incredible though it seems, never did happen, death making an end of all these exquisite preparations. Instead Vanessa was first baffled by her mother's death, and the unnatural life which for a time was entailed upon us, and now again, Stella's death set her among entirely new surroundings.

People who must follow obvious tokens, such as the colour of the eye, the shape of the nose, and love to invent a melodramatic fitness in life, as though it were a sensational novel, acclaimed her now the divinely appointed inheritor of all womanly virtues, and with a certain haziness forgot your grandmother's sharp features and Stella's vague ones, and created a model of them for Vanessa to follow, beautiful on the surface, but fatally insipid within. Once again we went through the same expressions of sympathy; we heard again and again that so great a tragedy had never happened; sometimes it appeared almost in the light of a work of art; more often it revealed a shapeless catastrophe, from which there could be no recovery. But happily it was time for us to leave London; we had taken a house at Painswick; and the ghastly mourners, the relations and friends, went back to their own homes.

But for us the tragedy was but just beginning; as in the case of other wounds the pain was drugged at the moment, and made itself felt afterwards when we began to move. There was pain in all our circumstances, or a dull discomfort, a kind of restlessness and aimlessness which was even worse. Misery of this kind tends to concentrate itself upon an object, if it can find one, and there was a figure, unfortunately, who would serve our purpose very well. Your grandfather showed himself strangely brisk, and so soon as we came to think, we fastened our eyes upon him, and found just cause for anger. We remembered how he had tasked Stella's strength, embittered her few months of joy, and now when he should be penitent, he showed less grief than anyone. On the contrary none was more vigorous, and there were signs at once which woke us to a sort of frenzy, that he was quite prepared to take Vanessa for his next victim. When he was sad, he explained, she should be sad; when he was angry, as he was periodically when she asked him for a cheque, she should weep; instead she stood before him like a stone. A girl who had character would not tolerate such speeches, and when she connected them with other words of the same kind, addressed to the sister lately dead, to her mother even, it was not strange that an uncompromising anger took possession of her. We made him the type of all that we hated in our lives; he was the tyrant of inconceivable selfishness, who had replaced the beauty and merriment of the dead with ugliness and gloom. We were bitter, harsh, and to a great extent, unjust; but even now it seems to me that there was some truth in our complaint; and sufficient reason why both parties should be unable at the time and without fault, to come to a good understanding. If he had been ten years younger, or we older, or had there been a mother or sister to intervene, much pain and anger and loneliness might have been spared. But again, death spoilt what should have been so fair.

There was also another cause to fret us and forbid us from judging clearly. Jack who was spending a terrible summer in London came to us regularly on Sunday. He was tired and morose, and it seemed that his only relief was to spend long hours with your mother or with me in a little summer house in the garden; he talked, when he talked, of Stella and the past; there were silences when no words seemed to have meaning; I remember the shape of a small tree which stood in a little hollow in front of us, and how, as I sat holding Jack's hand, I came to conceive this tree as the symbol of sorrow, for it was silent, enduring and without fruit. But now and then Jack would say something bitter though restrained, about your grandfather and his behaviour to Stella, and how her death had not saddened him. That was enough to sharpen all our feelings against him; for we had an enthusiastic wish to help Jack, and in truth he seemed the person who best understood our misery. But although I shared these vigils equally at first with Vanessa she, by degrees, began to have more of Jack's favour and confidence than I did; and directly any such favour is shown it becomes more marked and endures. She was the natural person to be with him, and also, as I have said, she had of old an affection for him, which although immature, was easily the starting point of much quicker and more fervent feelings, and the incentive now was urgent.

Profoundly gloomy as this all was, the intolerable part of it was the feeling of difference of temper and aim revealed day by day, among people who must live together. For Stella had united many things otherwise incompatible. We, (in future this 'we' must stand for your mother and me) walked alone when we could, and discussed the state of the different parties, and how they threatened to meet in conflict over her body. So far they did not more than threaten; but a man, or woman, of the world, George, for example or Kitty Maxse, might already foretell the supreme struggle of the future. Decency at present forbade open speech, but no doubt the suspicion was alive, and made itself felt in an unrest and intensity of feeling on George's part which we saw, but failed as yet to interpret. George indeed had become and was to remain, a very important figure. He had advanced so suddenly into the closest intimacy with us, that it was not strange if in our blindfold state we made rash and credulous judgements about him. He had been once, when we were children, a hero to us; strong and handsome and just; he taught us to hold our bats straight and to tell the truth, and we blushed with delight if he praised. All the world so far as we could tell, applauded him too. Your grandmother showed keen delight in his presence, and, sentimental as children are, we believed that he was like her dead husband, and perhaps we were not wrong. His triumphs over Italian Countesses and watchmakers in the slums, who all revealed to him at once their inmost hearts, were part of our daily legend; and then he would play with us in the back garden, and pretend, for we guessed that it was pretence, that he read our school stories. His affections, his character, his soul, as we understood, were immaculate; and daily achieved that uncomfortable and mysterious victory which virtue, in books, achieves over intellect. Gerald, strange though it may seem, represented intellect in the contest. George was in truth, a stupid, good natured young man, of profuse, voluble affections, which during his mother's lifetime were kept in check. When she died however, some restraint seemed to burst; he showed himself so sad, so affectionate, so boundlessly unselfish in his plans, that the voices of all women cried aloud in his praise, and men were touched by his modest virtues, at the same time that they were puzzled. What was it that made him so different from other men? Stupid he was, and good natured; but such qualities were not simple; they were modified, confused, distorted, exalted, set swimming in a sea of racing emotions until you were completely at a loss to know where you stood. Nature, we may suppose, had supplied him with abundant animal vigour, but she had neglected to set an efficient brain in control of it. The result was that all the impressions which the good priggish boy took in at school and college remained with him when he was a man; they were not extended, but were liable to be expanded into enormous proportions by violent gusts of passion and [he] proved more and more incapable of containing them. Thus, under the name of unselfishness he allowed himself to commit acts which a cleverer man would have called tyrannical; and, profoundly believing in the purity of his love, he behaved little better than a brute. How far he wilfully deceived himself, how far he was capable of understanding, what juggleries went on in that obscure mind, is a problem which we at any rate could never solve. But the combination of something like reason and much unlike anything but irrational instinct was for ever confusing us, deceiving us and leading us alternately to trust and suspect him, until his marriage happily made such speculations but an occasional diversion for the intellect.* But at the moment his position seemed perfectly accountable; he was the simple domestic creature, of deep feeling, who, from native goodness now that his chief joy was gone, was setting himself to do all he could to be mother and sister and brother to us in one. He spent his holiday with us and was always ready to take your grandfather for a walk, to discuss her difficulties with Vanessa, to arrange little plans for our amusement. Who shall say that there was not some real affection in this? some effort to do what he thought right against his will? But who again can distinguish the good from the bad, the feeling from the sentiment, the truth from the pose? We however were simply credulous, and ready to impose our conventional heroic shape upon the tumult of his character. Virtue it seemed was always victorious. Such were the figures that seemed unnaturally brought together in the great whirlpool; and it did not need the eye of a seer to foretell collision, fracture, and at length a sundering of the parts. Where are we today, indeed, who used to stand so close?

* George was married to Lady Margaret Herbert on 10 September 1904.

At the end of the summer Jack pressed us very hard to spend a week at Corby; we were to soothe the first shock of his home-coming, or to know something which we could not know else; for when you examine feelings with the intense microscope that sorrow lends, it is amazing how they stretch, like the finest goldbeater's skin, over immense tracts of substance. And we, poor children that we were, conceived it to be our duty evermore to go searching for these atoms, wherever they might lie sprinkled about the surface, the great mountains and oceans, of the world. It is pitiable to remember the hours we spent in such minute speculations. Either Jack expressed some wish, or we thought we guessed it, and then we must devise the appropriate solace, the tiny, but to us gigantic, inflection this way or that, of the course of events. And so some grain would be saved, or some pin-point closed, and our immense task of piecing together all the torn fragments of his life would progress by the breadth of an atom. Jack himself could not recognize what we were doing for him in its detail; but he certainly had come to realize the mass of our, say rather of Vanessa's, endeavour. He began to take a regular and unthinking satisfaction in being with her, without I suppose, for I was sometimes jealous, perceiving a single one of the multitude of fine adjustments that composed her presence. But that was proof, like a healthy sleep, that the healing process was well begun. We went to Corby and spent there one of the most acutely miserable weeks of our lives; and perhaps something of our misery came from the suspicion that Jack did not see all our efforts, and the outer world was grossly ignorant of them. Now and again I rebelled in the old way against him, but with an instant sense of treason, when I realized with what silence, as of one possessed of incommunicable knowledge, Vanessa met my plaints.*

* Jack Hills was elected to Parliament in 1906. In 1931 he married Mary Grace Ashton.

The Memoir Club Contributions

22 Hyde Park Gate

A S I have said, the drawing room at Hyde Park Gate was divided by
black folding doors picked out with thin lines of raspberry red. We
were still much under the influence of Titian. Mounds of plush, Watts'
portraits, busts shrined in crimson velvet, enriched the gloom of a room
naturally dark and thickly shaded in summer by showers of Virginia
Creeper.

But it is of the folding doors that I wish to speak. How could family life
have been carried on without them? As soon dispense with water-closets or
bathrooms as with folding doors in a family of nine men and women, one of
whom into the bargain was an idiot. Suddenly there would be a crisis – a
servant dismissed, a lover rejected, pass books opened, or poor Mrs Tyndall
who had lately poisoned her husband by mistake come for consolation. On
one side of the door Cousin Adeline, Duchess of Bedford, perhaps would be
on her knees – the Duke had died tragically at Woburn; Mrs Dolmetsch
would be telling how she had found her husband in bed with the parlour-
maid or Lisa Stillman would be sobbing that Walter Headlam had chalked
her nose with a billiard cue – "which", she cried, "is what comes of smoking
a pipe before gentlemen" – and my mother had much ado to persuade her
that life had still to be faced, and the flower of virginity was still unplucked
in spite of a chalk mark on the nose.

Though dark and agitated on one side, the other side of the door,
especially on Sunday afternoons, was cheerful enough. There round the oval
tea table with its pink china shell full of spice buns would be found old
General Beadle, talking of the Indian Mutiny; or Mr Haldane, or Sir
Frederick Pollock – talking of all things under the sun; or old C. B. Clarke,
whose name is given to three excessively rare Himalayan ferns; and
Professor Wolstenholme, capable, if you interrupted him, of spouting two
columns of tea not unmixed with sultanas through his nostrils; after which he
would relapse into a drowsy ursine torpor, the result of eating opium to
which he had been driven by the unkindness of his wife and the untimely
death of his son Oliver who was eaten, somewhere off the coast of
Coromandel, by a shark. These gentlemen came and came again; and they

were often reinforced by Mr Frederick Gibbs, sometime tutor to the Prince of Wales, whose imperturbable common sense and fund of information about the colonies in general and Canada in particular were a perpetual irritation to my father who used to wonder whether a brain fever at college in the year 1863 had not something to do with it. These old gentlemen were generally to be found, eating very slowly, staying very late and making themselves agreeable at Christmas-time with curious presents of Indian silver work, and hand bags made from the skin of the ornithorhynchus – as I seem to remember.

The tea table however was also fertilized by a ravishing stream of female beauty – the three Miss Lushingtons, the three Miss Stillmans, and the three Miss Montgomeries – all triplets, all ravishing, but of the nine the paragon for wit, grace, charm and distinction was undoubtedly the lovely Kitty Lushington – now Mrs Leo Maxse. (Their engagement under the jackmanii in the Love Corner at St Ives was my first introduction to the passion of love.)* At the time I speak of she was in process of disengaging herself from Lord Morpeth, and had, I suspect, to explain her motives to my mother, a martinet in such matters, for first promising to marry a man and then breaking it off. My mother believed that all men required an infinity of care. She laid all the blame, I feel sure, upon Kitty. At any rate I have a picture of her as she issued from the secret side of the folding doors bearing on her delicate pink cheeks two perfectly formed pear-shaped crystal tears. They neither fell nor in the least dimmed the lustre of her eyes. She at once became the life and soul of the tea table – perhaps Leo Maxse was there – perhaps Ronny Norman – perhaps Esmé Howard – perhaps Arthur Studd, for the gentlemen were not all old, or all professors by any means – and when my father groaned beneath his breath but very audibly, "Oh Gibbs, what a bore you are!" it was Kitty whom my mother instantly threw back into the breach. "Kitty wants to tell you how much she loved your lecture", my mother would cry, and Kitty still with the tears on her cheeks would improvise with the utmost gallantry some compliment or opinion which pacified my father who was extremely sensitive to female charm and largely depended upon female praise. Repenting of his irritation he would press poor Gibbs warmly by the hand and beg him to come soon again – which needless to say, poor Gibbs did.

And then there would come dancing into the room rubbing his hands, wrinkling his forehead, the most remarkable figure, as I sometimes think,

* In describing the love between Stella and Jack Hills she wrote: "And it was through that engagement that I had my first vision – so intense, so exciting, so rapturous was it that the word vision applies – my first vision then of love between man and woman." See p. 113.

that our household contained. I have alluded to a grisly relic of another age which we used to disinter from the nursery wardrobe – Herbert Duckworth's wig. (Herbert Duckworth had been a barrister.) Herbert Duckworth's son – George Herbert – was by no means grisly. His hair curled naturally in dark crisp ringlets; he was six foot high; he had been in the Eton Eleven; he was now cramming at Scoones' in the hope of passing the Foreign Office examination. When Miss Willett of Brighton saw him 'throwing off his ulster' in the middle of her drawing room she was moved to write an Ode Comparing George Duckworth to the Hermes of Praxiteles – which Ode my mother kept in her writing table drawer, along with a little Italian medal that George had won for saving a peasant from drowning. Miss Willett was reminded of the Hermes; but if you looked at him closely you noticed that one of his ears was pointed; and the other round; you also noticed that though he had the curls of a God and the ears of a faun he had unmistakably the eyes of a pig. So strange a compound can seldom have existed. And in the days I speak of, God, faun and pig were all in all alive, all in opposition, and in their conflicts producing the most astonishing eruptions.

To begin with the God – well, he was only a plaster cast perhaps of Miss Willett's Hermes, but I cannot deny that the benign figure of George Duckworth teaching his small half-brothers and sisters by the hour on a strip of coco-nut matting to play forward with a perfectly straight bat had something Christlike about it. He was certainly Christian rather than Pagan in his divinity, for it soon became clear that this particular forward stroke to be applied to every ball indifferently, was a symbol of moral rectitude, and that one could neither slog nor bowl a sneak without paltering rather dangerously (as poor Gerald Duckworth used to do) with the ideals of a sportsman and an English gentleman. Then, he would run miles to fetch cushions; he was always shutting doors and opening windows; it was always George who said the tactful thing, and broke bad news, and braved my father's irritation, and read aloud to us when we had the whooping cough, and remembered the birthdays of aunts, and sent turtle soup to the invalids, and attended funerals, and took children to the pantomime – oh yes, whatever else George might be he was certainly a saint.

But then there was the faun. Now this animal was at once sportive and demonstrative and thus often at variance with the self-sacrificing nature of the God. It was quite a common thing to come into the drawing room and find George on his knees with his arms extended, addressing my mother, who might be adding up the weekly books, in tones of fervent adoration. Perhaps he had been staying with the Chamberlains for the week-end. But he lavished caresses, endearments, enquiries and embraces as if, after forty years in the Australian bush, he had at last returned to the home of his youth and found an aged mother still alive to welcome him. Meanwhile we gathered round – the dinner bell had already rung – awkward, but appreciative. Few families, we felt, could exhibit such a scene as this. Tears rushed to his eyes with equal abandonment. For example when he had a tooth out he flung himself into the cook's arms in a paroxysm of weeping. When Judith Blunt refused him he sat at the head of the table sobbing loudly, but continuing to eat. He cried when he was vaccinated. He was fond of sending telegrams which began "My darling mother" and went on to say that he would be dining out. (I copied this style of his, I regret to say, with disastrous results on one celebrated occasion. "She is an angel" I wired, on hearing that Flora Russell had accepted him, and signed my nickname 'Goat'. "She is an aged Goat" was the version that arrived, at Islay, and had something to do, George said, with Flora's reluctance to ally herself with the Stephen family.) But all this exuberance of emotion was felt to be wholly to George's credit. It proved not only how deep and warm his feelings were, but how marvellously he had kept the open heart and simple manners of a child.

But when nature refused him two pointed ears and gave him only one she knew, I think, what she was about. In his wildest paroxysms of emotion, when he bellowed with grief, or danced round the room, leaping like a kid, and flung himself on his knees before the Dowager Lady Carnarvon there was always something quite conscious, a little uneasy about him, as though he were not quite sure of the effect – as though the sprightly faun had somehow been hobbled together with a timid and conventional old sheep.

It is true that he was abnormally stupid. He passed the simplest examinations with incredible difficulty. For years he was crammed by Mr Scoones; and again and again he failed to pass the Foreign Office examination. He had existed all his life upon jobs found for him by his friends. His small brown eyes seemed perpetually to be boring into something too hard for them to penetrate. But when one compares them to the eyes of a pig, one is alluding not merely to their stupidity, or to their greed – George, I have been told, had the reputation of being the greediest young man in London ball-rooms – but to something obstinate and pertinacious in their expression as if the pig were grouting for truffles with his snout and would by sheer persistency succeed in unearthing them. Never shall I forget the pertinacity with which he learnt "Love in the Valley" by heart in order to impress Flora Russell; or the determination with which he mastered the first volume of *Middlemarch* for the same purpose; and how immensely he was relieved when he left the second volume in a train and got my father, whose set was ruined, to declare that in his opinion one volume of *Middlemarch* was enough. Had his obstinacy been directed solely to self-improvement there would have been no call for us to complain. I myself might even have been of use to him. But it gradually became clear that he was muddling out a scheme, a plan of campaign, a system of life – I scarcely know what to call it – and then we had every reason to feel the earth tremble beneath our feet and the heavens darken. For George Duckworth had become after my mother's death, for all practical purposes, the head of the family. My father was deaf, eccentric, absorbed in his work, and entirely shut off from the world. The management of affairs fell upon George. It was usually said that he was father and mother, sister and brother in one – and all the old ladies of Kensington and Belgravia added with one accord that Heaven had blessed those poor Stephen girls beyond belief, and it remained for them to prove that they were worthy of such devotion.

But what was George Duckworth thinking and what was there alarming in the sight of him as he sat in the red leather arm-chair after dinner, mechanically stroking the dachshund Schuster, and lugubriously glancing at the pages of George Eliot? Well, he might be thinking about the crest on the post office notepaper, and how nice it would look picked out in red (he was now Austen Chamberlain's private secretary) or he might be thinking how the Duchess of St Albans had given up using fish knives at dinner; or how Mrs Grenfell had asked him to stay and he had created as he thought a good impression by refusing; at the same time he was revolving in the slow whirlpool of his brain schemes of the utmost thoughtfulness – plans for sending us for treats; for providing us with riding lessons; for finding jobs for some of poor Augusta Croft's innumerable penniless children. But the alarming thing was that he looked not merely muddled and emotional but obstinate. He looked as if he had made up his mind about something and would refuse to budge an inch. At the time it was extremely difficult to say what he had made up his mind to, but after the lapse of many years I think it may be said brutally and baldly, that George had made up his mind to rise in the social scale. He had a curious inborn reverence for the British aristocracy; the beauty of our great aunts had allied us in the middle of the nineteenth century with, I think I am right in saying, two dukes and quite a number of earls and countesses. They naturally showed no particular wish to remember the connection but George did his best to live up to it. His reverence for the symbols of greatness now that he was attached to a Cabinet Minister had fuller scope. His talk was all of ivory buttons that the coachmen of Cabinet Ministers wear in their coats; of having the entrée at Court; of baronies descending in the female line; of countesses secreting the diamonds of Marie Antoinette in black boxes under their beds. His secret dreams as he sat in the red leather chair stroking Schuster were all of marrying a wife with diamonds, and having a coachman with a button, and having the entrée at Court. But the danger was that his dreams were secret even to himself. Had you told him – and I think Vanessa did once – that he was a snob, he would have burst into tears. What he liked, he explained, was to know 'nice people'; Lady Jeune was nice; so were Lady Sligo, Lady Carnarvon and Lady

Leitrim. Poor Mrs Clifford, on the other hand, was not; nor was old Mrs Wolstenholme; of all our old friends, Kitty Maxse, who might have been Lady Morpeth, came nearest to his ideal. It was not a question of birth or wealth; it was – and then if you pressed him further he would seize you in his arms and cry out that he refused to argue with those he loved. "Kiss me, kiss me, you beloved", he would vociferate; and the argument was drowned in kisses. Everything was drowned in kisses. He lived in the thickest emotional haze, and as his passions increased and his desires became more vehement – he lived, Jack Hills assured me, in complete chastity until his marriage – one felt like an unfortunate minnow shut up in the same tank with an unwieldy and turbulent whale.

Nothing stood in the way of his advancement. He was a bachelor of prepossessing appearance though inclined to fat, aged about thirty years, with an independent income of something over a thousand a year. As private secretary to Austen Chamberlain he was as a matter of course invited to all the great parties of all the great peers. Hostesses had no time to remember, if they had ever known, that the Duckworths had made their money in cotton, or coal, not a hundred years ago, and did not really rank, as George made out, among the ancient families of Somersetshire. For I have it on the best authority that when the original Duckworth acquired Orchardleigh about the year 1810 he filled it with casts from the Greek to which he had attached not merely fig leaves for the Gods but aprons for the Goddesses – much to the amusement of the Lords of Longleat who never forgot that old Duckworth had sold cotton by the yard and probably bought his aprons cheap. George, as I say, could have mounted alone to the highest pinnacles of London society. His mantelpiece was a gallery of invitation cards from every house in London. Why then did he insist upon cumbering himself with a couple of half-sisters who were more than likely to drag him down? It is probably useless to enquire. George's mind swam and steamed like a cauldron of rich Irish stew. He believed that aristocratic society was possessed of all the virtues and all the graces. He believed that his family had been entrusted to his care. He believed that it was his sacred duty – but when he reached that point his emotions overcame him; he began to sob; he flung himself on his knees; he seized Vanessa in his arms; he implored her in the name of her mother, of her grandmother, by all that was sacred in the female sex and holy in the traditions of our family to accept Lady Arthur Russell's invitation to dinner, to spend the week-end with the Chamberlains at Highbury.

I cannot conceal my own opinion that Vanessa was to blame; not indeed that she could help herself, but if, I sometimes think, she had been born with one shoulder higher than another, with a limp, with a squint, with a large mole on her left cheek, both our lives would have been changed for the better. As it was, George had a good deal of reason on his side. It was plain that Vanessa in her white satin dress made by Mrs Young, wearing a single flawless amethyst round her neck, and a blue enamel butterfly in her hair – the gifts, of course, of George himself – beautiful, motherless, aged only eighteen, was a touching spectacle, an ornament for any dinner table, a potential peeress, anything might be made of such precious material as she was – outwardly at least; and to be seen hovering round her, providing her with jewels, and Arab horses, and expensive clothes, whispering encouragement, lavishing embraces which were not entirely concealed from the eyes of strangers, redounded to the credit of George himself and invested his figure with a pathos which it would not otherwise have had in the eyes of the dowagers of Mayfair. Unfortunately, what was inside Vanessa did not altogether correspond with what was outside. Underneath the necklaces and the enamel butterflies was one passionate desire – for paint and turpentine, for turpentine and paint. But poor George was no psychologist. His perceptions were obtuse. He never saw within. He was completely at a loss when Vanessa said she did not wish to stay with the Chamberlains at Highbury; and would not dine with Lady Arthur Russell – a rude, tyrannical old woman, with a bloodstained complexion and the manners of a turkey cock. He argued, he wept, he complained to Aunt Mary Fisher, who said that she could not believe her ears. Every battery was turned upon Vanessa. She was told that she was selfish, unwomanly, callous and incredibly ungrateful considering the treasures of affection that had been lavished upon her – the Arab horse she rode and the slabs of bright blue enamel which she wore.* Still she persisted. She did not wish to dine with Lady Arthur Russell. As the season wore on, every morning brought its card of invitation for Mr Duckworth and Miss Stephen; and every evening witnessed a battle between them. For the first year or so George, I suppose, was usually the victor. Off they went, in the hansom cab of those days and late at night Vanessa would come into my room complaining that she had been dragged from party to party, where she knew no one, and had been bored to death by the civilities of young men from the Foreign Office and the condescensions of old ladies of title. The more Vanessa resisted, the more George's natural obstinacy persisted. At last there was a crisis. Lady Arthur Russell was giving a series of select parties on Thursday evenings in South Audley Street. Vanessa had sat through one entire evening without opening her lips. George insisted that she must go next week and make amends, or he said, "Lady Arthur will never ask you to her house again." They argued until it was getting too late to dress. At last Vanessa, more in desperation than in concession, rushed

---

* The A.15 revision of A.14, pp. 1-11, ends in the middle of this sentence. From this point the text follows the less revised A.14 ts. See Editor's Note, p. 171.

upstairs, flung on her clothes and announced that she was ready to go. Off they went. What happened in the cab will never be known. But whenever they reached 2 South Audley Street – and they reached it several times in the course of the evening – one or the other was incapable of getting out. George refused to enter with Vanessa in such a passion; and Vanessa refused to enter with George in tears. So the cabman had to be told to drive once more round the Park. Whether they ever managed to alight I do not know.

But next morning as I was sitting spelling out my Greek George came into my room carrying in his hand a small velvet box. He presented me with the jewel it contained – a Jews' harp made of enamel with a pinkish blob of matter swinging in the centre which I regret to say only fetched a few shillings when I sold it the other day. But his face showed that he had come upon a different errand. His face was sallow and scored with innumerable wrinkles, for his skin was as loose and flexible as a pug dog's, and he would express his anguish in the most poignant manner by puckering lines, folds, and creases from forehead to chin. His manner was stern. His bearing rigid. If Miss Willett of Brighton could have seen him then she would certainly have compared him to Christ on the cross. After giving me the Jews' harp he stood before the fire in complete silence. Then, as I expected, he began to tell me his version of the preceding night – wrinkling his forehead more than ever, but speaking with a restraint that was at once bitter and manly. Never, never again, he said, would he ask Vanessa to go out with him. He had seen a look in her eyes which positively frightened him. It should never be said of him that he made her do what she did not wish to do. Here he quivered, but checked himself. Then he went on to say that he had only done what he knew my mother would have wished him to do. His two sisters were the most precious things that remained to him. His home had always meant more to him – more than he could say, and here he became agitated, struggled for composure, and then burst into a statement which was at once dark and extremely lurid. We were driving Gerald from the house, he cried – when a young man was not happy at home – he himself had always been content – but if his sisters – if Vanessa refused to go out with him – if he could not bring his friends to the house – in short, it was clear that the chaste, the immaculate George Duckworth would be forced into the arms of whores. Needless to say he did not put it like that; and I could only conjure up in my virgin consciousness, dimly irradiated by having read the "Symposium" with Miss Case, horrible visions of the vices to which young men were driven whose sisters did not make them happy at home. So we went on talking for an hour or two. The end of it was that he begged me, and I agreed, to go a few nights later to the Dowager Marchioness of Sligo's ball. I had already been to May Week at Cambridge, and my recollections of gallopading round the room with Hawtrey, or sitting on the stairs and quizzing the dancers with Clive,* were such as to make me wonder why Vanessa found dances in London so utterly detestable. A few nights later I discovered for myself. After two hours of standing about in Lady Sligo's ball-room, of waiting to be introduced to strange young men, of dancing a round with Conrad Russell or with Esmé Howard, of dancing very badly, of being left without a partner, of being told by George that I looked lovely but must hold myself upright, I retired to an ante-room and hoped that a curtain concealed me. For some time it did. At length old Lady Sligo discovered me, judged the situation for herself and being a kind old peeress with a face like a rubicund sow's carried me off to the dining room, cut me a large slice of iced cake, and left me to devour it by myself in a corner.

On that occasion George was lenient. We left about two o'clock, and on the way home he praised me warmly, and assured me that I only needed practice to be a great social success. A few days later he told me that the Dowager Countess of Carnarvon particularly wished to make my acquaintance, and had invited me to dinner. As we drove across the Park he stroked my hand, and told me how he hoped that I should make friends with Elsie – for so both he and Vanessa had called her for some time at her own request – how I must not be frightened – how though she had been vice-reine of Canada and vice-reine of Ireland she was simplicity itself – always since the death of her husband dressed in black – refused to wear any of her jewels though she had inherited the diamonds of Marie Antoinette – and was the one woman, he said, with a man's sense of honour. The portrait he drew was of great distinction and bereavement. There would also be present her sister, Mrs Popham of Littlecote, a lady also of distinction and also bereaved, for her husband, Dick Popham of Littlecote, came of an ancient unhappy race, cursed in the reign of Henry the Eighth, since which time the property had never descended from father to son. Sure enough Mary Popham was childless, and Dick Popham was in a lunatic asylum. I felt that I was approaching the house of grandeur and desolation, and was not a little impressed. But I could see nothing alarming either in Elsie Carnarvon or in Mrs Popham of Littlecote. They were a couple of spare prim little women, soberly dressed in high black dresses, with grey hair strained off their foreheads, rather prominent blue eyes, and slightly protruding front teeth. We sat down to dinner.

The conversation was mild and kindly. Indeed I soon felt that I could not only reply to their questions – was I fond of painting? – was I fond of reading? – did I help my father in his work? – but could initiate remarks of

* Ralph Hawtrey and Clive Bell.

my own. George had always complained of Vanessa's silence. I would prove that I could talk. So off I started. Heaven knows what devil prompted me – or why to Lady Carnarvon and Mrs Popham of Littlecote of all people in the world I, a chit of eighteen, should have chosen to discourse upon the need of expressing the emotions! That, I said, was the great lack of modern life. The ancients, I said, discussed everything in common. Had Lady Carnarvon ever read the dialogues of Plato? "We – both men and women—" once launched it was difficult to stop, nor was I sure that my audacity was not holding them spell-bound with admiration. I felt that I was earning George's gratitude for ever. Suddenly a twitch, a shiver, a convulsion of amazing expressiveness, shook the Countess by my side; her diamonds, of which she wore a chaste selection, flashed in my eyes; and stopping, I saw George Duckworth blushing crimson on the other side of the table. I realised that I had committed some unspeakable impropriety. Lady Carnarvon and Mrs Popham began at once to talk of something entirely different; and directly dinner was over George, pretending to help me on with my cloak, whispered in my ear in a voice of agony, "They're not used to young women saying anything—." And then as if to apologize to Lady Carnarvon for my ill breeding, I saw him withdraw with her behind a pillar in the hall, and though Mrs Popham of Littlecote tried to attract my attention to a fine specimen of Moorish metal work which hung on the wall, we both distinctly heard them kiss. But the evening was not over. Lady Carnarvon had taken tickets for the French actors, who were then appearing in some play whose name I have forgotten. We had stalls of course, and filed soberly to our places in the very centre of the crowded theatre. The curtain went up. Snubbed, shy, indignant, and uncomfortable, I paid little attention to the play. But after a time I noticed that Lady Carnarvon on one side of me, and Mrs Popham on the other, were both agitated by the same sort of convulsive twitching which had taken them at dinner. What could be the matter? They were positively squirming in their seats. I looked at the stage. The hero and heroine were pouring forth a flood of voluble French which I could not disentangle. Then they stopped. To my great astonishment the lady leapt over the back of a sofa; the gentleman followed her. Round and round the stage they dashed, the lady shrieking, the man groaning and grunting in pursuit. It was a fine piece of realistic acting. As the pursuit continued, the ladies beside me held to the arms of their stalls with claws of iron. Suddenly, the actress dropped exhausted upon the sofa, and the man with a howl of gratification, loosening his clothes quite visibly, leapt on top of her. The curtain fell. Lady Carnarvon, Mrs Popham of Littlecote and George Duckworth rose simultaneously. Not a word was said. Out we filed. And as our procession made its way down the stalls I saw Arthur Cane leap up in his seat like a jack-in-the-box, amazed and considerably amused that George Duckworth and Lady Carnarvon of all people should have taken a girl of eighteen to see the French actors copulate upon the stage.

The brougham was waiting, and Mrs Popham of Littlecote, without speaking a word or even looking at me, immediately secreted herself inside it. Nor could Lady Carnarvon bring herself to face me. She took my hand, and said in a tremulous voice – her elderly cheeks were flushed with emotion – "I do hope, Miss Stephen, that the evening has not tired you very much." Then she stepped into the carriage, and the two bereaved ladies returned to Bruton Street. George meanwhile had secured a cab. He was much confused, and yet very angry. I could see that my remarks at dinner upon the dialogues of Plato rankled bitterly in his mind. And he told the cabman to go, not back to Hyde Park Gate as I hoped, but on to Melbury Road.

"It's quite early still", he said in his most huffy manner as he sat down. "And I think you want a little practice in how to behave to strangers.* It's not your fault of course, but you have been out much less than most girls of your age." So it appeared that my education was to be continued, and that I was about to have another lesson in the art of behaviour at the house of Mrs Holman Hunt. She was giving a large evening party. Melbury Road was lined with hansoms, four-wheelers, hired flies, and an occasional carriage drawn by a couple of respectable family horses. "A very *dritte* crowd", said George disdainfully as we took our place in the queue. Indeed all our old family friends were gathered together in the Moorish Hall,† and directly I came in I recognised the Stillmans, the Lushingtons, the Montgomeries, the Morrises, the Burne-Joneses – Mr Gibbs, Professor Wolstenholme and General Beadle would certainly have been there too had they not all been sleeping for many years beneath the sod. The effect of the Moorish Hall, after Bruton Street, was garish, a little eccentric, and certainly very dowdy. The ladies were intense and untidy; the gentlemen had fine foreheads and short evening trousers, in some cases revealing a pair of bright red Pre-Raphaelite socks. George stepped among them like a Prince in disguise. I soon attached myself to a little covey of Kensington ladies who were being conveyed by Gladys Holman Hunt across the Moorish Hall to the studio. There we found old Holman Hunt himself dressed in a long Jaeger dressing gown, holding forth to a large gathering about the ideas which had inspired him in painting "The Light of the World", a copy of which stood upon an easel. He sipped cocoa and stroked his flowing beard as he talked, and we sipped cocoa and

* There are three to four short illegible words written above 'how to behave' which is itself an interlinear correction; 'in' is a doubtful reading.

† VW appears to have confused the Moorish Hall in nearby Leighton House with the Moorish decorations in Hunt's house. For a description of the latter, see *My Grandmothers and I* (London, 1960) by Diana Holman-Hunt.

shifted our shawls – for the room was chilly – as we listened. Occasionally some of us strayed off to examine with reverent murmurs other bright pictures upon other easels, but the tone of the assembly was devout, high-minded, and to me after the tremendous experiences of the evening, soothingly and almost childishly simple. George was never lacking in respect for old men of recognised genius, and he now advanced with his opera hat pressed beneath his arm; drew his feet together, and made a profound bow over Holman Hunt's hand. Holman Hunt had no notion who he was, or indeed who any of us were; but went on sipping his cocoa, stroking his beard, and explaining what ideas had inspired him in painting "The Light of the World", until we left.

At last – at last – the evening was over.

I went up to my room, took off my beautiful white satin dress, and unfastened the three pink carnations which had been pinned to my breast by the Jews' harp. Was it really possible that tomorrow I should open my Greek dictionary and go on spelling out the dialogues of Plato with Miss Case? I felt I knew much more about the dialogues of Plato than Miss Case could ever do. I felt old and experienced and disillusioned and angry, amused and excited, full of mystery, alarm and bewilderment. In a confused whirlpool of sensation I stood slipping off my petticoats, withdrew my long white gloves, and hung my white silk stockings over the back of a chair. Many different things were whirling round in my mind – diamonds and countesses, copulations, the dialogues of Plato, Mad Dick Popham and "The Light of the World". Ah, how pleasant it would be to stretch out in bed, fall asleep and forget them all!

Sleep had almost come to me. The room was dark. The house silent. Then, creaking stealthily, the door opened; treading gingerly, someone entered. "Who?" I cried. "Don't be frightened", George whispered. "And don't turn on the light, oh beloved. Beloved—" and he flung himself on my bed, and took me in his arms.

Yes, the old ladies of Kensington and Belgravia never knew that George Duckworth was not only father and mother, brother and sister to those poor Stephen girls; he was their lover also.

Old Bloomsbury

AT Molly's command I have had to write a memoir of Old Bloomsbury — of Bloomsbury from 1904 to 1914.* Naturally I see Bloomsbury only from my own angle – not from yours. For this I must ask you to make allowances. From my angle then, one approaches Bloomsbury through Hyde Park Gate – that little irregular cul-de-sac which lies next to Queen's Gate and opposite to Kensington Gardens. And we must look for a moment at that very tall house on the left hand side near the bottom which begins by being stucco and ends by being red brick; which is so high and yet – as I can say now that we have sold it – so rickety that it seems as if a very high wind would topple it over.

I was undressing at the top of that house when my last memoir ended, in my bedroom at the back. My white satin dress was on the floor. The faint smell of kid gloves was in the air. My necklace of seed-pearls was tangled with hairpins on the dressing table. I had just come back from a party – from a series of parties indeed, for it was a memorable night in the height of the season of 1903. I had dined with Lady Carnarvon in Bruton Street; I had seen George undoubtedly kiss her among the pillars in the hall; I had talked much too much – about my emotions on hearing music – at dinner; Lady Carnarvon, Mrs Popham, George and myself had then gone to the most indecent French play I have ever seen. We had risen like a flock of partridges at the end of the first act. Mrs Popham's withered cheeks had burnt crimson. Elsie's grey locks had streamed in the wind. We had parted, with great embarrassment on their side, on the pavement, and Elsie had said she did hope I wasn't tired – which meant, I felt, she hoped I wouldn't lose my virginity or something like that. And then we had gone on – George and I in a hansom together to another party, for George said, to my intense shame, I had talked much too much and I must really learn how to behave – we had gone on to the Holman Hunts, where "The Light of the World" had just come back from its mission to the chief cities of the British Empire, and Mr Edward Clifford, Mrs Russell Barrington, Mrs Freshfield and I know not what distinguished old gentlemen with black ribbons attached to their

* Molly MacCarthy, wife of Desmond, was an original member of the Memoir Club and secretary when this paper was presented.

43

eyeglasses and elderly ladies with curious vertebrae showing through their real but rather ragged old lace had talked in hushed voices of the master's art while the master himself sat in a skull cap drinking, in spite of the June night, hot cocoa from a mug.

It was long past midnight that I got into bed and sat reading a page or two of *Marius the Epicurean* for which I had then a passion. There would be a tap at the door; the light would be turned out and George would fling himself on my bed, cuddling and kissing and otherwise embracing me in order, as he told Dr Savage later, to comfort me for the fatal illness of my father – who was dying three or four storeys lower down of cancer.

But it is the house that I would ask you to imagine for a moment for, though Hyde Park Gate seems now so distant from Bloomsbury, its shadow falls across it. 46 Gordon Square could never have meant what it did had not 22 Hyde Park Gate preceded it. It was a house of innumerable small oddly shaped rooms built to accommodate not one family but three. For besides the three Duckworths and the four Stephens there was also Thackeray's grand-daughter, a vacant-eyed girl whose idiocy was becoming daily more obvious, who could hardly read, who would throw the scissors into the fire, who was tongue-tied and stammered and yet had to appear at table with the rest of us.* To house the lot of us, now a storey would be thrown out on top, now a dining room flung out at bottom. My mother, I believe, sketched what she wanted on a sheet of notepaper to save the architect's fees. These three families had poured all their possessions into this one house. One never knew when one rummaged in the many dark cupboards and wardrobes whether one would disinter Herbert Duckworth's barrister's wig, my father's clergyman's collar, or a sheet scribbled over with drawings by Thackeray which we afterwards sold to Pierpont Morgan for a considerable sum.† Old letters filled dozens of black tin boxes. One opened them and got a terrific whiff of the past. There were chests of heavy family plate. There were hoards of china and glass. Eleven people aged between eight and sixty lived there, and were waited upon by seven servants, while various old women and lame men did odd jobs with rakes and pails by day.

The house was dark because the street was so narrow that one could see Mrs Redgrave washing her neck in her bedroom across the way; also because

* Laura Stephen (see footnote on p. 6). She died, at seventy-four, in The Priory, Roehampton, in February 1945. See Lee, p. 102, and p. 780, note 32.

† In a letter to Violet Dickinson (22 July 1906), Virginia writes, "Thoby made £1000. *one thousand pounds* by selling 10 pages of Thackeray's Lord Bateman. George sold it to Pierpont Morgan." (*Letters*, I, No. 279.)

my mother who had been brought up in the Watts-Venetian-Little Holland House tradition had covered the furniture in red velvet and painted the woodwork black with thin gold lines upon it. The house was also completely quiet. Save for an occasional hansom or butcher's cart nothing ever passed the door. One heard footsteps tapping down the street before we saw a top hat or a bonnet; one almost always knew who it was that passed; it might be Sir Arthur Clay; the Muir-MacKenzies or the white-nosed Miss or the red-nosed Mrs Redgrave. Here then seventeen or eighteen people lived in small bedrooms with one bathroom and three water-closets between them. Here the four of us were born; here my grandmother died; here my mother died; here my father died; here Stella became engaged to Jack Hills* and two doors further down the street after three months of marriage she died too. When I look back upon that house it seems to me so crowded with scenes of family life, grotesque, comic and tragic; with the violent emotions of youth, revolt, despair, intoxicating happiness, immense boredom, with parties of the famous and the dull; with rages again, George and Gerald; with love scenes with Jack Hills; with passionate affection for my father alternating with passionate hatred of him, all tingling and vibrating in an atmosphere of youthful bewilderment and curiosity – that I feel suffocated by the recollection. The place seemed tangled and matted with emotion. I could write the history of every mark and scratch in my room, I wrote later. The walls and the rooms had in sober truth been built to our shape. We had permeated the whole vast fabric – it has since been made into an hotel – with our family history. It seemed as if the house and the family which had lived in it, thrown† together as they were by so many deaths, so many emotions, so many traditions, must endure for ever. And then suddenly in one night both vanished.

When I recovered from the illness which was not unnaturally the result of all these emotions and complications, 22 Hyde Park Gate no longer existed.‡ While I had lain in bed at the Dickinsons' house at Welwyn thinking that the birds were singing Greek choruses and that King Edward was using the foulest possible language among Ozzie Dickinson's azaleas, Vanessa had wound up Hyde Park Gate once and for all. She had sold; she had burnt; she

---

* Stella and Jack became engaged at Hindhead, but Stella lived at Hyde Park Gate during the engagement.

† 'thrown' is a doubtful reading.

‡ This was Virginia's second serious breakdown, which began in May 1904. She spent almost three months at Burnham Wood, Welwyn, where she made an attempt at suicide. She was cared for by Violet Dickinson, a family friend of the Duckworths, particularly of Stella's, who, since 1902, had been Virginia's most intimate friend. Ozzie is Violet's brother.

had sorted; she had torn up. Sometimes I believe she had actually to get men with hammers to batter down – so wedged into each other had the walls and the cabinets become. But now all the rooms stood empty. Furniture vans had carted off all the different belongings.* For not only had the furniture been dispersed. The family which had seemed equally wedged together had broken apart too. George had married Lady Margaret. Gerald had taken a bachelor flat in Berkeley Street. Laura had been finally incarcerated with a doctor in an asylum; Jack Hills had entered on a political career. The four of us were therefore left alone. And Vanessa – looking at a map of London and seeing how far apart they were – had decided that we should leave Kensington and start life afresh in Bloomsbury.

It was thus that 46 Gordon Square came into existence. When one sees it today, Gordon Square is not one of the most romantic of the Bloomsbury squares. It has neither the distinction of Fitzroy Square nor the majesty of Mecklenburgh Square. It is prosperous middle class and thoroughly mid-Victorian. But I can assure you that in October 1904 it was the most beautiful, the most exciting, the most romantic place in the world. To begin with it was astonishing to stand at the drawing room window and look into all those trees; the tree which shoots its branches up into the air and lets them fall in a shower; the tree which glistens after rain like the body of a seal – instead of looking at old Mrs Redgrave washing her neck across the way. The light and the air after the rich red gloom of Hyde Park Gate were a revelation. Things one had never seen in the darkness there – Watts pictures, Dutch cabinets, blue china – shone out for the first time in the drawing room at Gordon Square. After the muffled silence of Hyde Park Gate the roar of traffic was positively alarming. Old characters, sinister, strange, prowled and slunk past our windows. But what was even more exhilarating was the extraordinary increase of space. At Hyde Park Gate one had only a bedroom in which to read or see one's friends. Here Vanessa and I each had a sitting room; there was the large double drawing room; and a study on the ground floor. To make it all newer and fresher, the house had been completely done up. Needless to say the Watts-Venetian tradition of red plush and black paint had been reversed; we had entered the Sargent-Furse era; white and green chintzes were everywhere; and instead of Morris wall-papers with their intricate patterns we decorated our walls with washes of plain distemper. We were full of experiments and reforms. We were going to do without table napkins, we were to have [large supplies of] Bromo instead; we were going to paint; to write; to have coffee after dinner instead of tea at nine

* In this sentence and the following the additions in the ms, in both pen and pencil, are confusing and incomplete and therefore have not been included.

o'clock. Everything was going to be new; everything was going to be different. Everything was on trial.

We were, it appears, extremely social. For some months in the winter of 1904–05 I kept a diary from which I find that we were for ever lunching and dining out and loitering about the book shops – "Bloomsbury is ever so much more interesting than Kensington", I wrote – or going to a concert or visiting a picture gallery and coming home to find the drawing room full of the oddest collections of people. "Cousin Henry Prinsep, Miss Millais, Ozzie Dickinson and Victor Marshall all came this afternoon and stayed late, so that we had only just time to rush off to a Mr Rutter's lecture on Impressionism at the Grafton Gallery . . . Lady Hylton, V. Dickinson and E. Coltman came to tea. We lunched with the Shaw Stewarts and met an art critic called Nicholls. Sir Hugh seemed nice but there isn't much in him . . . I lunched with the Protheroes and met the Bertrand Russells. It was very amusing. Thoby and I dined with the Cecils and went on to the St Loe Stracheys where we knew a great many people . . . I called for Nessa and Thoby at Mrs Flower's and we went on to a dance at the Hobhouses'. Nessa was in a state of great misery today waiting for Mr Tonks who came at one to criticise her pictures. He is a man with a cold bony face, prominent eyes and a look of serenity and boredom. Meg Booth and Sir Fred Pollock came to tea . . ." So it goes on; but among all these short records of parties, of how the chintzes came home and how we went to the Zoo and how we went to *Peter Pan*, there are a few entries which bear on Bloomsbury. On Thursday March 2nd 1905 Violet Dickinson brought a clergyman's wife to tea and Sydney-Turner and Strachey came after dinner and we talked till twelve. On Wednesday the 8th of March: "Margaret* sent round her new motor car this afternoon and we took Violet to pay a series of calls, but we, of course, forgot our cards. Then I went on to the Waterloo Road and lectured (a class of working men and women) on the Greek Myths.† Home and found Bell, and we talked about the nature of good till almost one!"

On the 16th [of] March Miss Power and Miss Malone dined with us. Sydney-Turner and Gerald came in after dinner – the first of our Thursday evenings. On the 23rd [of] March nine people came to our evening and stayed till one.

A few days later I went to Spain, and the duty which I laid on myself of recording every sight and sound, every wave and hill, sickened me with diary writing so that I stopped – with this last entry: May the 11th –

---

* Lady Margaret Duckworth.

† Virginia lectured at Morley College, which was then located in the Waterloo Road, from 1905 to the end of 1907.

"Our evening: gay Bell, D. MacCarthy and Gerald – who shocked the cultured."

So my diary ends just as it might have become interesting. Yet I think it is clear even in this brief record in which every sort of doing is piled up higgledy-piggledy that these few meetings of Bloomsbury in its infancy differed from the rest. These are the only occasions when I do not merely say I had met so and so and thought him long-faced like Reginald Smith or pompous like Moorsom, or quite easy to get on with, but nothing much in him, like Sir Hugh Shaw Stewart. I say we talked to Strachey and Sydney-Turner. I add with a note of exclamation that we talked with Bell about the nature of good till one! And I did not use notes of exclamation often – and once more indeed – when I say that I smoked a cigarette with Beatrice Thynne!*

These Thursday evening parties were, as far as I am concerned, the germ from which sprang all that has since come to be called – in newspapers, in novels, in Germany, in France – even, I daresay, in Turkey and Timbuktu – by the name of Bloomsbury. They deserve to be recorded and described. Yet how difficult – how impossible. Talk – even the talk which had such tremendous results upon the lives and characters of the two Miss Stephens – even talk of this interest and importance is as elusive as smoke. It flies up the chimney and is gone.

In the first place it is not true to say that when the door opened and with a curious hesitation and self-effacement Turner† or Strachey glided in – that they were complete strangers to us. We had met them – and Bell, Woolf, Hilton Young‡ and others in Cambridge at May Week before my father died. But what was of much greater importance, we had heard of them from Thoby. Thoby possessed a great power of romanticizing his friends. Even when he was a little boy at a private school there was always some astonishing fellow, whose amazing character and exploits he would describe hour after hour when he came home for the holidays. These stories had the greatest fascination for me. I thought about Pilkington or Sidney Irwin or the Woolly Bear whom I never saw in the flesh as if they were characters in Shakespeare. I made up stories about them myself. It was a kind of saga that went on year after year. And now just as I had heard of Radcliffe, Stuart, or whoever it might be, I began to hear of Bell, Strachey, Turner, Woolf. We

---

* The first half of the next page in the ts was deleted by VW; some of the material appears elsewhere. This deletion together with the irregular pagination points to the existence of another, possibly incomplete, version of the present text.

† Saxon Sydney-Turner.

‡ Edward Hilton Young was President of the Union of Cambridge, a future politician, who is supposed to have proposed marriage to Virginia in 1909.

talked of them by the hour, rambling about the country or sitting over the fire in my bedroom.

"There's an astonishing fellow called Bell", Thoby would begin directly he came back. "He's a sort of mixture between Shelley and a sporting country squire."

At this of course I pricked up my ears and began to ask endless questions. We were walking over a moor somewhere, I remember. I got a fantastic impression that this man Bell was a kind of Sun God – with straw in his hair. He was an [illegible] of innocence and enthusiasm. Bell had never opened a book till he came to Cambridge, Thoby said. Then he suddenly discovered Shelley and Keats and went nearly mad with excitement. He did nothing but spout poetry and write poetry. Yet he was a perfect horseman – a gift which Thoby enormously admired – and kept two or three hunters up at Cambridge.

"And is Bell a great poet?" I asked.

No, Thoby wouldn't go so far as to say that; but it was quite on the cards that Strachey was. And so we discussed Strachey – or 'the Strache', as Thoby called him. Strachey at once became as singular, as fascinating as Bell. But it was in quite a different way. 'The Strache' was the essence of culture. In fact I think his culture a little alarmed Thoby. He had French pictures in his rooms. He had a passion for Pope. He was exotic, extreme in every way – Thoby described him – so long, so thin that his thigh was no thicker than Thoby's arm. Once he burst into Thoby's rooms, cried out, "Do you hear the music of the spheres?" and fell in a faint. Once in the midst of a dead silence, he piped up – and Thoby could imitate his voice perfectly – "Let's all write Sonnets to Robertson."* He was a prodigy of wit. Even the tutors and the dons would come and listen to him. "Whatever they give you, Strachey," Dr Jackson had said when Strachey was in for some examination, "it won't be good enough." And then Thoby, leaving me enormously impressed and rather dazed, would switch off to tell me about another astonishing fellow – a man who trembled perpetually all over. He was as eccentric, as remarkable in his way as Bell and Strachey in theirs. He was a Jew. When I asked why he trembled, Thoby somehow made me feel that it was part of his nature – he was so violent, so savage; he so despised the whole human race. "And after all," Thoby said, "it is a pretty feeble affair, isn't it?" Nobody was much good after twenty-five, he said. But most people, I gathered, rather rubbed along, and came to terms with things. Woolf did not and Thoby thought it sublime. One night he dreamt he was throttling a man

---

* A. J. Robertson, a freshman at Trinity at the same time as Bell, Woolf, Strachey, Sydney-Turner and Thoby Stephen.

and he dreamt with such violence that when he woke up he had pulled his own thumb out of joint. I was of course inspired with the deepest interest in that violent trembling misanthropic Jew who had already shaken his fist at civilisation and was about to disappear into the tropics so that we should none of us ever see him again.* And then perhaps the talk got upon Sydney-Turner. According to Thoby, Sydney-Turner was an absolute prodigy of learning. He had the whole of Greek literature by heart. There was practically nothing in any language that was any good that he had not read. He was very silent and thin and odd. He never came out by day. But late at night if he saw one's lamp burning he would come and tap at the window like a moth. At about three in the morning he would begin to talk. His talk was then of astonishing brilliance. When later I complained to Thoby that I had met Turner and had not found him brilliant Thoby severely supposed that by brilliance I meant wit; he on the contrary meant truth. Sydney-Turner was the most brilliant talker he knew because he always spoke the truth.

Naturally then, when the bell rang and these astonishing fellows came in, Vanessa and I were in a twitter of excitement. It was late at night; the room was full of smoke; buns, coffee and whisky were strewn about; we were not wearing white satin or seed-pearls; we were not dressed at all.† Thoby went to open the door; in came Sydney-Turner; in came Bell; in came Strachey.

They came in hesitatingly, self-effacingly, and folded themselves up quietly [in] the corners of sofas. For a long time they said nothing. None of our old conversational openings seemed to do. Vanessa and Thoby and Clive, if Clive were there – for Clive‡ was always ready to sacrifice himself in the cause of talk – would start different subjects. But they were almost always answered in the negative. "No", was the most frequent reply. "No, I haven't seen it"; "No, I haven't been there." Or simply, "I don't know." The conversation languished in a way that would have been impossible in the drawing room at Hyde Park Gate. Yet the silence was difficult, not dull. It seemed as if the standard of what was worth saying had risen so high that it was better not to break it unworthily. We sat and looked at the ground. Then at last Vanessa, having said perhaps that she had been to some picture show, incautiously used the word "beauty". At that, one of the young men would lift his head slowly and say, "It depends what you mean by beauty." At once all our ears were pricked. It was as if the bull had at last been turned into the ring.

* Leonard Woolf was a civil servant in Ceylon from 1904 to 1911.
† Two or three illegible words are written in the margin.
‡ To accommodate the interlinear correction which is set off by dashes it was necessary to delete: (for Clive) 'differed in many ways from the others'.

The bull might be 'beauty', might be 'good', might be 'reality'. Whatever it was, it was some abstract question that now drew out all our forces. Never have I listened so intently to each step and half-step in an argument. Never have I been at such pains to sharpen and launch my own little dart. And then what joy it was when one's contribution was accepted.* No praise has pleased me more than Saxon's saying – and was not Saxon infallible after all? – that he thought I had argued my case very cleverly. And what strange cases those were! I remember trying to persuade Hawtrey† that there is such a thing as atmosphere in literature. Hawtrey challenged me to prove it by pointing out in any book any one word which had this quality apart from its meaning. I went and fetched *Diana of the Crossways*. The argument, whether it was about atmosphere or the nature of truth, was always tossed into the middle of the party. Now Hawtrey would say something; now Vanessa; now Saxon; now Clive; now Thoby. It filled me with wonder to watch those who were finally left in the argument piling stone upon stone, cautiously, accurately, long after it had completely soared above my sight. But if one could not say anything, one could listen. One had glimpses of something miraculous happening high up in the air. Often we would still be sitting in a circle at two or three in the morning. Still Saxon would be taking his pipe from his mouth as if to speak, and putting it back again without having spoken. At last, rumpling his hair back, he would pronounce very shortly some absolutely final summing up. The marvellous edifice was complete, one could stumble off to bed feeling that something very important had happened. It had been proved that beauty was – or beauty was not – for I have never been quite sure which – part of a picture.

From such discussions Vanessa and I got probably much the same pleasure that undergraduates get when they meet friends of their own for the first time. In the world of the Booths and the Maxses we were not asked to use our brains much. Here we used nothing else. And part of the charm of those Thursday evenings was that they were astonishingly abstract. It was not only that Moore's book‡ had set us all discussing philosophy, art, religion; it was that the atmosphere – if in spite of Hawtrey I may use that word – was abstract in the extreme. The young men I have named had no

---

* 'When after a silence, some one said' has been pencilled in above a deleted line of type following 'accepted', leaving the sentence incomplete. It has therefore been deleted.

† Ralph Hawtrey, educated at Trinity College, Cambridge, as a mathematician, was a member of the 'Apostles' at the same time as Woolf, Strachey and Sydney-Turner. He later became well known as an economist.

‡ G. E. Moore's *Principia Ethica* (1903).

'manners' in the Hyde Park Gate sense. They criticised our arguments as severely as their own. They never seemed to notice how we were dressed or if we were nice looking or not. All that tremendous encumbrance of appearance and behaviour which George had piled upon our first years vanished completely. One had no longer to endure that terrible inquisition after a party – and be told, "You looked lovely." Or, "You did look plain." Or, "You must really learn to do your hair." Or, "Do try not to look so bored when you dance." Or, "You did make a conquest", or, "You <u>were</u> a failure." All this seemed to have no meaning or existence in the world of Bell, Strachey, Hawtrey and Sydney-Turner. In that world the only comment as we stretched ourselves after our guests had gone, was, "I must say you made your point rather well"; "I think you were talking rather through your hat." It was an immense simplification. And for my part it went deeper than this. The atmosphere of Hyde Park Gate had been full of love and marriage. George's engagement to Flora Russell, Stella's to Jack Hills, Gerald's innumerable flirtations were all discussed either in private or openly with the greatest interest. Vanessa was already supposed to have attracted Austen Chamberlain. My Aunt Mary Fisher, poking about as usual in nooks and corners, had discovered that there were six drawings of him in Vanessa's sketchbook and [had] come to her own conclusions. George rather suspected that Charles Trevelyan was in love with her. But at Gordon Square love was never mentioned. Love had no existence. So lightly was it treated that for years I believed that Desmond had married an old Miss Cornish, aged about sixty, with snow-white hair. One never took the trouble to find out. It seemed incredible that any of these young men should want to marry us or that we should want to marry them. Secretly I felt that marriage was a very low down affair, but that if one practised it, one practised it – it is a serious confession I know – with young men who had been in the Eton Eleven and dressed for dinner. When I looked round the room at 46 I thought – if you will excuse me for saying so – that I had never seen young men so dingy, so lacking in physical splendour as Thoby's friends. Kitty Maxse who came in once or twice sighed afterwards, "I've no doubt they're very nice, but, oh darling, how awful they do look!" Henry James, on seeing Lytton and Saxon at Rye, exclaimed to Mrs Prothero, "Deplorable! Deplorable! How could Vanessa and Virginia have picked up such friends? How could Leslie's daughters have taken up with young men like that?" But it was precisely this lack of physical splendour, this shabbiness! that was in my eyes a proof of their superiority. More than that, it was, in some obscure way, reassuring; for it meant that things could go on like this, in abstract argument, without dressing for dinner, and never revert to the ways, which I had come to think so distasteful, at Hyde Park Gate.

I was wrong. One afternoon that first summer Vanessa said to Adrian and me and I watched her, stretching her arms above her head with a gesture that was at once reluctant and yielding, in the great looking-glass as she said it – "Of course, I can see that we shall all marry. It's bound to happen" – and as she said it I could feel a horrible necessity impending over us; a fate would descend and snatch us apart just as we had achieved freedom and happiness. She, I felt, was already aware of some claim, some need which I resented and tried to ignore. A few weeks later indeed Clive proposed to her. "Yes," said Thoby grimly when I murmured something to him very shyly about Clive's proposal, "That's the worst of Thursday evenings!" And her marriage in the beginning of 1907 was in fact the end of them. With that, the first chapter of Old Bloomsbury came to an end. It had been very austere, very exciting, of immense importance. A small concentrated world dwelling inside the much larger and looser world of dances and dinners had come into existence. It had already begun to colour that world and still I think colours the much more gregarious Bloomsbury which succeeded it.

But it could not have gone on. Even if Vanessa had not married, even if Thoby had lived,* change was inevitable. We could not have gone on discussing the nature of beauty in the abstract for ever. The young men, as we used to call them, were changing from the general to the particular. They had ceased to be Mr Turner, Mr Strachey, Mr Bell. They had become Saxon, Lytton, Clive. Then too one was beginning to criticise, to distinguish, to compare. Those old flamboyant portraits were being revised. One could see that Walter Lamb whom Thoby had compared to a Greek boy playing a flute in a vineyard was in fact rather bald, and rather dull; one could wish that Saxon could be induced either to go or to say something perhaps that was not strictly true; one could even doubt, when *Euphrosyne* was published, whether as many of the poems in that famous book were sure of immortality as Thoby made out.† But there was something else that made for a change though I at least did not know what it was. Perhaps if I read you a passage from another diary which I kept intermittently for a month or two in the year 1909 you will guess what it was. I am describing a tea-party in James Strachey's rooms at Cambridge.‡

"His rooms," I wrote, "though they are lodgings, are discreet and dim. French pastels hang upon the walls and there are cases of old books. The

* Thoby Stephen died in November 1906 of typhoid fever.

† A volume of poems privately published in 1905 to which Bell, Strachey, Sydney-Turner, Woolf, Walter Lamb and others contributed.

‡ James Strachey was the younger brother of Lytton who became the translator and general editor of the standard English edition of Freud, published by The Hogarth Press.

three young men – Norton,* Brooke and James Strachey – sat in deep chairs; and gazed with soft intent eyes into the fire. Mr Norton knew that he must talk; he and I talked laboriously. The others were silent. I should like to account for this silence, but time presses and I am puzzled. For the truth is that these young men are evidently respectable; they are not only able but their views seem to me honest and simple. They lack all padding; so that one has convictions to disagree with if one disagrees. Yet we had nothing to say to each other and I was conscious that not only my remarks but my presence was criticised. They wished for the truth and doubted if I could speak it or be it. I thought this courageous of them but unsympathetic. I admired the atmosphere – was it more? – and felt in some respects at ease in it. Yet why should intellect and character be so barren? It seems as if the highest efforts of the most intelligent people produce a negative result; one cannot honestly be anything."

There is a great change there from what I should have written two or three years earlier. In part, of course, the change was due to circumstances; I lived alone with Adrian now in Fitzroy Square; and we were the most incompatible of people.† We drove each other perpetually into frenzies of irritation or into the depths of gloom. We still went to a great many parties: but the combination of the two worlds which I think was so [illegible] was far more difficult. I could not reconcile the two. True, we still had Thursday evenings as before. But they were always strained and often ended in dismal failure. Adrian stalked off to his room, I to mine, in complete silence. But there was more in it than that. What it was I was not altogether certain. I knew theoretically, from books, much more than I knew practically from life. I knew that there were buggers in Plato's Greece; I suspected – it was not a question one could just ask Thoby – that there were buggers in Dr Butler's Trinity [College], Cambridge; but it never occurred to me that there were buggers even now in the Stephens' sitting room at Gordon Square. It never struck me that the abstractness, the simplicity which had been so great a relief after Hyde Park Gate were largely due to the fact that the majority of the young men who came there were not attracted by young women. I did not realise that love, far from being a thing they never mentioned, was in fact a thing which they seldom ceased to discuss. Now I had begun to be puzzled. Those long sittings, those long silences, those long arguments – they still went on in Fitzroy Square as they had done in Gordon Square. But now I found them of the most perplexing nature. They still excited me much more

* H. T. J. Norton, a Cambridge mathematician, associated with the inner circle of pre-war Bloomsbury; Rupert Brooke, the poet, who died in 1915.

† Adrian and Virginia moved to 29 Fitzroy Square after Vanessa's marriage to Clive Bell.

than any men I met with in the outer world of dinners and dance – and yet I was, dared I say it or think it even? – intolerably bored. Why, I asked, had we nothing to say to each other? Why were the most gifted of people also the most barren? Why were the most stimulating of friendships also the most deadening? Why was it all so negative? Why did these young men make one feel that one could not honestly be anything? The answer to all my questions was, obviously – as you will have guessed – that there was no physical attraction between us.

The society of buggers has many advantages – if you are a woman. It is simple, it is honest, it makes one feel, as I noted, in some respects at one's ease. But it has this drawback – with buggers one cannot, as nurses say, show off. Something is always suppressed, held down. Yet this showing off, which is not copulating, necessarily, nor altogether being in love, is one of the great delights, one of the chief necessities of life. Only then does all effort cease; one ceases to be honest, one ceases to be clever. One fizzes up into some absurd delightful effervescence of soda water or champagne through which one sees the world tinged with all the colours of the rainbow. It is significant of what I had come to desire that I went straight – on almost the next page of my diary indeed – from the dim and discreet rooms of James Strachey at Cambridge to dine with Lady Ottoline Morrell at Bedford Square.* Her rooms, I noted without drawing any inferences, seemed to me instantly full of "lustre and illusion".

So one changed. But these changes of mine were part of a much bigger change. The headquarters of Bloomsbury have always been in Gordon Square. Now that Vanessa and Clive were married, now that Clive had shocked the Maxses, the Booths, the Cecils, the Protheroes, irretrievably, now that the house was done up once more, now that they were giving little parties with their beautiful brown table linen and their lovely eighteenth-century silver, Bloomsbury rapidly lost the monastic character it had had in Chapter One; the character of Chapter Two was superficially at least to be very different.

Another scene has always lived in my memory – I do not know if I invented it or not – as the best illustration of Bloomsbury Chapter Two. It was a spring evening. Vanessa and I were sitting in the drawing room. The drawing room had greatly changed its character since 1904. The Sargent-

---

* Lady Ottoline Morrell was the daughter of General Arthur Bentinck and Lady Bolsover. She rebelled against her upper class, philistine background and in marrying Philip Morrell, who later became a Liberal member of Parliament, she was able to make an escape. She entertained a wide circle of distinguished people, including many artists and writers, at 44 Bedford Square in London, at Garsington Manor in Oxfordshire and, after the war, at 10 Gower Street in London.

Furse age was over. The age of Augustus John was dawning. His "Pyramus" filled one entire wall. The Watts' portraits of my father and my mother were hung downstairs if they were hung at all. Clive had hidden all the match boxes because their blue and yellow swore with the prevailing colour scheme. At any moment Clive might come in and he and I should begin to argue – amicably, impersonally at first; soon we should be hurling abuse at each other and pacing up and down the room. Vanessa sat silent and did something mysterious with her needle or her scissors. I talked, egotistically, excitedly, about my own affairs no doubt. Suddenly the door opened and the long and sinister figure of Mr Lytton Strachey stood on the threshold. He pointed his finger at a stain on Vanessa's white dress.

"Semen?" he said.

Can one really say it? I thought and we burst out laughing. With that one word all barriers of reticence and reserve went down. A flood of the sacred fluid seemed to overwhelm us. Sex permeated our conversation. The word bugger was never far from our lips. We discussed copulation with the same excitement and openness that we had discussed the nature of good. It is strange to think how reticent, how reserved we had been and for how long. It seems a marvel now that so late as the year 1908 or 9 Clive had blushed and I had blushed too when I asked him to let me pass to go to the lavatory on the French Express. I never dreamt of asking Vanessa to tell me what happened on her wedding night. Thoby and Adrian would have died rather than discuss the love affairs of undergraduates. When all intellectual questions had been debated so freely, sex was ignored. Now a flood of light poured in upon that department too. We had known everything but we had never talked. Now we talked of nothing else. We listened with rapt interest to the love affairs of the buggers. We followed the ups and downs of their chequered histories; Vanessa sympathetically; I – had I not written in 1905, women are so much more amusing than men* – frivolously, laughingly. "Norton tells me", Vanessa would say, "that James is in utter despair. Rupert has been twice to bed with Hobhouse" and I would cap her stories with some equally thrilling piece of gossip; about a divine undergraduate with a head like a Greek God – but alas his teeth were bad – called George Mallory.

All this had the result that the old sentimental views of marriage in which we were brought up were revolutionized. I should be sorry to tell you how old I was before I saw that there is nothing shocking in a man's having a mistress, or in a woman's being one. Perhaps the fidelity of our parents was

---

* The first (deleted) version of the phrase set off by dashes was: 'it is one of the differences between us'. In her diary for 20 January 1905, she wrote: 'Men are not so amusing as women.' *A Passionate Apprentice: The Early Journals of Virginia Woolf*, ed. Mitchell Leaska, The Hogarth Press, 1990, p. 225.

not the only or inevitably the highest form of married life. Perhaps indeed that fidelity was not so strict as one had supposed. "Of course Kitty Maxse has two or three lovers", said Clive – Kitty Maxse, the chaste, the exquisite, the devoted! Again, the whole aspect of life was changed.

So there was now nothing that one could not say, nothing that one could not do, at 46 Gordon Square. It was, I think, a great advance in civilisation. It may be true that the loves of buggers are not – at least if one is of the other persuasion – of enthralling interest or paramount importance. But the fact that they can be mentioned openly leads to the fact that no one minds if they are practised privately. Thus many customs and beliefs were revised. Indeed the future of Bloomsbury was to prove that many variations can be played on the theme of sex, and with such happy results that my father himself might have hesitated before he thundered out the one word which he thought fit to apply to a bugger or an adulterer; which was Blackguard!

Here I come to a question which I must leave to some other memoir writer to discuss – that is to say, if we take it for granted that Bloomsbury exists, what are the qualities that admit one to it, what are the qualities that expel one from it? Now at any rate between 1910 and 1914 many new members were admitted. It must have been in 1910 I suppose that Clive one evening rushed upstairs in a state of the highest excitement. He had just had one of the most interesting conversations of his life. It was with Roger Fry. They had been discussing the theory of art for hours. He thought Roger Fry the most interesting person he had met since Cambridge days. So Roger appeared. He appeared, I seem to think, in a large ulster coat, every pocket of which was stuffed with a book, a paint box or something intriguing; special tips which he had bought from a little man in a back street; he had canvases under his arms; his hair flew; his eyes glowed. He had more knowledge and experience than the rest of us put together. [His mind seemed hooked on to life] by an extraordinary number of attachments. We started talking about *Marie-Claire*.* And at once we were all launched into a terrific argument about literature; adjectives?† associations? overtones? We had down Milton; we re-read Wordsworth. We had to think the whole thing over again. The old skeleton arguments of primitive Bloomsbury about art and beauty put on flesh and blood. There was always some new idea afoot; always some new picture standing on a chair to be looked at, some new poet fished out from obscurity and stood in the light of day. Odd people wandered through 46; Rothenstein, Sickert, Yeats, Tonks – Tonks who could, I suppose, make Vanessa miserable no more. And sometimes

* An autobiographical novel by Marguerite Audoux, a seamstress. It was widely acclaimed when it was published in 1910 in France.

† Three or four illegible words were written in pen above 'adjectives'.

one began to meet a queer faun-like figure, hitching his clothes up, blinking his eyes, stumbling oddly over the long words in his sentences. A year or two before, Adrian and I had been standing in front of a certain gold and black picture in the Louvre when a voice said: "Are you Adrian Stephen? I'm Duncan Grant." Duncan now began to haunt the purlieus of Bloomsbury. How he lived I do not know. He was penniless. Uncle Trevor* indeed said he was mad. He lived in a studio in Fitzroy Square with an old drunken charwoman called Filmer and a clergyman who frightened girls in the street by making faces at them. Duncan was on the best of terms with both. He was rigged out by his friends in clothes which seemed always to be falling to the floor. He borrowed old china from us to paint; and my father's old trousers to go to parties in. He broke the china and he ruined the trousers by jumping into the Cam to rescue a child who was swept into the river by the rope of Walter Lamb's barge, the 'Aholibah'. Our cook Sophie called him "that Mr Grant" and complained that he had been taking things again as if he were a rat in her larder. But she succumbed to his charm. He seemed to be vaguely tossing about in the breeze; but he always alighted exactly where he meant to.

And once at least Morgan flitted through Bloomsbury lodging for a moment in Fitzroy Square on his way even then to catch a train.† He carried, I think, the same black bag with the same brass label on it that is now in the hall outside at this moment. I felt as if a butterfly – by preference a pale blue butterfly – had settled on the sofa; if one raised a finger or made a movement the butterfly would be off. He talked of Italy and the Working Men's College. And I listened – with the deepest curiosity, for he was the only novelist I knew – except Henry James and George Meredith; the only one anyhow who wrote about people like ourselves. But I was too much afraid of raising my hand and making the butterfly fly away to say much. I used to watch him from behind a hedge as he flitted through Gordon Square, erratic, irregular, with his bag, on his way to catch a train.

These, with Maynard – very truculent, I felt, very formidable, like a portrait of Tolstoy as a young man to look at, able to rend any argument that came his way with a blow of his paw, yet concealing, as the novelists say, a kind and even simple heart under that immensely impressive armour of intellect – and Norton; Norton who was the essence of all I meant by Cambridge; so able; so honest; so ugly; so dry; Norton with whom I spent a whole night once talking and with whom I went at dawn to Covent Garden, whom I still see in memory scowling in his pince-nez – yellow and severe

---

* Trevor Grant, uncle of both Duncan Grant and Lytton Strachey.
† E. M. Forster.

against a bank of roses and carnations – these I think were the chief figures in Bloomsbury before the war.

But here again it becomes necessary to ask – where does Bloomsbury end? What is Bloomsbury? Does it for instance include Bedford Square? Before the war, I think we should most of us have said 'Yes'. When the history of Bloomsbury is written – and what better subject could there be for Lytton's next book? – there will have to be a chapter, even if it is only in the appendix, devoted to Ottoline. Her first appearance among us was, I think, in 1908 or 9. I find from my diary that I dined with her on March the 30th 1909 – I think for the first time. But a few weeks before this, she had swooped down upon one of my own Thursday evenings with Philip, Augustus John and Dorelia in tow: she had written the next morning to ask me to give her the names and addresses of all "my wonderful friends". This was followed by an invitation to come to Bedford Square any Thursday about ten o'clock and bring any one I liked. I took Rupert Brooke. Soon we were all swept into that extraordinary whirlpool where such odd sticks and straws were brought momentarily together. There was Augustus John, very sinister in a black stock and a velvet coat; Winston Churchill, very rubicund, all gold lace and medals, on his way to Buckingham Palace; Raymond Asquith crackling with epigrams; Francis Dodd telling me most graphically how he and Aunt Susie* had killed bugs: she held the lamp; he a basin of paraffin; bugs crossed the ceiling in an incessant stream. There was Lord Henry Bentinck at one end of the sofa and perhaps Nina Lamb at the other. There was Philip fresh from the House of Commons humming and hawing on the hearth-rug. There was Gilbert Cannan who was said to be in love with Ottoline. There was Bertie Russell, whom she was said to be in love with. Above all, there was Ottoline herself.

"Lady Ottoline", I wrote in my diary, "is a great lady who has become discontented with her own class and is trying to find what she wants among artists and writers. For this reason, as if they were inspired with something divine, she approaches them in a deferential way and they see her as a disembodied spirit escaping from her world into one where she can never take root. She is remarkable to look at if not beautiful. Like most passive people she is very careful and elaborate in her surroundings. She takes the utmost pains to set off her beauty as though it were some rare object picked up in a dusky Florentine back street. It always seems possible that the rich American women who finger her Persian cloak and call it 'very good' may go on to finger her face and call it a fine work in the late renaissance style; the

---

* Aunt Susie (Isabel Dacre) was a close friend of Francis Dodd, etcher, painter and later Royal Academician.

brow and eyes magnificent, the chin perhaps restored. The pallor of her cheeks, the way she has of drawing back her head and looking at you blankly gives her the appearance of a marble Medusa. She is curiously passive." And then I go on to exclaim rather rhapsodically that the whole place was full of "lustre and illusion".

When indeed one remembers that drawing room full of people, the pale yellows and pinks of the brocades, the Italian chairs, the Persian rugs, the embroideries, the tassels, the scent, the pomegranates, the pugs, the pot-pourri and Ottoline bearing down upon one from afar in her white shawl with the great scarlet flowers on it and sweeping one away out of the large room and the crowd into a little room with her alone, where she plied one with questions that were so intimate and so intense, about life and one's friends, and made one sign one's name in a little scented book – it was only last week that I signed my name in another little scented book in Gower Street – I think my excitement may be excused.*

Indeed lustre and illusion tinged Bloomsbury during those last years before the war. We were not so austere; we were not so exalted. There were quarrels and intrigues. Ottoline may have been a Medusa; but she was not a passive Medusa. She had a great gift for drawing people under. Even Middleton Murry, it is said, was pulled down by her among the vegetables at Garsington. And by this time we were far from drab. Thursday evenings with their silences and their arguments were a thing of the past. Their place was taken by parties of a very different sort. The Post-Impressionist movement had cast – not its shadow – but its bunch of variegated lights upon us. We bought poinsettias made of scarlet plush; we made dresses of the printed cotton that is specially loved by negroes; we dressed ourselves up as Gauguin pictures and careered round Crosby Hall.† Mrs Whitehead was scandalized.‡ She said that Vanessa and I were practically naked. My mother's ghost was invoked once more – by Violet Dickinson – to deplore the fact that I had taken a house in Brunswick Square and had asked young men to share it.§ George Duckworth came all the way from Charles Street to

---

* Presumably Ottoline kept a visitor's book at 10 Gower Street, where the Morrells moved after the war, as she had done at Bedford Square. The paragraph that follows – up to 'The Post-Impressionist movement' – is from the mutilated fragment in the Berg Collection.

† At the Ball to celebrate the end of the Second Post-Impressionist Exhibition (1912).

‡ The wife of Alfred North Whitehead, Cambridge philosopher and mathematician.

§ Virginia shared 38 Brunswick Square with Adrian, Maynard Keynes, Duncan Grant and Leonard Woolf, 1911–12.

beg Vanessa to make me give up the idea and was not comforted perhaps when she replied that after all the Foundling Hospital was handy. Stories began to circulate about parties at which we all undressed in public. Logan Pearsall Smith told Ethel Sands that he knew for a fact that Maynard had copulated with Vanessa on a sofa in the middle of the drawing room. It was a heartless, immoral, cynical society it was said; we were abandoned women and our friends were the most worthless of young men.

Yet in spite of Logan, in spite of Mrs Whitehead, in spite of Vanessa and Maynard and what they did on the sofa at Brunswick Square. Old Bloomsbury still survives. If you seek proof – look around.

Am I a Snob?

Molly* has very unfairly, I think, laid upon me the burden of providing a memoir tonight. We all forgive Molly everything of course because of her insidious, her devastating charm. But it is unfair. It is not my turn; I am not the oldest of you. I am not the most widely lived or the most richly memoried. Maynard, Desmond, Clive and Leonard all live stirring and active lives; all constantly brush up against the great; all constantly affect the course of history one way or another. It is for them to unlock the doors of their treasure-houses and to set before us those gilt and gleaming objects which repose within. Who am I that I should be asked to read a memoir? A mere scribbler; what's worse, a mere dabbler in dreams; one who is not fish, flesh, fowl or good red herring. My memoirs, which are always private, and at their best only about proposals of marriage, seductions by half-brothers, encounters with Ottoline and so on, must soon run dry. Nobody now asks me to marry them; for many years nobody has attempted to seduce me. Prime Ministers never consult me. Twice I have been to Hendon, but each time the aeroplane refused to mount into the air. I have visited most of the capitals of Europe, it is true; I can speak a kind of dog French and mongrel Italian; but so ignorant am I, so badly educated, that if you ask me the simplest question – for instance, where is Guatemala? – I am forced to turn the conversation.

Yet Molly has asked me to write a paper. What can it be about? That is the question I asked myself, and it seemed to me, as I sat brooding, that the time has come when we old fogies – we ignorant and private living old fogies – must face this question – what are our memoirs to be about, if the Memoir Club is to go on meeting, and if half the members are people like myself to whom nothing ever happens? Dare I suggest that the time has come when we must interpret Molly's commands rather liberally, and instead of sweeping the lamp of memory over the adventures and excitement of real life, must turn that beam inwards and describe ourselves?

Am I speaking for myself only when I say that though nothing worth calling an adventure has befallen me since I last occupied this thorny and prominent chair I still seem to myself a subject of inexhaustible and

* MacCarthy. See p. 43n.

fascinating anxiety? – a volcano in perpetual eruption? Am I alone in my egotism when I say that never does the pale light of dawn filter through the blinds of 52 Tavistock Square but I open my eyes and exclaim, "Good God! Here I am again!" – not always with pleasure, often with pain; sometimes with a spasm of acute disgust – but always, always with interest?

Myself then might be the subject of this paper; but there are drawbacks. It would run to so many volumes – that single subject – that those of us who have hair; those whose hair is still capable of growth – would find it tickling their toes before I had done. I must break off one tiny fragment of this vast subject; I must give one brief glance at one small corner of this universe – which still to me seems as trackless and tiger-haunted as that other upon which is written – where I know not – the word Guatemala; I must, I say, choose one aspect only; and ask one question only; and this is it – Am I a snob?

As I try to answer it, I may perhaps turn up a memory or two; I may perhaps revive certain of your own memories; at any rate, I will try to give you facts; and though of course I shall not tell the whole truth, perhaps I shall tell enough to set you guessing. But in order to answer that question, I must begin by asking – what is a snob? And since I have no skill in analysis – since my education was neglected – I shall take the obvious course of trying to find some object against which I can measure myself: with which to compare myself. Desmond, for instance. Naturally I take Desmond first. Is he a snob?

He ought to be. He was educated at Eton, then went to Cambridge. We all know the old tag about grateful science adoring the aristocracy. But whatever Eton and Cambridge did to encourage snobbery in him, nature did far more. She gave him all the gifts that a grateful aristocracy adores in science; a golden tongue; perfect manners; complete self-possession; boundless curiosity, mixed with sympathy; he can also sit a horse and shoot a pheasant at a pinch. As for poverty, since Desmond has never minded how he dresses, no one else has ever given the matter a thought. So here then, undoubtedly, is my pattern; let me compare my case with his.

We were standing, when I thought this, at a window in the drawing room at Tavistock Square. Desmond had lunched with us, we had spent the afternoon talking; suddenly he remembered that he was dining somewhere. But where? "Now where am I dining?" he said and took out his pocket book. Something distracted his attention for a moment, and I looked over his shoulder. Hastily, furtively, I ran my eye over his engagements. Monday Lady Bessborough 8:30. Tuesday Lady Ancaster 8:30. Wednesday Dora Sanger seven sharp. Thursday Lady Salisbury ten o'clock. Friday lunch Wolves and dine Lord Revelstoke. White waistcoat. White waistcoat was twice underlined. Years later I discovered the reason – he was to meet our king, our late lamented George. Well, he glanced at his engagements; shut the book and made off. Not a word did he say about the peerage. He never brought the conversation round to Revelstoke; white waistcoats were unmentioned. "No," I said to myself with a keen pang of disappointment as he shut the door, "Desmond, alas, is not a snob."

I must seek another pattern. Take Maynard now. He too was at Eton and at Cambridge. Since then he has been concerned in so many great affairs that were he to rattle his engagements under our noses we should be fairly deafened with the clink of coronets and dazed with the glitter of diamonds. But are we deafened? Are we dazed? Alas, no. Dominated, I suspect by the iron rod of old Cambridge, dominated too by that moral sense which grows stronger in Maynard the older he gets, that stern desire to preserve our generation in its integrity, and to protect the younger generation from its folly, Maynard never boasts. It is for me to inform you that he lunched today with the Prime Minister. Poor old Baldwin with the tears running down his cheeks marched him up and down – up and down beneath the celebrated pictures of Pitt and Peel. "If only", he kept on saying, "you would take a seat in the Cabinet, Keynes; or a peerage, Keynes . . ." It is for me to tell you that story. Maynard never mentioned it. Pigs, plays, pictures – he will talk of them all. But never of Prime Ministers and peerages. Alas and alas – Maynard is not a snob. I am foiled again.

All the same, I have made one discovery. The essence of snobbery is that you wish to impress other people. The snob is a flutter-brained, hare-brained creature so little satisfied with his or her own standing that in order to consolidate it he or she is always flourishing a title or an honour in other people's faces so that they may believe, and help him to believe what he does not really believe – that he or she is somehow a person of importance.

This is a symptom that I recognise in my own case. Witness this letter. Why is it always on top of all my letters? Because it has a coronet – if I get a letter stamped with a coronet that letter miraculously floats on top. I often ask – why? I know perfectly well that none of my friends will ever be, or ever has been impressed by anything I do to impress them. Yet I do it – here is the letter – on top. This shows, like a rash or a spot, that I have the disease. And I go on to ask when and how did I catch it?

When I was a girl I had certain opportunities for snobbery, because though outwardly an intellectual family, very nobly born in a bookish sense, we had floating fringes in the world of fashion. We had George Duckworth to begin with. But George Duckworth's snobbery was of so gross and palpable a texture that I could smell it and taste it from afar. I did not like that smell and taste. My temptation reached me in subtler ways – through Kitty Maxse originally, I think – a lady of the most delicate charm, of the most ethereal grace so that the great, whom she introduced, were sprayed and disinfected and robbed of their grossness. Who could call the Marchioness of Bath gross, or her daughters, the Ladies Katherine and Beatrice Thynne? It was unthinkable. Beautiful they were and stately; they dressed disgracefully, but they held themselves superbly. When we dined or lunched with old Lady Bath I sat there shivering with ecstasy – an ecstasy that was wholly snobbish perhaps but made up of different parts – of pleasure, terror, laughter and amazement. There Lady Bath sat at the end of the table on a chair stamped with the coronet and arms of the Thynnes; and on the table beside her on two cushions lay two Waterbury watches. These she consulted from time to time. But why? I do not know. Had time any special significance for her? She seemed to have endless leisure. Often she would nod off to sleep. Then she would wake and look at her watches. She looked at them because she liked looking at them. Her indifference to public opinion intrigued and delighted me. So too did her conversation with her butler Middleton.

A carriage would pass the window.

"Who's that driving by?" she would say suddenly.

"Lady Suffield, my lady", Middleton would reply. And Lady Bath would look at her watches. Once I remember the word 'marl' cropped up in conversation.

"What's marl, Middleton?" Lady Bath asked.

"A mixture of earth and carbonate of lime, my lady", Middleton informed me. Meanwhile Katie had seized a bloody bone from the plate and was feeding the dogs. As I sat there I felt these people don't care a snap what anyone thinks. Here is human nature in its uncropped, unpruned, natural state. They have a quality which we in Kensington lack. Perhaps I am only finding excuses for myself, but that was the origin of the snobbery which now leads me to put this letter on top of the pack – the aristocrat is freer, more natural, more eccentric than we are. Here I note that my snobbery is not of the intellectual kind. Lady Bath was simple in the extreme. Neither Katie nor Beatrice could spell. Will Rothenstein and Andrew Lang were the brightest lights in their intellectual world. Neither Rothenstein or Andrew Lang impressed me. If you ask me would I rather meet Einstein or the Prince of Wales, I plump for the Prince without hesitation.

I want coronets; but they must be old coronets; coronets that carry land with them and country houses; coronets that breed simplicity, eccentricity, ease; and such confidence in your own state that you can surround your plate with Waterbury watches and feed dogs with bloody bones with your own hands. No sooner have I said this than I am forced to qualify this statement. This letter rises up in witness against me. It has a coronet on top but it is not an old coronet; it is from a lady whose birth is no better – perhaps worse – than my own. Yet when I received this letter I was all in a flutter. I will read it to you.

Dear Virginia
I am not very young and since ALL my friends are either dead or dying I would much like to see you and ask you a great favour. You will laugh when I tell you what it is but in case you would lunch here alone with me on [the] 12th or 13th, 17th or 18th, I will tell you what it is. No, I won't. I will wait to know if on any one of these dates you can see your admirer

Margot Oxford*

I wrote at once – though I seldom write at once – to say that I was entirely at Lady Oxford's service. Whatever she asked, I would do. I was not left in doubt very long. Soon came this second letter.

Dear Virginia,
I think I should warn you of the favour which I want you to do for me. All my friends are either dying or dead and I am aware that my own time is closing round me. The greatest compliment ever paid me – among few – was when you said I was a good writer. This, coming from you, might have turned my head as you are far the greatest female writer living. When I die, I would like you to write a short notice in *The Times* to say you admired my writing, and thought that journalists should have made more use of me. I am not at all vain, but I have been hurt by being first employed and then turned down by editors of newspapers. This may seem trivial to you – as indeed it is – but I would like you to give me to the Press. Do not give another thought to this if it bothers you, but praise from you would delight my family when I am dead.

Your ever admiring

Margot Oxford

You could send it to Editor of *The Times* as Dawson† keeps and values all contributions upon those who are dead.

---

* Margot Asquith, Lady Oxford, second wife of Herbert Asquith, Earl of Oxford (Prime Minister 1908–16).

† Geoffrey Dawson, twice editor of *The Times*, 1912–19, 1923–41.

Now I was not, I think, flattered to be the greatest female writer in Lady Oxford's eyes; but I was flattered to be asked to lunch with her alone. "Of course," I replied, "I will come and lunch with you alone." And I was pleased when on the day in question Mabel, our dour cook, came to me, and said, "Lady Oxford has sent her car for you, ma'am." Obviously she was impressed by me; I was impressed by myself. I rose in my own esteem because I rose in Mabel's.

When I reached Bedford Square there was a large lunch party; Margot was rigged up in her finery; a ruby cross set with diamonds blazed on her breast; she was curled and crisp like a little Greek horse; tart and darting like an asp or an adder. Philip Morrell was the first to feel her sting. He was foolish and she snubbed him. But then she recovered her temper. She was very brilliant. She rattled off a string of anecdotes about the Duke of Beaufort and the Badminton hunt; how she had got her blue; how she had [heard] about Lady Warwick and the [Prince of Wales?,]* about Lady Ripon, Lady Bessborough; L[ord] Balfour and 'the Souls'.† As for age, death and obituary articles, *The Times*, nothing was said of them. I am sure she had forgotten that such things existed. So had I. I was enthralled. I embraced her warmly in the hall; and the next thing I remember is that I found myself pacing along the Farringdon Road talking aloud to myself, and seeing the butchers' shops and the trays of penny toys through an air that seemed made of gold dust and champagne.

Now no party of intellectuals has ever sent me flying down the Farringdon Road. I have dined with H. G. Wells to meet Bernard Shaw, Arnold Bennett and Granville Barker and I have only felt like an old washerwoman toiling step by step up a steep and endless staircase.

Thus I seem to have arrived at the conclusion that I am not only a coronet snob; but also a lit up drawing room snob; a social festivity snob. Any group of people if they are well dressed, and socially sparkling and unfamiliar will do the trick; sends up that fountain of gold and diamond dust which I suppose obscures the solid truth. Here is another letter which perhaps will throw more light upon other angles of the problem.

It must have been about twelve years ago, for we were still living in Richmond,‡ that I received one of those flyaway missives with which we are

---

* 'the' is the last word of the line of type that trails off the page. The Countess of Warwick was a celebrated beauty and member of the Prince of Wales' circle. It is only a possibility that the Prince of Wales was intended here, however.

† The ts has 'La Balfour' but 'Lord' must surely have been intended. Arthur James Balfour, philosopher and statesman, Prime Minister 1902–5, was the central figure of the exclusive, aristocratic and intellectual coterie known as 'the Souls'.

‡ The Woolfs lived in Richmond from 1914–24.

now all so familiar – a yellow sheet upon which a hand bowls like an intoxicated hoop; and finally curls itself into a scrawl which reads Sibyl Colefax.* "It would give me so much pleasure", it read, "if you would come to tea" – here followed a variety of dates – "to meet Paul Valéry." Now as I have always met Paul Valéry or his equivalent since I can remember, to be asked out to tea to meet him by a Sibyl Colefax whom I did not know – I had never met her – was no lure to me. If it had been, it was counteracted by another fact about myself to which I have some shyness in alluding; my dress complex; my suspenders complex in particular. I hate being badly dressed; but I hate buying clothes. In particular I hate buying suspenders. It is partly, I think, that in order to buy suspenders you must visit the most private room in the heart of a shop; you must stand in your chemise.† Shiny black satin women pry and snigger. Whatever the confession reveals, and I suspect it is something discreditable, I am very shy under the eyes of my own sex when in my chemise. But in those days twelve years ago skirts were short; stockings had to be neat; my suspenders were old; and I could not face buying another pair – let alone hat and coat. So I said, "No, I will not come to tea to meet Paul Valéry." Invitations then showered; how many tea parties I was asked to I cannot remember; at last the situation became desperate; I was forced to buy suspenders; and I accepted – shall I say the fiftieth – invitation to Argyll House. This time it was to meet Arnold Bennett.

The very night before the party a review of one of my books by Arnold Bennett appeared in the *Evening Standard*. It was *Orlando*, I think. He attacked it violently. He said it was a worthless book, which had dashed every hope he might have had of me as a writer. His whole column was devoted to trouncing me. Now though very vain – unlike Lady Oxford – my vanity as a writer is purely snobbish. I expose a large surface of skin to the reviewer but very little flesh and blood. That is, I mind good reviews and bad reviews only because I think my friends think I mind them. But as I know that my friends almost instantly forget reviews, whether good or bad, I too forget them in a few hours. My flesh and blood feelings are not touched. The only criticisms of my books that draw blood are those that are unprinted; those that are private.

Thus as twenty four hours had passed since I read the review, I went into the drawing room at Argyll House far more concerned with my appearance

---

* Lady Colefax of Argyll House was a well-known London hostess. Leonard Woolf described her as 'an unabashed hunter of lions'.

† 'you must undress' was typed after 'shop' then deleted; it was then written in and partially deleted. The present phrase was the last addition made in the margin.

as a woman than with my reputation as a writer. Now I saw Sibyl for the first time and I likened her to a bunch of red cherries on a hard black straw hat. She came forward and led me up to Arnold Bennett as a lamb is led to the butcher.

"Here is Mrs Woolf!" she said with a smile. As a hostess she was gloating. She was thinking, now there will be a scene which will redound to the credit of Argyll House. Other people were there – they too seemed expectant; they all smiled. But Arnold Bennett, I felt, was uncomfortable. He was a kind man; he took his own reviews seriously; here he was shaking hands with a woman whom he had 'slanged', as he called it, only the evening before.

"I am sorry, Mrs Woolf," he began, "that I slanged your book last night . . ."

He stammered. And I blurted out, quite sincerely, "If I choose to publish books, that's my own look out. I must take the consequences."

"Right – right", he stammered. I think he approved. "I didn't like your book", he went on. "I thought it a very bad book . . ." He stammered again.

"You can't hate my books more than I hate yours, Mr Bennett", I said. I don't know if he altogether approved of that; but we sat down together and talked and got on very well indeed. I was pleased to find in some letters of his that have been published that he commended me for bearing him no grudge; he said that we got on finely.

But that is not my point. My point is that this little scene pleased Sibyl, and was the foundation of what I suppose I must call, subject to qualifications, my intimacy with her. I was instantly promoted from tea to meat. It was lunch to begin with; then when I refused lunch, it was dinner. I went – I went several times. But I found by degrees that I was always asked to meet writers; and I did not want to meet writers; and then that if I had Noel Coward on my left, I always had Sir Arthur on my right.* Sir Arthur was very kind; he did his best to entertain me; but why he thought that I was primarily interested in the Dye-stuffs Bill I have never found out. So it was, however. Our talk always drifted that way. At one time I was the second leading authority in England on that measure. But at last, what with Noel Coward on my left and Sir Arthur on my right, I felt I could no longer bring myself to dine with Sibyl. I excused myself. The more I excused myself the more she persisted. Then she suggested that she should come and see me. She came. Again my snobbery asserted itself. I bought iced cakes; tidied up the room; threw away Pinker's bones, and pulled covers over the holes in the chairs. Soon I realised that her snobbery demanded nothing but a burnt bun; as untidy a room as possible; and if my

---

* Sir Arthur Colefax, husband of Sibyl.

fingers were covered with ink stains it was all to the good. We struck up an intimacy on those lines. She would exclaim, "Oh how I long to be a writer!" And I would reply, "Oh Sibyl, if only I could be [a] great hostess like you!" Her anecdotes of the great world amused me very much; and I drew lurid if fanciful pictures of my own struggles with English prose. As we became – shall I call it intimate? – can snobs be intimate? – she would sit on the floor, pull up her skirts, adjust her knickers – she only wears one undergarment, I may tell you; it is of silk – and pour out her grievances. She would complain almost with tears in her eyes – how Osbert Sitwell had laughed at her; how people called her a climber, a lion hunter. How vilely untrue this was . . . how all she wanted was that Argyll House should be a centre where interesting people could meet interesting people. And yet she was laughed at . . . abused. Once in the middle of one of these confidences – and they flattered me very much – the telephone rang; and Lady Cunard's butler asked me to dine with her ladyship – whom I had never met. Sibyl, when I explained the situation, was furious. "I've never heard of such insolence!" she exclaimed. Her face was contorted with a look that reminded me of the look on a tigress's face when someone snatches a bone from its paws. She abused Lady Cunard. Nothing she could say was bad enough for her. She was [a] mere lion hunter; a snob. Again, there was Lady Cholmondeley. She asked me to go and see her. "And who is Lady Cholmondeley?" I asked. Never shall I forget the careful and vindictive way in which she pulled that lady's character to pieces. She couldn't understand, I remember she said, anybody being so insolent as to ask another person to dine when they did not know them. She strongly advised me to have nothing to do either with Lady Cunard or Lady Cholmondeley. Yet she had done the very same thing herself. What was the difference between them?

In short there was much to interest me in our intimacy; such as it was. It developed. Soon she suggested a plan which I have never had the courage to make public. It was that there should be fortnightly parties – now at Tavistock Square, now at Argyll House; we were to ask four of our friends; she was to ask four of hers; Bloomsbury and the great world were to mix; she, I rather think, delicately intimated that she would stand the cost. But even I, even at my most intoxicated, saw that this would never do. Once we provided Lytton* for her; the party was a deadly failure. Lytton was very good and very patient; but he said to me at leaving, "Please don't ask me to meet Colefax again."

We reached a kind of frankness. Time after time she threw me over

---

* Strachey.

shamelessly; time after time I found out that her excuse only meant that she had a better engagement elsewhere. For example – here is one of those excuses – she had invited herself for a particular day: it was inconvenient; but I had kept it free.

Dearest Virginia,

I had an unpleasant week of going to my business at 10 instead of 9 and coming back to bed at 6. I thought this would have mended me by Tuesday instead of which I was summoned by a difficult lady to see bedroom curtains in Piccadilly at 5:30 and the interview, prolonged till 6:15, sent me to bed altogether! Now I've mended and now you are engaged. Could I come on the 18th or would you come here on the 16th at 6? If not the 18th then the 23rd, if you'll have me.

Ever your devoted
Sibyl

The day after I met someone who had been at a cocktail party at Madame d'Erlanger's and had met Sibyl. "Was there any talk of bedroom curtains?" I asked. Apparently there was none.*

I used to tax her with it; she scarcely prevaricated. But once when I played the same trick on her – throwing over an engagement, but giving her three weeks' notice – I got a series of letters which in the violence of their abuse, in the sincerity of their rage – for she imputed to me the vilest motives – I had been seduced by a better engagement – I had been dining, she was sure, with Lady Cunard or Lady Cholmondeley – reached a pitch of eloquence that was really impressive. The light all this threw on her psychology, on my psychology – on the snob psychology generally, was very interesting. Why did we go on seeing each other? I wondered. What was in fact the nature of our relation? Light was to be thrown on it in a startling way.

One morning last February the telephone rang soon after breakfast, and Leonard answered it. I saw his face change as he listened.

"Good God!" he exclaimed. "You don't say so!" Then he turned to me and said, "Arthur Colefax is dead!"†

Harold Nicolson was on the telephone; he had rung up to say that Arthur Colefax had died suddenly the afternoon before; he had only been ill one day; Sibyl, he said, was distracted. Sir Arthur was dead! A clap struck me full in the face. A clap of genuine surprise and sympathy. It was not for Sir Arthur.

---

* Typographical errors plus incomplete deletions make this paragraph a 'doubtful reading'. However, the meaning is clear.

† He died on 19 February 1936.

For him I felt what one feels for an old cabinet that has always stood in the middle of a drawing room. The cabinet had gone – it was surprising – it was sad. But I had never been intimate with the cabinet. For Sibyl my feeling was different – with her I had been – I was intimate. And for her I felt, as I say, a clap of genuine, unadulterated sympathy. No sooner had I felt it than it split into several pieces. I was very sorry; but I was also very curious. What did she feel – what did she really feel about Arthur?

Now when a feeling is thus mixed it is very difficult to put it into words. In proof of this, when it came to writing a letter of sympathy, I boggled. No words that I could find seemed right. I wrote and rewrote; finally I tore up what I had written. We were going down to Monks House for the week-end; I picked three flowers; tied them up with a card on which I wrote 'For Sibyl. With love from Leonard and Virginia.' As we passed Argyll House Leonard rang the bell of that now shrouded mansion and gave the flowers into the hand of the weeping Fielding. She at least seemed genuinely heart-broken. That was my solution of the problem.

And it seemed to be amazingly successful. That is, I received a four page letter* a few days later, a heart-broken letter – a letter about Arthur and their happiness; about the old days when they had sat on Greek islands in the sun; about the perfection of their marriage; and her present solitude. It read sincerely; it read as if she were telling the truth; and I was a little flattered that she should tell it so openly, so intimately, even so gushingly, to me.†

When I heard later that she had written letters very like the one she sent me to people whom she scarcely knew at all, I was not so well pleased. When I heard that she had dined out every night since his death, and read in the papers that Lady Colefax had been at this great party and at that first night, I was baffled. Did she feel less than she made out? Or was she being very brave? Was she so tanned and leathered by society that the only thing she could not face was solitude? It was an interesting problem in the psychology of snobbery.

She wrote to me several times. She told me she was leaving Argyll House. She asked me to come and see the May in flower for the last time; I did not go; then she asked me to come and see the tulips in flower for the

* This letter is included in the 'Monks House Papers' at the University of Sussex Library.

† The following passage is deleted in the ts: "Yet when she asked me to dine with her alone, I could not face it. Again the feeling seemed to break into three separate bits, and when I thought of spending a whole evening alone with her talking about Arthur I shirked it. I thought no. I shall be found out. I made some excuse, and waited till time had passed, and the need for genuine feeling should be less pressing."

last time. We were away, and I did not go. Then when I came back in October, she wrote and said that unless I came on Tuesday the 27th of October I should never see Argyll House again. On the 30th she was leaving for ever. She particularly wanted, she said, to see me alone. I was flattered. I said I would come; and on the morning of Tuesday Fielding rang up to remind me; and to say that her ladyship wanted me to come at 4:45 punctually.

It was a wet and windy evening; leaves swirled along the pavement of the King's Road; and I had a feeling of chaos and desolation. At 4:45 precisely I rang the bell of Argyll House for the last time. The door was opened not by a Fielding but by a seedy man in a brown suit who looked like a bailiff. He was surly.

"You're too late", he said, shaking his head and holding the door only half open, as if to stop me.

"But Lady Colefax told me to come at a quarter to five", I said.

That rather stumped him.

"I don't know anything about that", he said. "But you'd better come this way."

And he led me not into the drawing room but into the pantry. It was odd to find oneself in the pantry of Argyll House – that pantry from which so many succulent dishes had issued. The pantry was full of kitchen tables; and on them were ranged dinner services, bunches of knives and forks, stacks of tumblers and wine glasses – all with tickets on them. Then I realised that the whole place was up for sale; the surly man was the auctioneer's agent. I stood there looking about me when Fielding hurried in from the kitchen, still in her grey dress and muslin apron, but so flustered and so distracted that I felt she was dressed in sack cloth and ashes. She waved her hands in despair.

"I don't know where Lady Colefax is", she moaned. "And I don't know where to put you. The people are still here. They ought to have gone at four – but still all over the place . . ."

"I'm so sorry, Fielding", I said. "This is very sad—"

Tears ran down her cheeks; were in her eyes; she moaned, as she waved her hands and led me in a fluttering, undecided way, first [into] a scullery, then into the dining room. I sat down on one of the brown chairs in that rich festive room. Last time I had sat there Sir Arthur was on my right; Noel Coward was on my left. Now the chairs were ticketed; there were tickets on the glass trees on the mantelpiece; on the chandelier; on the candlesticks. A man in a black overcoat was strolling about the room, picking up now a candlestick, now a cigarette box, as if calculating what they were worth. Then two furtive fashionable ladies came in. One of them held out her hand to me.

"Have you come to see the furniture?" she said to me, in a low tone, as if she were at a funeral. I recognised Ava Bodley – Mrs Ralph Wigram.*

"No. I've come to see Sibyl", I said.

I thought I detected a shade of envy in her face; I was a friend; she was a mere sightseer. She strolled off, and began looking at the furniture. Then, as I sat there, trying to fix my mind on Sir Arthur and the kindness which he had always shown me – the door half opened; round the edge peered Sibyl who beckoned, silently, as if she were afraid to show herself in her own dining room. I followed her, and she took me into the drawing room and shut the door.

"Who was that?" she said to me anxiously.

"Mrs Wigram", I replied. She wrung her hands.

"Oh I hope she didn't see me", she murmured. "They ought to have gone at four. But they're still all over the place."

The drawing room however was empty; though there were tickets on the chairs and tables. We sank down side by side on the sofa. I used to liken her to a bunch of glossy red cherries on a hard straw hat. But now the cherries were pale. The dye had run. The black brim was soppy with water. She looked old and ill and haggard lines were grooved as if with a chisel on either side of her nose. I felt extremely sorry for her. We were like two survivors clinging to a raft. This was the end of all her parties; we were sitting in the ruins of that magnificent structure which had borne so lately the royal crown on top. I put my bare hand on her bare hand and felt, "This is genuine. There can be no mistake about this."

Then Fielding brought in tea – the kind of tea people have when they are starting on a journey; a few slices of thin bread and butter and three parliament biscuits. Sibyl apologized for the tea. "What a horrid tea!" Then she began to talk rather distractedly; she told me about her operation; how the doctors said she ought to take a six months' holiday. "Am I Greta Garbo?" she said. Then how she had bought a house in North Street; how she was going to stay with the Clarkes . . . She was always breaking off and saying, "Oh but don't let's go into that." It was as if she wanted to say something, but could not. After all, she had asked me to come to see her alone.

At last I said, "I'm so sorry, Sibyl . . ."

The tears came to her eyes. "Oh it's been awful! You can't think what it's like", she began. Then she stopped. The tears did not fall. "You see I'm not a person who can say what they feel", she said. "I can't talk. I've not talked to anybody. If I did, I couldn't go on. And I've got to go on . . ." and again

* Wife of Ralph Follet Wigram, CMG, counsellor in the Foreign Office.

she began telling me how she had bought a house in North Street, from a madman; the house was very dirty . . . Then the door opened and Fielding beckoned.

"Mrs Wigram wants to speak to you, milady", she said. Sibyl sighed; but she got up and went.

On the whole I admired her very much. I thought, as I sat there, how brave she was. Was she not giving a supper party that very night, here, in the midst of the ruins, in the midst of the chairs and tables that were all up for sale? But here she came back.

"How I loathe that woman!" she exclaimed.

And she told me as she began to eat her bread and butter how Mrs Wigram was a mere climber; the sort of woman who pushed and shoved and she had just played, too, a dirty trick on her. When she heard that Sibyl wanted the house in North Street, she had told the Lyttons, who had bid against her. But she had got the house in spite of them; and very cheap too; for seven hundred pounds less than she expected – "Oh but don't let's talk about that", she broke off. And again I tried to be intimate. I said something rather commonplace and awkward about leaving houses – how much one minded it and so on. Then again tears came into her eyes. "Yes", she said, looking around her. "I've always had a passion for this house. I've felt about it as a lover feels . . ."

Again the door opened.

"Lady Mary Cholmondeley on the telephone, milady", said Fielding.

"Tell her I'm engaged", said Sibyl angrily. Fielding went.

"Who can she mean?" Sibyl asked. "I don't know any Lady Mary Cholmondeley. Can it be . . . Oh dear," she sighed getting up, "I must go and see for myself. Fielding's the bane of my life", she sighed. "First she cries, then she laughs; and she won't wear spectacles though she's as blind as a bat. I must go and see for myself."

Again she left me. Another illusion had gone, I thought. I had always thought Fielding a treasure – an old servant to whom Sibyl was devoted. But no; first she cried; then she laughed; and she was as blind as a bat. This was another peep into the pantry at Argyll House.

As I sat there waiting I thought of the times I had sat on that sofa – with Sir Arthur; with Arnold Bennett; with George Moore; with old Mr Birrell; with Max Beerbohm. It was in this room that Olga Lynn threw down her music in a rage because people talked; and here that I saw Sibyl glide across the room and lead Lord Balfour, beaming benevolence and distinction, to soothe the angry singer . . . But Sibyl came back again, and again took up her bread and butter.

"What were we talking about", she said, "before Fielding interrupted? And what am I to do about Fielding?" she added. "I can't send her away.

She's been with us all these years. But she's such an awful . . . but don't let's go into that," she broke off again.

Again I made an effort to talk more intimately. "I've been thinking of all the people I've met here", I said. "Arnold Bennett. George Moore. Max Beerbohm . . ."

She smiled. I saw that I had given her pleasure. "That's what I like you to say", she said. "That's what I've wanted – that the people I like should meet the people I like. That's what I tried to do—" "And that's what you've done", I said, warming up. I felt very grateful to her, although in fact I had never much enjoyed meeting other writers, still she had kept open house; she had worked very hard; it had been a great achievement in its way. I tried to tell her so.

"I have enjoyed myself in this room so much", I said. "D'you remember the party when Olga Lynn threw down her music? And then, that time I met Arnold Bennett. And then – Henry James . . ." I stopped. I had never met Henry James at Argyll House. That was before my time.

"Did you know him?" I said, quite innocently.

"Know Henry James!" Sibyl exclaimed. Her face lit up. It was as if I had touched on a nerve, the wrong nerve, I rather felt. She became the old Sibyl again – the hostess.

"Dear H.J.! I should think I did! I shall never forget", she began, "how when Wolcott Balestier died in Vienna – he was Rudyard Kipling's brother-in-law, you know—"* Here the door opened again; and again Fielding – Fielding who was as blind as a bat and the curse of Sibyl's life – peered in.

"The car's at the door, milady", she said.

Sibyl turned to me. "I've a tiresome engagement in Mount Street", she said. "I must go. But I'll give you a lift."

She got up and we went into the hall. The door was open. The Rolls Royce was waiting at the door behind the gate. This is my farewell, I said to myself, pausing for a moment, and looked, as one looks for the last time, at the Italian pots, at the looking-glasses, all with their tickets on them, that stood in the hall. I wanted to say something to show that I minded leaving Argyll House for the last time. But Sibyl seemed to have forgotten all about it. She looked animated. The colour had come back into the cherries; the straw hat was hard again. "I was just telling you", she resumed. "When Wolcott Balestier died in Vienna, Henry James came to see me, and he said, 'Dear Sibyl, there are those two poor women alone with the corpse of that dear young man in Vienna, and I feel that it is my duty—'" By this time we were walking down the flagged pathway to the car.

---

* Balestier died in 1891; Kipling married his sister Caroline in 1892.

"Mount Street", she said to the chauffeur and got in. "H.J. said to me," she resumed, "'I feel it is my duty to go to Vienna in case I can be of any assistance to those two bereaved ladies . . .'" And the car drove off, and she sat by my side, trying to impress me with the fact that she had known Henry James.

Sketch of the Past

TWO days ago – Sunday 16th April 1939 to be precise – Nessa said that if I did not start writing my memoirs I should soon be too old. I should be eighty-five, and should have forgotten – witness the unhappy case of Lady Strachey.* As it happens that I am sick of writing Roger's life, perhaps I will spend two or three mornings making a sketch.† There are several difficulties. In the first place, the enormous number of things I can remember; in the second, the number of different ways in which memoirs can be written. As a great memoir reader, I know many different ways. But if I begin to go through them and to analyse them and their merits and faults, the mornings – I cannot take more than two or three at most – will be gone. So without stopping to choose my way, in the sure and certain knowledge that it will find itself – or if not it will not matter – I begin: the first memory.

This was of red and purple flowers on a black ground – my mother's dress; and she was sitting either in a train or in an omnibus, and I was on her lap. I therefore saw the flowers she was wearing very close; and can still see purple and red and blue, I think, against the black; they must have been anemones, I suppose. Perhaps we were going to St Ives; more probably, for from the light it must have been evening, we were coming back to London. But it is more convenient artistically to suppose that we were going to St Ives, for that will lead to my other memory, which also seems to be my first memory, and in fact it is the most important of all my memories. If life has a base that it stands upon, if it is a bowl that one fills and fills and fills – then my bowl without a doubt stands upon this memory. It is of lying half asleep, half awake, in bed in the nursery at St Ives. It is of hearing the waves breaking, one, two, one, two, and sending a splash of water over the beach; and then breaking, one, two, one, two, behind a yellow blind. It is of hearing the blind draw its little acorn across the floor as the wind blew the blind out. It is of lying and hearing this splash and seeing this light, and feeling, it is

---

* Lady Strachey, mother of Lytton, died at the age of eighty-nine, in 1928. In old age she wrote "Some Recollections of a Long Life" which were very short – less than a dozen pages in *Nation and Athenaeum*. This may indicate, as Michael Holroyd has suggested, that by the early 1920s she had forgotten more than she remembered.

† VW was at work on *Roger Fry: A Biography* (The Hogarth Press; London, 1949).

almost impossible that I should be here; of feeling the purest ecstasy I can conceive.

I could spend hours trying to write that as it should be written, in order to give the feeling which is even at this moment very strong in me. But I should fail (unless I had some wonderful luck); I dare say I should only succeed in having the luck if I had begun by describing Virginia herself.

Here I come to one of the memoir writer's difficulties – one of the reasons why, though I read so many, so many are failures. They leave out the person to whom things happened. The reason is that it is so difficult to describe any human being. So they say: "This is what happened"; but they do not say what the person was like to whom it happened. And the events mean very little unless we know first to whom they happened. Who was I then? Adeline Virginia Stephen, the second daughter of Leslie and Julia Prinsep Stephen, born on 25th January 1882, descended from a great many people, some famous, others obscure; born into a large connection, born not of rich parents, but of well-to-do parents, born into a very communicative, literate, letter writing, visiting, articulate, late nineteenth century world; so that I could if I liked to take the trouble, write a great deal here not only about my mother and father but about uncles and aunts, cousins and friends. But I do not know how much of this, or what part of this, made me feel what I felt in the nursery at St Ives. I do not know how far I differ from other people. That is another memoir writer's difficulty. Yet to describe oneself truly one must have some standard of comparison; was I clever, stupid, good looking, ugly, passionate, cold—? Owing partly to the fact that I was never at school, never competed in any way with children of my own age, I have never been able to compare my gifts and defects with other people's. But of course there was one external reason for the intensity of this first impression: the impression of the waves and the acorn on the blind; the feeling, as I describe it sometimes to myself, of lying in a grape and seeing through a film of semi-transparent yellow – it was due partly to the many months we spent in London. The change of nursery was a great change. And there was the long train journey; and the excitement. I remember the dark; the lights; the stir of the going up to bed.

But to fix my mind upon the nursery – it had a balcony; there was a partition, but it joined the balcony of my father's and mother's bedroom. My mother would come out on to her balcony in a white dressing gown. There were passion flowers growing on the wall; they were great starry blossoms, with purple streaks, and large green buds, part empty, part full.

If I were a painter I should paint these first impressions in pale yellow, silver, and green. There was the pale yellow blind; the green sea; and the silver of the passion flowers. I should make a picture that was globular; semi-transparent. I should make a picture of curved petals; of shells; of things that were semi-transparent; I should make curved shapes, showing the light through, but not giving a clear outline. Everything would be large and dim; and what was seen would at the same time be heard; sounds would come through this petal or leaf – sounds indistinguishable from sights. Sound and sight seem to make equal parts of these first impressions. When I think of the early morning in bed I also hear the caw of rooks falling from a great height. The sound seems to fall through an elastic, gummy air; which holds it up; which prevents it from being sharp and distinct.* The quality of the air above Talland House seemed to suspend sound, to let it sink down slowly, as if it were caught in a blue gummy veil. The rooks cawing is part of the waves breaking – one, two, one, two – and the splash as the wave drew back and then it gathered again, and I lay there half awake, half asleep, drawing in such ecstasy as I cannot describe.

The next memory – all these colour-and-sound memories hang together at St Ives – was much more robust; it was highly sensual. It was later. It still makes me feel warm; as if everything were ripe; humming; sunny; smelling so many smells at once; and all making a whole that even now makes me stop – as I stopped then going down to the beach; I stopped at the top to look down at the gardens. They were sunk beneath the road. The apples were on a level with one's head. The gardens gave off a murmur of bees; the apples were red and gold; there were also pink flowers; and grey and silver leaves. The buzz, the croon, the smell, all seemed to press voluptuously against some membrane; not to burst it; but to hum round one such a complete rapture of pleasure that I stopped, smelt; looked. But again I cannot describe that rapture. It was rapture rather than ecstasy.

The strength of these pictures – but sight was always then so much mixed with sound that picture is not the right word – the strength anyhow of these impressions makes me again digress. Those moments – in the nursery, on the road to the beach – can still be more real than the present moment. This I have just tested. For I got up and crossed the garden. Percy was digging the asparagus bed; Louie was shaking a mat in front of the bedroom door.† But I was seeing them through the sight I saw here – the nursery and the road to the beach. At times I can go back to St Ives more completely than I can this morning. I can reach a state where I seem to be watching things happen as if I were there. That is, I suppose, that my memory supplies what I had forgotten, so that it seems as if it were happening independently, though I am

---

* VW has written 'made it seem to fall from a great height' above 'prevents . . . distinct.'

† The gardener and daily help, respectively, at Monks House, the country home of the Woolfs in Rodmell, Sussex, from 1919.

really making it happen. In certain favourable moods, memories – what one has forgotten – come to the top. Now if this is so, is it not possible – I often wonder – that things we have felt with great intensity have an existence independent of our minds; are in fact still in existence? And if so, will it not be possible, in time, that some device will be invented by which we can tap them? I see it – the past – as an avenue lying behind; a long ribbon of scenes, emotions. There at the end of the avenue still, are the garden and the nursery. Instead of remembering here a scene and there a sound, I shall fit a plug into the wall; and listen in to the past. I shall turn up August 1890. I feel that strong emotion must leave its trace; and it is only a question of discovering how we can get ourselves again attached to it, so that we shall be able to live our lives through from the start.

But the peculiarity of these two strong memories is that each was very simple. I am hardly aware of myself, but only of the sensation. I am only the container of the feeling of ecstasy, of the feeling of rapture. Perhaps this is characteristic of all childhood memories; perhaps it accounts for their strength. Later we add to feelings much that makes them more complex; and therefore less strong; or if not less strong, less isolated, less complete. But instead of analysing this, here is an instance of what I mean – my feeling about the looking-glass in the hall.

There was a small looking-glass in the hall at Talland House. It had, I remember, a ledge with a brush on it. By standing on tiptoe I could see my face in the glass. When I was six or seven perhaps, I got into the habit of looking at my face in the glass. But I only did this if I was sure that I was alone. I was ashamed of it. A strong feeling of guilt seemed naturally attached to it. But why was this so? One obvious reason occurs to me – Vanessa and I were both what was called tomboys; that is, we played cricket, scrambled over rocks, climbed trees, were said not to care for clothes and so on. Perhaps therefore to have been found looking in the glass would have been against our tomboy code. But I think that my feeling of shame went a great deal deeper. I am almost inclined to drag in my grandfather – Sir James, who once smoked a cigar, liked it, and so threw away his cigar and never smoked another. I am almost inclined to think that I inherited a streak of the puritan, of the Clapham Sect.* At any rate, the looking-glass shame has lasted all my life, long after the tomboy phase was over. I cannot now powder my nose in public. Everything to do with dress – to be fitted, to come into a room wearing a new dress – still frightens me; at least makes me shy, self-conscious, uncomfortable. "Oh to be able to run, like Julian Morrell, all over

* In marrying Jane Catherine Venn, James Stephen had allied himself with the very heart of the Clapham Sect.

the garden in a new dress", I thought not many years ago at Garsington; when Julian undid a parcel and put on a new dress and scampered round and round like a hare.* Yet femininity was very strong in our family. We were famous for our beauty – my mother's beauty, Stella's beauty, gave me as early as I can remember, pride and pleasure. What then gave me this feeling of shame, unless it were that I inherited some opposite instinct? My father was spartan, ascetic, puritanical. He had I think no feeling for pictures; no ear for music; no sense of the sound of words. This leads me to think that my – I would say 'our' if I knew enough about Vanessa, Thoby and Adrian – but how little we know even about brothers and sisters – this leads me to think that my natural love for beauty was checked by some ancestral dread. Yet this did not prevent me from feeling ecstasies and raptures spontaneously and intensely and without any shame or the least sense of guilt, so long as they were disconnected with my own body. I thus detect another element in the shame which I had in being caught looking at myself in the glass in the hall. I must have been ashamed or afraid of my own body. Another memory, also of the hall, may help to explain this. There was a slab outside the dining room door for standing dishes upon. Once when I was very small Gerald Duckworth lifted me on to this, and as I sat there he began to explore my body. I can remember the feel of his hand going under my clothes; going firmly and steadily lower and lower. I remember how I hoped that he would stop; how I stiffened and wriggled as his hand approached my private parts. But it did not stop. His hand explored my private parts too. I remember resenting, disliking it – what is the word for so dumb and mixed a feeling? It must have been strong, since I still recall it. This seems to show that a feeling about certain parts of the body; how they must not be touched; how it is wrong to allow them to be touched; must be instinctive. It proves that Virginia Stephen was not born on the 25th January 1882, but was born many thousands of years ago; and had from the very first to encounter instincts already acquired by thousands of ancestresses in the past.

And this throws light not merely on my own case, but upon the problem that I touched on the first page; why it is so difficult to give any account of the person to whom things happen. The person is evidently immensely complicated. Witness the incident of the looking-glass. Though I have done my best to explain why I was ashamed of looking at my own face I have only been able to discover some possible reasons; there may be others; I do not suppose that I have got at the truth; yet this is a simple incident; and it happened to me personally; and I have no motive for lying about it. In spite

* Julian Morrell was the daughter of Ottoline and Philip Morrell; Garsington Manor was their house in Oxfordshire.

of all this, people write what they call 'lives' of other people; that is, they collect a number of events, and leave the person to whom it happened unknown. Let me add a dream; for it may refer to the incident of the looking-glass. I dreamt that I was looking in a glass when a horrible face – the face of an animal – suddenly showed over my shoulder. I cannot be sure if this was a dream, or if it happened. Was I looking in the glass one day when something in the background moved, and seemed to me alive? I cannot be sure. But I have always remembered the other face in the glass, whether it was a dream or a fact, and that it frightened me.

These then are some of my first memories. But of course as an account of my life they are misleading, because the things one does not remember are as important; perhaps they are more important. If I could remember one whole day I should be able to describe, superficially at least, what life was like as a child. Unfortunately, one only remembers what is exceptional. And there seems to be no reason why one thing is exceptional and another not. Why have I forgotten so many things that must have been, one would have thought, more memorable than what I do remember? Why remember the hum of bees in the garden going down to the beach, and forget completely being thrown naked by father into the sea? (Mrs Swanwick says she saw that happen.)*

This leads to a digression, which perhaps may explain a little of my own psychology; even of other people's. Often when I have been writing one of my so-called novels I have been baffled by this same problem; that is, how to describe what I call in my private shorthand – "non-being". Every day includes much more non-being than being. Yesterday for example, Tuesday the 18th of April, was [as] it happened a good day; above the average in "being". It was fine; I enjoyed writing these first pages; my head was relieved of the pressure of writing about Roger; I walked over Mount Misery† and along the river; and save that the tide was out, the country, which I notice very closely always, was coloured and shaded as I like – there were the willows, I remember, all plumy and soft green and purple against the blue. I also read Chaucer with pleasure; and began a book – the memoirs of Madame de la Fayette – which interested me. These separate moments of being were however embedded in many more moments of non-being. I have already forgotten what Leonard and I talked about at lunch; and at tea; although it

---

* Mrs Swanwick was the only daughter of Oswald and Eleanor Sickert. In her autobiography, *I Have Been Young* (London, 1935), she recalls having known Leslie Stephen at St Ives: "We watched with delight his naked babies running about the beach or being towed into the sea between his legs, and their beautiful mother."

† Two cottages on the down between Southease and Piddinghoe known locally as Mount Misery.

was a good day the goodness was embedded in a kind of nondescript cotton wool. This is always so. A great part of every day is not lived consciously. One walks, eats, sees things, deals with what has to be done; the broken vacuum cleaner; ordering dinner; writing orders to Mabel; washing; cooking dinner; bookbinding. When it is a bad day the proportion of non-being is much larger. I had a slight temperature last week; almost the whole day was non-being. The real novelist can somehow convey both sorts of being. I think Jane Austen can; and Trollope; perhaps Thackeray and Dickens and Tolstoy. I have never been able to do both. I tried – in *Night and Day*; and in *The Years*. But I will leave the literary side alone for the moment.

As a child then, my days, just as they do now, contained a large proportion of this cotton wool, this non-being. Week after week passed at St Ives and nothing made any dint upon me. Then, for no reason that I know about, there was a sudden violent shock; something happened so violently that I have remembered it all my life. I will give a few instances. The first: I was fighting with Thoby on the lawn. We were pommelling each other with our fists. Just as I raised my fist to hit him, I felt: why hurt another person? I dropped my hand instantly, and stood there, and let him beat me. I remember the feeling. It was a feeling of hopeless sadness. It was as if I became aware of something terrible; and of my own powerlessness. I slunk off alone, feeling horribly depressed. The second instance was also in the garden at St Ives. I was looking at the flower bed by the front door; "That is the whole", I said. I was looking at a plant with a spread of leaves; and it seemed suddenly plain that the flower itself was a part of the earth; that a ring enclosed what was the flower; and that was the real flower; part earth; part flower. It was a thought I put away as being likely to be very useful to me later. The third case was also at St Ives. Some people called Valpy had been staying at St Ives, and had left. We were waiting at dinner one night, when somehow I overheard my father or my mother say that Mr Valpy had killed himself. The next thing I remember is being in the garden at night and walking on the path by the apple tree. It seemed to me that the apple tree was connected with the horror of Mr Valpy's suicide. I could not pass it. I stood there looking at the grey-green creases of the bark – it was a moonlit night – in a trance of horror. I seemed to be dragged down, hopelessly, into some pit of absolute despair from which I could not escape. My body seemed paralysed.

There are three instances of exceptional moments. I often tell them over, or rather they come to the surface unexpectedly. But now that for the first time I have written them down, I realise something that I have never realised before. Two of these moments ended in a state of despair. The other ended, on the contrary, in a state of satisfaction. When I said about the flower "That is the whole," I felt that I had made a discovery. I felt that I had put away in my mind something that I should go back [to], to turn over and explore. It strikes me now that this was a profound difference. It was the difference in the first place between despair and satisfaction. This difference I think arose from the fact that I was quite unable to deal with the pain of discovering that people hurt each other; that a man I had seen had killed himself. The sense of horror held me powerless. But in the case of the flower I found a reason; and was thus able to deal with the sensation. I was not powerless. I was conscious – if only at a distance – that I should in time explain it. I do not know if I was older when I saw the flower than I was when I had the other two experiences. I only know that many of these exceptional moments brought with them a peculiar horror and a physical collapse; they seemed dominant; myself passive. This suggests that as one gets older one has a greater power through reason to provide an explanation; and that this explanation blunts the sledge-hammer force of the blow. I think this is true, because though I still have the peculiarity that I receive these sudden shocks, they are now always welcome; after the first surprise, I always feel instantly that they are particularly valuable. And so I go on to suppose that the shock-receiving capacity is what makes me a writer. I hazard the explanation that a shock is at once in my case followed by the desire to explain it. I feel that I have had a blow; but it is not, as I thought as a child, simply a blow from an enemy hidden behind the cotton wool of daily life; it is or will become a revelation of some order; it is a token of some real thing behind appearances; and I make it real by putting it into words. It is only by putting it into words that I make it whole; this wholeness means that it has lost its power to hurt me; it gives me, perhaps because by doing so I take away the pain, a great delight to put the severed parts together. Perhaps this is the strongest pleasure known to me. It is the rapture I get when in writing I seem to be discovering what belongs to what; making a scene come right; making a character come together. From this I reach what I might call a philosophy; at any rate it is a constant idea of mine; that behind the cotton wool is hidden a pattern; that we – I mean all human beings – are connected with this; that the whole world is a work of art; that we are parts of the work of art. *Hamlet* or a Beethoven quartet is the truth about this vast mass that we call the world. But there is no Shakespeare, there is no Beethoven; certainly and emphatically there is no God; we are the words; we are the music; we are the thing itself. And I see this when I have a shock.

This intuition of mine – it is so instinctive that it seems given to me, not made by me – has certainly given its scale to my life ever since I saw the flower in the bed by the front door at St Ives. If I were painting myself I should have to find some – rod, shall I say – something that would stand for the conception. It proves that one's life is not confined to one's body and what one says or does; one is living all the time in relation to certain background rods or conceptions. Mine is that there is a pattern hid behind the cotton wool. And this conception affects me every day. I prove this, now, by spending the morning writing, when I might be walking, running a shop, or learning to do something that will be useful if war comes. I feel that by writing I am doing what is far more necessary than anything else.

All artists I suppose feel something like this. It is one of the obscure elements in life that has never been much discussed. It is left out in almost all biographies and autobiographies, even of artists. Why did Dickens spend his entire life writing stories? What was his conception? I bring in Dickens partly because I am reading *Nicholas Nickleby* at the moment; also partly because it struck me, on my walk yesterday, that these moments of being of mine were scaffolding in the background; were the invisible and silent part of my life as a child. But in the foreground there were of course people; and these people were very like characters in Dickens. They were caricatures; they were very simple; they were immensely alive. They could be made with three strokes of the pen, if I could do it. Dickens owes his astonishing power to make characters alive to the fact that he saw them as a child sees them; as I saw Mr Wolstenholme; C. B. Clarke, and Mr Gibbs.

I name these three people because they all died when I was a child. Therefore they have never been altered. I see them exactly as I saw them then. Mr Wolstenholme was a very old gentleman who came every summer to stay with us. He was brown; he had a beard and very small eyes in fat cheeks; and he fitted into a brown wicker beehive chair as if it had been his nest. He used to sit in this beehive chair smoking and reading. He had only one characteristic – that when he ate plum tart he spurted the juice through his nose so that it made a purple stain on his grey moustache. This seemed enough to cause us perpetual delight. We called him 'The Woolly One'. By way of shading him a little I remember that we had to be kind to him because he was not happy at home; that he was very poor, yet once gave Thoby half a crown; that he had a son who was drowned in Australia; and I know too that he was a great mathematician. He never said a word all the time I knew him. But he still seems to me a complete character; and whenever I think of him I begin to laugh.

Mr Gibbs was perhaps less simple. He wore a tie ring; had a bald, benevolent head; was dry; neat; precise; and had folds of skin under his chin. He made father groan – "why can't you go – why can't you go?" And he gave Vanessa and myself two ermine skins, with slits down the middle out of which poured endless wealth – streams of silver. I also remember him lying in bed, dying; husky; in a night shirt; and showing us drawings by Retzsch.*

---

* Friedrich Retzsch (1779–1857), a German engraver widely known in Germany and England. The ts has 'Ketsch' which is obviously a typing error.

The character of Mr Gibbs also seems to me complete and amuses me very much.

As for C. B. Clarke, he was an old botanist; and he said to my father "All you young botanists like Osmunda." He had an aunt aged eighty who went for a walking tour in the New Forest. That is all – that is all I have to say about these three old gentlemen. But how real they were! How we laughed at them! What an immense part they played in our lives!

One more caricature comes into my mind; though pity entered into this one. I am thinking of Justine Nonon. She was immensely old. Little hairs sprouted on her long bony chin. She was a hunchback; and walked like a spider, feeling her way with her long dry fingers from one chair to another. Most of the time she sat in the arm-chair beside the fire. I used to sit on her knee; and her knee jogged up and down; and she sang in a hoarse cracked voice "Ron ron ron – et plon plon plon—" and then her knee gave and I was tumbled on to the floor. She was French; she had been with the Thackerays. She only came to us on visits. She lived by herself at Shepherd's Bush; and used to bring Adrian a glass jar of honey. I got the notion that she was extremely poor; and it made me uncomfortable that she brought this honey, because I felt she did it by way of making her visit acceptable. She said no: "I have come in my carriage and pair" – which meant the red omnibus. For this too I pitied her; also because she began to wheeze; and the nurses said she would not live much longer; and soon she died. That is all I know about her; but I remember her as if she were a completely real person, with nothing left out, like the three old men.

2nd May . . . I write the date, because I think that I have discovered a possible form for these notes. That is, to make them include the present – at least enough of the present to serve as platform to stand upon. It would be interesting to make the two people, I now, I then, come out in contrast. And further, this past is much affected by the present moment. What I write today I should not write in a year's time. But I cannot work this out; it had better be left to chance, as I write by fits and starts by way of a holiday from Roger. I have no energy at the moment to spend upon the horrid labour that it needs to make an orderly and expressed work of art; where one thing follows another and all are swept into a whole. Perhaps one day, relieved from making works of art, I will try to compose this.

But to continue – the three old men and the one old woman are complete, as I was saying, because they died when I was a child. They none of them lived on to be altered as I altered – as others, like the Stillmans or the Lushingtons, lived on and were added to and filled and left finally incomplete. The same thing applies to places. I cannot see Kensington Gardens as I saw it as a child because I saw it only two days ago – on a chill afternoon, all the cherry trees lurid in the cold yellow light of a hail storm. I know that it was very much larger in 1890 when I was seven than it is now. For one thing, it was not connected with Hyde Park. Now I walk from one to the other. We drive in our car; and leave it by the new kiosk. But then there was the Broad Walk, the Round Pond, and the Flower Walk. Then – I will try to get back to then – there were two gates, one opposite Gloucester Road, the other opposite Queen's Gate. At each gate sat an old woman. The Queen's Gate old woman was an elongated, emaciated figure with a goat-like face, yellow and pockmarked. She sold nuts and boot-laces, I think. And Kitty Maxse said of her: "Poor things, it's drink that makes them like that." She always sat, and wore a shawl and had to me a faint, obliterated, debased likeness to Granny; whose face was elongated too, but she wore a very soft shawl, like tapioca pudding, over her head, and it was fastened by an amethyst brooch set in pearls. The other old woman was round and squat. To her was attached a whole wobbling balloon of air-balls. She held this billowing, always moving, most desirable mass by one string. They glowed in my eyes always red and purple, like the flower my mother wore; and they were always billowing in the air. For a penny, she would detach one from the bellying soft mass, and I would dance away with it. She too wore a shawl and her face was puckered, as the air-balls puckered in the nursery if they survived to be taken home. I think Nurse and Sooney were on speaking terms with her; but I never heard what she said. Anemones, the blue and purple bunches that are now being sold, always bring back that quivering mound of air-balls outside the gate of Kensington Gardens.

Then we went up the Broad Walk. The Broad Walk had a peculiar property – when we took our first walk there after coming back from St Ives, we always abused it; it was not a hill at all, we said. By degrees as the weeks passed the hill became steeper and steeper until by the summer it was a hill again. The swamp – as we called the rather derelict ground behind the Flower Walk – had to Adrian and myself at least the glamour of the past on it. When Nessa and Thoby were very small, that is to say, it had been, they told us, a real swamp; they had found the skeleton of a dog there. And it must have been covered with reeds and full of pools, we thought, for we believed that the dog had been starved and drowned. In our day it had been drained, though it was still muddy. But it had a past always to us. And we compared it, of course, with Halestown Bog* near St Ives. Halestown bog where the Osmunda grew; and those thick ferns with bulbous roots that had trees marked on them, if you cut them across. I brought some home every autumn to make into pen holders. It was natural always to compare Kensington Gardens with St Ives, always of course to the disadvantage of London. That

---

* Halse Town Bog which the Stephens always called 'Halestown Bog'.

was one of the pleasures of scrunching the shells with which now and then the Flower Walk was strewn. They had little ribs on them like the shells on the beach. On the other hand the crocodile tree was itself; and is still there – the tree on the Speke Monument path;* which has a great root exposed; and the root is polished, partly by the friction of our hands, for we used to scramble over it.

As we walked, to beguile the dulness [of] innumerable winter walks we made up stories, long long stories that were taken up at the same place and added to each in turn. There was the Jim Joe and Harry Hoe story; about three brothers who had herds of animals and adventures – I have forgotten what. But there again, the Jim Joe and Harry Hoe story was a London story; and inferior to the Talland House garden story about Beccage and Hollywinks; spirits of evil who lived on the rubbish heap; and disappeared through a hole in the escallonia hedge – as I remember telling my mother and Mr Lowell.† Walks in Kensington Gardens were dull. Non-being made up a great proportion of our time in London. The walks – twice every day in Kensington Gardens – were so monotonous. Speaking for myself, non-being lay thick over those years. Past the thermometer we went – sometimes it was below the little freezing bar but not often save in the great 1894–5 winter when we skated every day; when I dropped my watch and the rough man gave it me; and asked for money; and a kind lady offered three coppers; and he said he would only take silver; and she shook her head and faded away – past the thermometer we went, past the gate-keeper in his green livery and his gold laced hat, up the Flower Walk, round the pond. We sailed boats of course. There was the great day when my Cornish lugger sailed perfectly to the middle of the pond and then with my eyes upon it, amazed, sank suddenly: "Did you see that?" my father cried, coming striding towards me. We had both seen it and both were amazed. To make the wonder complete, many weeks later in the spring, I was walking by the pond and a man in a flat-boat was dredging the pond of duckweed, and to my unspeakable excitement, up he brought my lugger in his dredging net; and I claimed it; and he gave it to me, and I ran home with this marvellous story to tell. Then my mother made new sails; and my father rigged it, and I remember seeing him fixing the sails to the yard-arm after dinner; and how interested he became and said, with his little snort, half laughing, something like "Absurd – what fun it is doing this!"

* The red granite obelisk in Kensington Gardens dedicated to the memory of the explorer John Hanning Speke.

† James Russell Lowell, the poet and critic, American Ambassador to the Court of St James 1880–5, and friend of Leslie Stephen, was Virginia's godfather.

I could collect a great many more floating incidents – scenes in Kensington Gardens; how if we had a penny we went to the white house near the palace and bought sweets from the smooth-faced, pink-cheeked woman in a grey cotton dress who used then to keep a sweet shop there; how on one day of the week we bought *Tit-Bits* and read the jokes – I liked the Correspondence best – sitting on the grass, breaking our chocolate into "Frys" as we called them, for a penny slab was divided into four; how we knocked into a lady racing our go-cart round a steep corner, and her sister scolded us violently; how we tied Shag to a railing, and some children told the Park Keeper that we were cruel – but the stories were not then very exciting; though they helped to break up the eternal round of Kensington Gardens.

What then has remained interesting? Again those moments of being. Two I always remember. There was the moment of the puddle in the path; when for no reason I could discover, everything suddenly became unreal; I was suspended; I could not step across the puddle; I tried to touch something . . . the whole world became unreal. Next, the other moment when the idiot boy sprang up with his hand outstretched mewing, slit-eyed, red-rimmed; and without saying a word, with a sense of the horror in me, I poured into his hand a bag of Russian toffee. But it was not over, for that night in the bath the dumb horror came over me. Again I had that hopeless sadness; that collapse I have described before; as if I were passive under some sledge-hammer blow; exposed to a whole avalanche of meaning that had heaped itself up and discharged itself upon me, unprotected, with nothing to ward it off, so that I huddled up at my end of the bath, motionless. I could not explain it; I said nothing even to Nessa sponging herself at the other end.

Looking back, then, at Kensington Gardens, though I can recover incidents, many more than I have patience to describe, I cannot recover, save by fits and starts, the focus, the proportions of the external world. It seems to me that a child must have a curious focus; it sees an air-ball or a shell with extreme distinctness; I still see the air-balls, blue and purple, and the ribs on the shells; but these points are enclosed in vast empty spaces. How large for instance was the space beneath the nursery table! I see it still as a great black space with the table-cloth hanging down in folds on the outskirts in the distance; and myself roaming about there, and meeting Nessa. "Have black cats got tails?" she asked, and I said "NO", and was proud because she had asked me a question. Then we roamed off again into that vast space. The night nursery was vast too. In winter I would slip in before bed to take a look at the fire. I was very anxious to see that the fire was low, because it frightened me if it burnt after we went to bed. I dreaded that little flickering flame on the walls; but Adrian liked it; and to make a compromise, Nurse folded a towel over the fender; but I could not help opening my eyes, and there often was the flickering flame; and I looked and looked and could not sleep; and in order to have company, said "What did you say, Nessa?" although she was asleep, to wake her and to hear someone's voice. These were early fears; for later, when Thoby had gone to school, leaving Nessa to take his monkey Jacko to bed with her, no sooner was the door shut than we began story-telling. The story always began thus: "Clémont* dear child, said Mrs Dilke," and it went on to tell wild stories of the Dilke family† and Miss Rosalba the governess; how they dug under the floor and discovered sacks of gold; and held great feasts and ate fried eggs "with plenty of frizzling", for the wealth of the Dilkes in real life compared with our own moderate means impressed us. We noticed how many new clothes Mrs Dilke wore; how seldom my mother bought a new dress.

Many bright colours; many distinct sounds; some human beings, caricatures; comic; several violent moments of being, always including a circle of the scene which they cut out: and all surrounded by a vast space – that is a rough visual description of childhood. This is how I shape it; and how I see myself as a child, roaming about, in that space of time which lasted from 1882 to 1895. A great hall I could liken it to; with windows letting in strange lights; and murmurs and spaces of deep silence. But somehow into that picture must be brought, too, the sense of movement and change. Nothing remained stable long. One must get the feeling of everything approaching and then disappearing, getting large, getting small, passing at different rates of speed past the little creature; one must get the feeling that made her press on, the little creature driven on as she was by growth of her legs and arms, driven without her being able to stop it, or to change it, driven as a plant is driven up out of the earth, up until the stalk grows, the leaf grows, buds swell. That is what is indescribable, that is what makes all images too static, for no sooner has one said this was so, than it was past and altered. How immense must be the force of life which turns a baby, who can just distinguish a great blot of blue and purple on a black background, into the child who thirteen years later can feel all that I felt on May 5th 1895 – now almost exactly to a day, forty-four years ago – when my mother died.

This shows that among the innumerable things left out in my sketch I have left out the most important – those instincts, affections, passions, attachments – there is no single word for them, for they changed month by month – which bound me, I suppose, from the first moment of consciousness to other

---

* In a paper written by Vanessa Bell for the Memoir Club ("Notes on Virginia's Childhood, a Memoir", ed. Richard Schaubeck, Jr: Frank Hallman; New York, 1974) 'Clémont' is spelled 'Clémenté'.

† Next-door neighbours.

people. If it were true, as I said above, that the things that ceased in childhood, are easy to describe because they are complete, then it should be easy to say what I felt for my mother, who died when I was thirteen. Thus I should be able to see her completely undisturbed by later impressions, as I saw Mr Gibbs and C. B. Clarke. But the theory, though true of them, breaks down completely with her. It breaks down in a curious way, which I will explain, for perhaps it may help to explain why I find it now so curiously difficult to describe both my feeling for her, and her herself.

Until I was in the forties – I could settle the date by seeing when I wrote *To the Lighthouse*, but am too casual here to bother to do it – the presence of my mother obsessed me.* I could hear her voice, see her, imagine what she would do or say as I went about my day's doings. She was one of the invisible presences who after all play so important a part in every life. This influence, by which I mean the consciousness of other groups impinging upon ourselves; public opinion; what other people say and think; all those magnets which attract us this way to be like that, or repel us the other and make us different from that; has never been analysed in any of those Lives which I so much enjoy reading, or very superficially.

Yet it is by such invisible presences that the "subject of this memoir" is tugged this way and that every day of his life; it is they that keep him in position. Consider what immense forces society brings to play upon each of us, how that society changes from decade to decade; and also from class to class; well, if we cannot analyse these invisible presences, we know very little of the subject of the memoir; and again how futile life-writing becomes. I see myself as a fish in a stream; deflected; held in place; but cannot describe the stream.

To return to the particular instance which should be more definite and more capable of description than for example the influence on me of the Cambridge Apostles,† or the influence of the Galsworthy, Bennett, Wells school of fiction, or the influence of the Vote, or of the War – that is, the influence of my mother. It is perfectly true that she obsessed me, in spite of the fact that she died when I was thirteen, until I was forty-four. Then one day walking round Tavistock Square I made up, as I sometimes make up my books, *To the Lighthouse*; in a great, apparently involuntary, rush.‡ One thing burst into another. Blowing bubbles out of a pipe gives the feeling of

* *To the Lighthouse* was begun in 1925 and published in 1927 when VW was forty-five.

† The popular name for the semi-secret 'Cambridge Conversazione Society' which was founded in the 1820s. All the young men who formed the nucleus of 'old Bloomsbury' belonged to it, except Clive Bell and Thoby Stephen.

‡ 52 Tavistock Square was the London home of the Woolfs from 1924 to 1939.

the rapid crowd of ideas and scenes which blew out of my mind, so that my lips seemed syllabling of their own accord as I walked. What blew the bubbles? Why then? I have no notion. But I wrote the book very quickly; and when it was written, I ceased to be obsessed by my mother. I no longer hear her voice; I do not see her.

I suppose that I did for myself what psycho-analysts do for their patients. I expressed some very long felt and deeply felt emotion. And in expressing it I explained it and then laid it to rest. But what is the meaning of "explained" it? Why, because I described her and my feeling for her in that book, should my vision of her and my feeling for her become so much dimmer and weaker? Perhaps one of these days I shall hit on the reason; and if so, I will give it, but at the moment I will go on, describing what I can remember, for it may be true that what I remember of her now will weaken still further. (This note is made provisionally, in order to explain in part why it is now so difficult to give any clear description of her.)

Certainly there she was, in the very centre of that great Cathedral space which was childhood; there she was from the very first. My first memory is of her lap; the scratch of some beads on her dress comes back to me as I pressed my cheek against it. Then I see her in her white dressing gown on the balcony; and the passion flower with the purple star on its petals. Her voice is still faintly in my ears – decided, quick; and in particular the little drops with which her laugh ended – three diminishing ahs . . . "Ah – ah – ah . . ." I sometimes end a laugh that way myself. And I see her hands, like Adrian's, with the very individual square-tipped fingers, each finger with a waist to it, and the nail broadening out. (My own are the same size all the way, so that I can slip a ring over my thumb.) She had three rings; a diamond ring, an emerald ring, and an opal ring. My eyes used to fix themselves upon the lights in the opal as it moved across the page of the lesson book when she taught us, and I was glad that she left it to me (I gave it to Leonard). Also I hear the tinkle of her bracelets, made of twisted silver, given her by Mr Lowell, as she went about the house; especially as she came up at night to see if we were asleep, holding a candle shaded; this is a distant memory, for, like all children, I lay awake sometimes and longed for her to come. Then she told me to think of all the lovely things I could imagine. Rainbows and bells . . . But besides these minute separate details, how did I first become conscious of what was always there   her astonishing beauty? Perhaps I never became conscious of it; I think I accepted her beauty as the natural quality that a mother – she seemed typical, universal, yet our own in particular – had by virtue of being our mother. It was part of her calling. I do not think that I separated her face from that general being; or from her whole body. Certainly I have a vision of her now, as she came up the path by the lawn at St Ives; slight, shapely – she held herself very straight. I was playing. I stopped, about to speak to her. But she half turned from us, and lowered her eyes. From that indescribably sad gesture I knew that Philips, the man who had been crushed on the line and whom she had been visiting, was dead. It's over, she seemed to say. I knew, and was awed by the thought of death. At the same time I felt that her gesture as a whole was lovely. Very early, through nurses or casual visitors, I must have known that she was thought very beautiful. But that pride was snobbish, not a pure and private feeling: it was mixed with pride in other people's admiration. It was related to the more definitely snobbish pride caused in me by the nurses who said one night talking together while we ate our supper: "They're very well connected. . . ."

But apart from her beauty, if the two can be separated, what was she herself like? Very quick; very direct; practical; and amusing, I say at once offhand. She could be sharp, she disliked affectation. "If you put your head on one side like that, you shan't come to the party," I remember she said to me as we drew up in a carriage in front of some house. Severe; with a background of knowledge that made her sad. She had her own sorrow waiting behind her to dip into privately. Once when she had set us to write exercises I looked up from mine and watched her reading – the Bible perhaps; and, struck by the gravity of her face, told myself that her first husband had been a clergyman and that she was thinking, as she read what he had read, of him. This was a fable on my part; but it shows that she looked very sad when she was not talking.

But can I get any closer to her without drawing upon all those descriptions and anecdotes which after she was dead imposed themselves upon my view of her? Very quick; very definite; very upright; and behind the active, the sad, the silent. And of course she was central. I suspect the word "central" gets closest to the general feeling I had of living so completely in her atmosphere that one never got far enough away from her to see her as a person. (That is one reason why I see the Gibbses and the Beadles and the Clarkes so much more distinctly.) She was the whole thing; Talland House was full of her; Hyde Park Gate was full of her. I see now, though the sentence is hasty, feeble and inexpressive, why it was that it was impossible for her to leave a very private and particular impression upon a child. She was keeping what I call in my shorthand the panoply of life – that which we all lived in common – in being. I see now that she was living on such an extended surface that she had not time, nor strength, to concentrate, except for a moment if one were ill or in some child's crisis, upon me, or upon anyone – unless it were Adrian. Him she cherished separately; she called him 'My Joy'. The later view, the understanding that I now have of her position must have its say; and it shows me that a woman of forty with seven children, some of them needing grown-up attention, and four still in the nursery; and an eighth, Laura, an idiot, yet living with us; and a husband fifteen years her elder, difficult, exacting, dependent on her; I see now that a woman who had to keep all this in being and under control must have been a general presence rather than a particular person to a child of seven or eight. Can I remember ever being alone with her for more than a few minutes? Someone was always interrupting. When I think of her spontaneously she is always in a room full of people; Stella, George and Gerald are there; my father, sitting reading with one leg curled round the other, twisting his lock of hair; "Go and take the crumb out of his beard," she whispers to me; and off I trot. There are visitors, young men like Jack Hills who is in love with Stella; many young men, Cambridge friends of George's and Gerald's; old men, sitting round the tea table talking – father's friends, Henry James, Symonds,* (I see him peering up at me on the broad staircase at St Ives with his drawn yellow face and a tie made of a yellow cord with two plush balls on it); Stella's friends – the Lushingtons, the Stillmans; I see her at the head of the table underneath the engraving of Beatrice given her by an old governess and painted blue; I hear jokes; laughter; the clatter of voices; I am teased; I say something funny; she laughs; I am pleased; I blush furiously; she observes; someone laughs at Nessa for saying that Ida Milman is her B.F.; Mother says soothingly, tenderly, "Best friend, that means." I see her going to the town with her basket; and Arthur Davies goes with her; I see her knitting on the hall step while we play cricket; I see her stretching her arms out to Mrs Williams when the bailiffs took possession of their house and the Captain stood at the window bawling and shying jugs, basins, chamber pots on to the gravel – "Come to us, Mrs Williams"; "No, Mrs Stephen," sobbed Mrs Williams, "I will not leave my husband." – I see her writing at her table in London and the silver candlesticks, and the high carved chair with the claws and the pink seat; and the three-cornered brass ink pot; I wait in agony peeping surreptitiously behind the blind for her to come down the street, when she has been out late the lamps are lit and I am sure that she has been run over. (Once my father found me peeping; questioned me; and said rather anxiously but reprovingly, "You shouldn't be so nervous, Jinny.") And there is my last sight of her; she was dying; I came to kiss her and as I crept out of the room she said: "Hold yourself straight, my little Goat." . . . What a jumble of things I can remember, if I let my mind run, about my mother; but they are all of her in company; of her surrounded; of her generalised; dispersed, omnipresent, of her as the creator of that crowded merry world which spun so gaily in the

---

* John Addington Symonds, man of letters, was the father of Katherine who married the artist Charles Furse and Margaret (Madge) who married William Wyamar Vaughan.

centre of my childhood. It is true that I enclosed that world in another made by my own temperament; it is true that from the beginning I had many adventures outside that world; and often went far from it; and kept much back from it; but there it always was, the common life of the family, very merry, very stirring, crowded with people; and she was the centre; it was herself. This was proved on May 5th 1895. For after that day there was nothing left of it. I leant out of the nursery window the morning she died. It was about six, I suppose. I saw Dr Seton walk away up the street with his head bent and his hands clasped behind his back. I saw the pigeons floating and settling. I got a feeling of calm, sadness, and finality. It was a beautiful blue spring morning, and very still. That brings back the feeling that everything had come to an end.

May 15th 1939. The drudgery of making a coherent life of Roger has once more become intolerable, and so I turn for a few days' respite to May 1895. The little platform of present time on which I stand is, so far as the weather is concerned, damp and chilly. I look up at my skylight – over the litter of *Athenaeum* articles, Fry letters – all strewn with the sand that comes from the house that is being pulled down next door – I look up and see, as if reflecting it, a sky the colour of dirty water. And the inner landscape is much of a piece. Last night Mark Gertler* dined here and denounced the vulgarity, the inferiority of what he called "literature"; compared with the integrity of painting. "For it always deals with Mr and Mrs Brown," – he said – with the personal, the trivial, that is; a criticism which has its sting and its chill, like the May sky. Yet if one could give a sense of my mother's personality one would have to be an artist. It would be as difficult to do that, as it should be done, as to paint a Cézanne.

One of the few things that is certain about her is that she married two very different men. If one looks at her not as a child, of seven or eight, but as a woman now older than she was when she died, there is something to take hold of in that fact. She was not so rubbed out and featureless, not so dominated by the beauty of her own face, as she has since become – and inevitably. For what reality can remain real of a person who died forty-five years ago† at the age of forty-nine, without leaving a book, or a picture, or any piece of work – apart from the three children who now survive and the memory of her that remains in their minds? There is the memory; but there is nothing to check that memory by; nothing to bring it to ground with.

There are however these two marriages; and they show that she was capable of falling in love with two very different men; one, to put it in a

* The artist who committed suicide in this same year, 23 June 1939.
† VW mistakenly typed '43 years ago'.

nutshell, the pink of propriety; the other, the pink of intellectuality. She could span them both. This must serve me by way of foot rule, in trying to measure her character.

The elements of that character, though, are formed in twilight. She was born, I think, in 1848;* I think in India; the daughter of Dr Jackson and his half-French wife. Not very much education came her way. An old governess – was she Mademoiselle Rose? did she give her the picture of Beatrice that hung in the dining room at Talland House? – taught her French, which she spoke with a very good accent; and she could play the piano and was musical. I remember that she kept De Quincey's *Opium Eater* on her table, one of her favourite books; and for a birthday present she chose all the works of Scott which her father gave her in the first edition – some remain; others are lost. For Scott she had a passion. She had an instinctive, not a trained mind. But her instinct, for books at least, seems to me to have been strong, and I liked it, for she gave a jump, I remember, when reading *Hamlet* aloud to her I misread 'sliver' 'silver' – she jumped as my father jumped at a false quantity when we read Virgil with him. She was her mother's favourite daughter of the three; and as her mother was an invalid even as a child she was used to nursing; to waiting on a sick bed. They had a house at Well Walk during the Crimean War; for there was an anecdote about watching the soldiers drill on the Heath. But her beauty at once came to the fore, even as a little girl; for there was another anecdote – how she could never be sent out alone, but must have Mary with her, to protect her from admiring looks: to keep her unconscious of that beauty – and she was, my father said, very little conscious of it. It was due to this beauty, I suspect, that she had that training which was much more important than any she had from governesses – the training of life at Little Holland House. She was a great deal at Little Holland House as a child, partly, I imagine, because she was acceptable to the painters, and the Prinseps – Aunt Sara and Uncle Thoby must have been proud of her.†

Little Holland House was her world then. But what was that world like? I think of it as a summer afternoon world. To my thinking Little Holland House is an old white country house, standing in a large garden. Long windows open on to the lawn. Through them comes a stream of ladies in crinolines and little straw hats; they are attended by gentlemen in peg-top trousers and whiskers. The date is round about 1860. It is a hot summer

---

* Julia was born in 1846, not in 1848.

† Julia's Aunt Sara, one of the seven Pattle sisters, married Thoby Prinsep. They settled in Little Holland House, Kensington, where they entertained an aristocracy of intellect in which the painters – Holman Hunt, Burne-Jones and, above all, G. F. Watts who was long a resident – played a dominant role.

day. Tea tables with great bowls of strawberries and cream are scattered about the lawn. They are "presided over" by some of the six lovely sisters;* who do not wear crinolines, but are robed in splendid Venetian draperies; they sit enthroned, and talk with foreign emphatic gestures – my mother too gesticulated, throwing her hands out – to the eminent men (afterwards to be made fun of by Lytton);† rulers of India, statesmen, poets, painters. My mother comes out of the window wearing that striped silk dress buttoned at the throat with a flowing skirt that appears in the photograph. She is of course "a vision" as they used to say; and there she stands, silent, with her plate of strawberries and cream; or perhaps is told to take a party across the garden to Signior's studio.‡ The sound of music also comes from those long low rooms where the great Watts pictures hang; Joachim playing the violin; also the sound of a voice reading poetry – Uncle Thoby would read his translations from the Persian poets. How easy it is to fill in the picture with set pieces that I have gathered from memoirs – to bring in Tennyson in his wideawake; Watts in his smock frock; Ellen Terry dressed as a boy; Garibaldi in his red shirt – and Henry Taylor turned from him to my mother – "the face of one fair girl was more to me" – so he says in a poem. But if I turn to my mother, how difficult it is to single her out as she really was; to imagine what she was thinking, to put a single sentence into her mouth! I dream; I make up pictures of a summer's afternoon.

But the dream is based upon one fact. Once when we were children, my mother took us to Melbury Road; and when we came to the street that had been built on the old garden she gave a little spring forward, clapped her hands, and cried "That was where it was!" as if a fairyland had disappeared. Thus I think it is true that Little Holland House was a summer afternoon world to her. As a fact too I know that she adored her Uncle Thoby. His walking stick, with a hole in the top through which a tassel must have hung, a beautiful eighteenth-century looking cane, always stood at the head of her bed at Hyde Park Gate. She was a hero worshipper, simple, uncritical, enthusiastic. She felt for Uncle Thoby, my father said, much more than she felt for her own father – "old Dr Jackson"; "respectable"; but, for all his good looks and the amazing mane of white hair that stood out like a three-cornered hat round his head, he was a commonplace prosaic old man; boring

---

* Although there were seven Pattle sisters, no one ever spoke of Julia (Cameron) as beautiful. However, F. W. Maitland in *The Life and Letters of Leslie Stephen* (London, 1906) makes the same error when referring to Maria Pattle as "one of six sisters" (p. 317n).

† Strachey.

‡ The studio of G. F. Watts.

people with his stories of a famous poison case in Calcutta; excluded from this poetical fairyland; and no doubt out of temper with it. My mother had no romance about him; but she derived from him, I suspect, the practicality, the shrewdness, which were among her qualities.

Little Holland House then was her education. She was taught there to take such part as girls did then in the lives of distinguished men; to pour out tea; to hand them their strawberries and cream; to listen devoutly, reverently to their wisdom; to accept the fact that Watts was the great painter; Tennyson the great poet; and to dance with the Prince of Wales. For the sisters, with the exception of my grandmother who was devout and spiritual, were worldly in the thoroughgoing Victorian way. Aunt Virginia, it is plain, put her own daughters, my mother's first cousins, through tortures compared with which the boot or the Chinese shoe is negligible, in order to marry one to the Duke of Bedford, the other to Lord Henry Somerset. (That is how we came to be, as the nurses said, so "well connected".) But here again I am dipping into memoirs, and leaving Julia Jackson, the real person, on one side. The only certainties I can lay hands on in those early years are that two men proposed to her (or to her parents on her behalf); one was Holman Hunt; the other Woolner, a sculptor.* Both proposals were made and refused when she was scarcely out of the nursery. I know too that she went once wearing a hat with grey feathers to a river party where Anny Thackeray† was; and Nun (that is Aunt Caroline, father's sister) saw her standing alone; and was amazed that she was not the centre of a bevy of admirers; "Where are they?" she asked Anny Thackeray; who said, "Oh they don't happen to be here today" – a little scene which makes me suspect that Julia aged seventeen or eighteen was aloof; and shed a certain silence round her by her very beauty.

That little scene is dated; she cannot have been more than eighteen; because she married when she was nineteen.‡ She was in Venice; met Herbert Duckworth; fell head over ears in love with him, he with her, and so they married. That is all I know, perhaps all that anyone now knows, of the most important thing that ever happened to her. How important it was is proved by the fact that when he died four years later she was "as unhappy as it is possible for a human being to be". That was her own saying; it came to me from Kitty Maxse. "I have been as unhappy and as happy as it is possible for a human being to be." Kitty remembered it, because though she was very

---

* Hunt and Thomas Woolner were founder members of the Pre-Raphaelite Brotherhood.

† Anne Thackeray was the elder daughter of the novelist W. M. Thackeray and sister of Leslie Stephen's first wife. She married her cousin, Richmond Ritchie.

‡ She was twenty-one when she married Herbert Duckworth.

intimate with my mother, this was the only time in all their friendship that she
ever spoke of what she had felt for Herbert Duckworth.

What my mother was like when she was as happy as anyone can be, I have
no notion. Not a sound or a scene has survived from those four years. They
were well off; lived in Bryanston Square; he practised not very seriously at
the Bar; (once they went on circuit; and a friend said to him, "I spent the
whole morning in Court looking at a beautiful face" – Herbert's wife);
George was born; then Stella; and Gerald was about to be born when Herbert
Duckworth died. They were staying with the Vaughans at Upton;* he
stretched to pick a fig for my mother; an abscess burst; and he died in a few
hours. Those are the only facts I know about those four happy years.

If it were possible to know what Herbert himself was like, some ray of light
might fall from him upon my mother. But, like all very handsome men who
die tragically, he left not so much a character behind him as a legend. Youth
and death shed a halo through which it is difficult to see a real face – a face
one might see today in the street or here in my studio. To Aunt Mary – my
mother's sister, likely thus to share some of her feelings – he was "Oh
darling, a beam of light . . . like no one I have ever met . . . When Herbert
Duckworth smiled . . . when Herbert Duckworth came into the room . . ."
here she broke off, shook her head quickly from side to side and screwed her
face up, as if he were ineffable; no words could describe him. And in this
spasmodic way she gave an echo of what must have been my mother's
feeling; only hers was much deeper, and stronger. He must have been to her
the perfect man; heroic; handsome; magnanimous; "the great Achilles,
whom we knew" – it seems natural to quote Tennyson – and also genial,
lovable, simple, and also her husband; and her children's father. It was thus
natural to her when she was a girl to love the simple, the genial, the normal
ordinary type of man, in preference to the queer, the uncouth artistic, the
intellectual, whom she had met and who had wished to marry her. Herbert
was the perfect type of public school boy and English gentleman, my father
said. She chose him and how completely he satisfied her is proved by the
collapse, the complete collapse into which she fell when he died. All her
gaiety, all her sociability left her. She was as unhappy as it is possible for
anyone to be. There is very little known of the years that were thus stamped.
Only that saying, and Stella once told me that she used to lie upon his grave
at Orchardleigh. As she was undemonstrative that seems a superlative
expression of grief.

* Julia's sister, Adeline, married Henry Halford Vaughan. Upton Castle, in
Pembrokeshire, was rented by the Vaughans.

What is known, and is much more remarkable, is that during those eight years spent, so far as she had time over from her children and house, 'doing good', nursing, visiting the poor, she lost her faith. This hurt her mother, a deeply religious woman, to whom she was devoted, and thus must have been a genuine conviction; something arrived at as the result of solitary and independent thinking. It proves that there was more in her than simplicity; enthusiasm; romance; and thus makes sense of her two incongruous choices: Herbert and my father. There was a complexity in her; great simplicity and directness combined with a sceptical, a serious spirit. Probably it was that combination that accounted for the great impression she made on people; the positive impression. Her character was sharpened by the mixture of simplicity and scepticism. She was sociable yet severe; very amusing; but very serious; extremely practical but with a depth in her . . . "She was a mixture of the Madonna and a woman of the world," is Miss Robins's description.*

The certain fact at any rate is that when at last she was left alone – "Oh the torture of never being left alone!" is a saying of hers, reported I forget by whom, that refers to her widowhood, and the fuss that friends and family made – when she was alone at last in Hyde Park Gate, she began to think out her position; and for this reason perhaps read something my father had written. She liked it (he says in the 'Mausoleum Book'), when she was not sure that she liked him. It is thus permissible to think of her sitting in the creeper-shaded drawing room at Hyde Park Gate in her widow's dress, alone, when the children had gone to bed, with a copy of the *Fortnightly*, trying to reason out the case for agnosticism. From that she would go on to think of Leslie Stephen, the gaunt bearded man who lived up the street, married to Minny Thackeray. He was in every way the opposite of Herbert Duckworth; but there was something in his mind that interested her. One evening she called on the Leslie Stephens, [and] found them sitting over the fire together; a happy married pair, with one child in the nursery, and another to be born soon. She sat talking; and then went home, envying them their happiness and comparing it with her own loneliness. Next day Minny died suddenly. And about two years later she married the gaunt bearded widower.†

"How did father ask you to marry him?" I once asked her, with my arm slipped in hers as we went down the twisted stairs into the dining room. She gave her little laugh, half surprised, half shocked. She did not answer. He

---

* Elizabeth Robins, the actress, had been a friend of Julia's.
† Minny died in 1875; Leslie Stephen married Julia in 1878.

asked her in a letter; and she refused him. Then one night when he had given up all thought of it, and had been dining with her, and asking her advice about a governess for Laura, she followed him to the door and said "I will try to be a good wife to you."

Perhaps there was pity in her love; certainly there was devout admiration for his mind; and so she spanned the two marriages with the two different men; and emerged from that corridor of the eight silent years to live fifteen years more;* to bear four children; and [to] die early on the morning of the 5th of May 1895. George took us down to say goodbye. My father staggered from the bedroom as we came. I stretched out my arms to stop him, but he brushed past me, crying out something I could not catch; distraught. And George led me in to kiss my mother, who had just died.

May 28th 1939. Led by George with towels wrapped round us and given each a drop of brandy in warm milk to drink, we were taken into the bedroom. I think candles were burning; and I think the sun was coming in. At any rate I remember the long looking-glass; with the drawers on either side; and the washstand; and the great bed on which my mother lay. I remember very clearly how even as I was taken to the bedside I noticed that one nurse was sobbing, and a desire to laugh came over me, and I said to myself as I have often done at moments of crisis since, "I feel nothing whatever". Then I stooped and kissed my mother's face. It was still warm. She [had] only died a moment before. Then we went upstairs into the day nursery.

Perhaps it was the next evening that Stella took me into the bedroom to kiss mother for the last time. She had been lying on her side before. Now she was lying straight in the middle of her pillows. Her face looked immeasurably distant, hollow and stern. When I kissed her, it was like kissing cold iron. Whenever I touch cold iron the feeling comes back to me – the feeling of my mother's face, iron cold, and granulated. I started back. Then Stella stroked her cheek, and undid a button on her nightgown. "She always liked to have it like that," she said. When she came up to the nursery later she said to me, "Forgive me. I saw you were afraid." She had noticed that I had started. When Stella asked me to forgive her for having given me that shock, I cried – we had been crying off and on all day – and said, "When I see mother, I see a man sitting with her." Stella looked at me as if I had frightened her. Did I say that in order to attract attention to myself? Or was it true? I cannot be sure, for certainly I had a great wish to draw attention to myself. But certainly it was true that when she said: "Forgive me," and thus

* After her marriage to Leslie Stephen, Julia lived seventeen years.

made me visualize my mother, I seemed to see a man sitting bent on the edge of the bed.

"It's nice that she shouldn't be alone", Stella said after a moment's pause.

Of course the atmosphere of those three or four days before the funeral was so melodramatic, histrionic and unreal that any hallucination was possible. We lived through them in hush, in artificial light. Rooms were shut. People were creeping in and out. People were coming to the door all the time. We were all sitting in the drawing room round father's chair sobbing. The hall reeked of flowers. They were piled on the hall table. The scent still brings back those days of astonishing intensity. But I have one memory of great beauty. A telegram had been sent to Thoby at Clifton. He was to arrive in the evening at Paddington. George and Stella whispered together in the hall, about who was to go and meet him. To my relief, Stella overcame some objection on George's part, and said, "But I think it would do her good to go"; and so I was taken in a cab with George and Nessa to meet Thoby at Paddington. It was sunset, and the great glass dome at the end of the station was blazing with light. It was glowing yellow and red and the iron girders made a pattern across it. I walked along the platform gazing with rapture at this magnificent blaze of colour, and the train slowly steamed into the station. It impressed and exalted me. It was so vast and so fiery red. The contrast of that blaze of magnificent light with the shrouded and curtained rooms at Hyde Park Gate was so intense. Also it was partly that my mother's death unveiled and intensified; made me suddenly develop perceptions, as if a burning glass had been laid over what was shaded and dormant. Of course this quickening was spasmodic. But it was surprising – as if something were becoming visible without any effort. To take another instance – I remember going into Kensington Gardens about that time. It was a hot spring evening, and we lay down – Nessa and I – in the long grass behind the Flower Walk. I had taken *The Golden Treasury* with me. I opened it and began to read some poem. And instantly and for the first time I understood the poem (which it was I forget). It was as if it became altogether intelligible; I had a feeling of transparency in words when they cease to be words and become so intensified that one seems to experience them; to foretell them as if they developed what one is already feeling. I was so astonished that I tried to explain the feeling. "One seems to understand what it's about", I said awkwardly. I suppose Nessa has forgotten; no one could have understood from what I said the queer feeling I had in the hot grass, that poetry was coming true. Nor does that give the feeling. It matches what I have sometimes felt when I write. The pen gets on the scent.

But though I remember so distinctly those two moments – the arch of glass burning at the end of Paddington Station and the poem I read in Kensington Gardens, those two clear moments are almost the only clear moments in the muffled dulness that then closed over us. With mother's death the merry, various family life which she had held in being shut for ever. In its place a dark cloud settled over us; we seemed to sit all together cooped up, sad, solemn, unreal, under a haze of heavy emotion. It seemed impossible to break through. It was not merely dull; it was unreal. A finger seemed laid on one's lips.

I see us now, all dressed in unbroken black, George and Gerald in black trousers, Stella with real crape deep on her dress, Nessa and myself with slightly modified crape, my father black from head to foot – even the notepaper was so black bordered that only a little space for writing remained – I see us emerging from Hyde Park Gate on a fine summer afternoon and walking in procession hand in hand, for we were always taking hands – I see us walking – I rather proud of the solemn blackness and the impression it must make – into Kensington Gardens; and how golden the laburnum shone. And then we sat silent under the trees. The silence was stifling. A finger was laid on our lips. One had always to think whether what one was about to say was the right thing to say. It ought to be a help. But how could one help? Father used to sit sunk in gloom. If he could be got to talk – and that was part of our duty – it was about the past. It was about "the old days". And when he talked, he ended with a groan. He was getting deaf, and his groans were louder than he knew. Indoors he would walk up and down the room, gesticulating, crying that he had never told mother how he loved her. Then Stella would fling her arms round him and protest. Often one would break in upon a scene of this kind. And he would open his arms and call one to him. We were his only hope, his only comfort, he would say. And there kneeling on the floor one would try – perhaps only to cry.

Stella of course bore the brunt. She grew whiter and whiter in her unbroken black dress. She would sit at her table with the black-edged notepaper before her writing, answering letters of sympathy. There was a photograph of mother in front of her; and sometimes she would cry, as she wrote. As the summer wore on, visitors came, sympathetic women, old friends. They were admitted to the back drawing room, where father sat like the Queen in Shakespeare – "here I and sorrow sit" – with the Virginia Creeper hanging a curtain of green over the window, so that the room was like a green cave. We in the front room sat crouched, hearing muffled voices, ready for the visitor to emerge with tears on tear-stained cheeks. The shrouded, cautious, dulled life took the place of all the chatter and laughter of the summer. There were no more parties; no more young men and women laughing. No more flashing visions of white summer dresses and hansoms dashing off to private views and dinner parties, none of that natural life and gaiety which my mother had created. The grown-up world into which I would dash for a moment and pick off some joke or little scene and dash back again upstairs to the nursery was ended. There were none of those snatched moments that were so amusing and for some reason so soothing and yet exciting when one ran downstairs to dinner arm in arm with mother; or chose the jewels she was to wear. There was none of that pride when one said something that amused her, or that she thought very remarkable. How excited I used to be when the 'Hyde Park Gate News' was laid on her plate on Monday morning, and she liked something I had written!* Never shall I forget my extremity of pleasure – it was like being a violin and being played upon – when I found that she had sent a story of mine to Madge Symonds; it was so imaginative, she said; it was about souls flying round and choosing bodies to be born into.

The tragedy of her death was not that it made one, now and then and very intensely, unhappy. It was that it made her unreal; and us solemn, and self-conscious. We were made to act parts that we did not feel; to fumble for words that we did not know. It obscured, it dulled. It made one hypocritical and immeshed in the conventions of sorrow. Many foolish and sentimental ideas came into being. Yet there was a struggle, for soon we revived, and there was a conflict between what we ought to be and what we were. Thoby put his into words. One day before he went back to school, he said: "It's silly going on like this . . .", sobbing, sitting shrouded, he meant. I was shocked at his heartlessness; yet he was right, I know; and yet how could we escape?

It was Stella who lifted the canopy again. A little light crept in.

June 20th 1939. I was thinking as I crossed the Channel last night of Stella; in a very jerky disconnected way, with people quarrelling outside the door; the boat train arriving; chains clanking; and the steamer giving those sudden stertorous snorts. And as the first morning after a broken night is distracted and broken, instead of beginning Roger again, as I ought, I will write down some of my distracted and disconnected thoughts; to serve, should the time come, for notes.

How many people are there still able to think about Stella on the 20th June 1939? Very few. Jack died last Christmas; George and Gerald a year or two ago; Kitty Maxse and Margaret Massingberd have been dead many years now. Susan Lushington and Lisa Stillman are still alive; but how they live and where, I know not. Perhaps thus I think of her less disconnectedly and more truly than anyone now living, save for Vanessa and Adrian; and

---

* The 'Hyde Park Gate News' appeared weekly, as far as is known, from 9 February 1891 until April 1895. The paper was at first the joint venture of Vanessa, Virginia and Thoby but gradually it became almost entirely Virginia's responsibility. See QB, I, pp. 28–32, and Lee, pp. 108–13.

perhaps old Sophie Farrell.* Of her childhood I know practically nothing. She was the only daughter of the handsome barrister Herbert Duckworth, but as he died when she was three or four, she did not remember him, or those years when her mother was as happy as anyone can be. I think, from stray anecdotes and from what I noticed myself, that when she came to consciousness as a child the unhappy years were at their height. That would account for some qualities in Stella. Her first memories were of a very sad widowed mother, who "went about doing good" – Stella wished to have that on the tombstone – visiting the slums, visiting too the Cancer Hospital in the Brompton Road. Our Quaker Aunt told me that this was her habit; for she said how one case there had "shocked her". Thus Stella as a child lived in the shade of that widowhood; saw that beautiful crape-veiled figure daily; and perhaps took then the ply that was so marked – that attitude of devotion, almost canine in its touching adoration, to her mother; that passive, suffering affection; and also that complete unquestioning dependence.

They were sun and moon to each other; my mother the positive and definite; Stella the reflecting and satellite. My mother was stern to her. All her devotion was given to George who was like his father; and her care was for Gerald, born posthumously and very delicate. Stella she treated severely; so much so that before their marriage my father ventured a protest. She replied that it might be true; she was hard on Stella because she felt Stella "part of myself". A pale silent child I imagine her; sensitive; modest; uncomplaining; adoring her mother, thinking only how she could help her, and without any ambition or even character of her own. And yet she had character. Very gentle, very honest, and in some way individual – so she made her own impression on people. Friends, like Kitty Maxse, the brilliant, the sparkling, loved her with a real laughing tenderness for her own sake. Her charm was great; it came partly from this modesty, from this honesty, from this perfectly simple unostentatious unselfishness; it came too from her lack of pose, her lack of snobbery; and from the genuineness, from something that was – could I put my finger on it – perfectly herself, individual. This unnamed quality – the sensitiveness to real things – was queer in the sister of George and Gerald, who were so opaque and conventional; who had so innate a respect for the conventions and respectabilities. By some odd fling in her birth, she had escaped all taint of Duckworth philistinism; she had none of their shrewd middle-class complacency. Instead of their little brown eyes that were so greedy and twinkling, hers were very large and rather a pale

---

* Sophie Farrell was the Stephens' cook at 22 Hyde Park Gate and at 46 Gordon Square, Bloomsbury. After Vanessa's marriage she went with Virginia and Adrian to 29 Fitzroy Square and later to George Duckworth.

blue. They were dreamy, candid eyes. She was without their instinctive worldliness. She was lovely too, in a far vaguer, less perfect way than my mother. She reminded me always of those large white flowers – elder-blossom, cow parsley, that one sees in the fields in June. Perhaps my mother's laughing nickname – 'Old Cow' – suggests the cow parsley. Or again, a white faint moon in a blue sky suggests her. Or those large white roses that have many petals and are semi-transparent. She had beautiful fair hair, growing in horns over her forehead; and no colour in her face at all. As for teaching – she had perhaps a governess; went to classes; was taught the violin by Arnold Dolmetsch and played in Mrs Marshall's orchestra. But there was a stoppage in her mind, a gentle impassivity about books and learning. As Jack told me after her death, she thought herself so stupid as to be almost wanting; and said that the rheumatic fever she had as a child had (I remember the word) 'touched' her. But again, what was remarkable considering the Duckworth strain – so boorish, so rustic, so philistine – is that however simple she was in brain, she was not, as George's sister might so well have been, a cheery ordinary English upper middle class girl with rosy cheeks and bright brown eyes. She was herself. She remains quite distinct in my mind. What is odd is that I cannot compare her either in character or face with anyone else. What she would have looked like now in a room full of other people I cannot imagine; or how she would have talked. I have never seen anyone who reminded me of her; and that is true too of my mother. They do not blend in the world of the living at all.

She was nineteen when I was six or seven; and as a girl could not then go about London alone, I used as a small child to be sent with her, as chaperone. Among my earliest memories is the memory of going out with her perhaps to shop, or to pay some call; and, the errand done, she would take me to a shop and give me a glass of milk and biscuits sprinkled with sugar on a marble table. And sometimes we went in hansoms. But she lived, of course, downstairs in the drawing room; pouring out tea; and there were many young men, it seemed when one dashed in for a second, sitting round her. Vaguely we knew that Arthur Studd was in love with her; and Ted Sanderson; and I think Richard Norton; and Jim Stephen.* That great figure with the deep voice and the wild eyes would come to the house looking for her, with his madness on him; and would burst into the nursery and spear the bread on his swordstick and at one time we were told to go out by the back door and if we met Jim we were to say that Stella was away.

* James Kenneth Stephen, second son of James Fitzjames Stephen, brother of Leslie.

*

19th July 1939. I was forced to break off again, and rather suspect that these breaks will be the end of this memoir.

I was thinking about Stella as we crossed the Channel a month ago. I have not given her a thought since. The past only comes back when the present runs so smoothly that it is like the sliding surface of a deep river. Then one sees through the surface to the depths. In those moments I find one of my greatest satisfactions, not that I am thinking of the past; but that it is then that I am living most fully in the present. For the present when backed by the past is a thousand times deeper than the present when it presses so close that you can feel nothing else, when the film on the camera reaches only the eye. But to feel the present sliding over the depths of the past, peace is necessary. The present must be smooth, habitual. For this reason – that it destroys the fullness of life – any break – like that of house moving – causes me extreme distress; it breaks; it shallows; it turns the depth into hard thin splinters. As I say to L[eonard]: "What's there real about this? Shall we ever live a real life again?" "At Monks House," he says. So I write this, taking a morning off from the word filing and fitting that my life of Roger means – I write this partly in order to recover my sense of the present by getting the past to shadow this broken surface. Let me then, like a child advancing with bare feet into a cold river, descend again into that stream.

. . . Jim Stephen was in love with Stella. He was mad then. He was in the exalted stage of his madness. He would dash up in a hansom; leave my father to pay it. The hansom had been driving him about London all day. The man wanted perhaps a sovereign. It was paid. For 'dear Jim' was a great favourite. Once, as I say, he dashed up [to] the nursery and speared the bread. Another time, off we went to his room in De Vere Gardens and he painted me on a small bit of wood. He was a great painter for a time. I suppose madness made him believe he was all powerful. Once he came in at breakfast, "Savage* has just told me I'm in danger of dying or going mad", he laughed. And soon he ran naked through Cambridge; was taken to an asylum; and died. This great mad figure with his broad shoulders and very clean cut mouth, and the deep voice and the powerful face – and the very blue eyes – this mad man would recite poetry to us; "The Burial of Sir John Moore", I remember; and he always brings to mind some tormented bull; and also Achilles – Achilles on his pressed bed lolling roars out a deep applause. He was in love with Stella – incongruously enough. And we had orders to tell him, if we met him in the

---

* Dr George Savage, later Sir George, was an old friend of the Stephen family. He was also one of Virginia's doctors.

street, that she was away, staying with the Lushingtons at Pyports. There was a great mystery about love then.

Jim was one of her lovers. The other – that is, the most important – was Jack Hills. It was at St Ives that she refused him; late one night we heard her sobbing through the attic wall. He had gone at once. A refusal in those days was catastrophic. It meant a complete breach. Human relations, at least between the sexes, were carried on as relations between countries are now – with ambassadors, and treaties. The parties concerned met on the great occasion of the proposal. If this were refused, a state of war was declared. That explains why she cried so bitterly. For she had done something of great practical as well as emotional importance. He went off at once – to Norway to fish; later perhaps they met in a completely formal way at parties. Negotiations were kept faintly alive through my mother; an interpreter was necessary. All this procedure gave love its solemnity. Feelings were banked up; silence interposed; there was in every family a code, a religious code, that penetrated, somehow or other, to the children. It was secret; but we guessed.

Thus, when my mother died, Stella was left without any negotiator, for my father did not fill the part. He must have come back – it proves how deep the feeling was to admit such a return – the night before my mother died. It was desperate but not hopeless.*

June 8th 1940. I have just found this sheaf of notes, thrown away into my waste-paper basket. I had been tidying up; and had cast all my life of Roger into that large basket, and with it, these sheets too. Now I am correcting the final page proofs of Roger; and it was to refresh myself from that antlike meticulous labour that I determined to look for these pages. Shall I ever finish these notes – let alone make a book from them? The battle is at its crisis; every night the Germans fly over England; it comes closer to this house daily. If we are beaten then – however we solve that problem, and one solution is apparently suicide (so it was decided three nights ago in London among us) – book writing becomes doubtful. But I wish to go on, not to settle down in that dismal puddle.

Jack Hills, I was saying, came back the night before my mother died, which shows that though the negotiations had been broken off, there must have been a connection, or how could he have come that night of great crisis?

* The source of the ambiguity of this passage can be traced to an earlier ms version (A.5c, p. 4, l.22–p. 5, l.3) which reads: "Thus when my mother died, Stella was left without any negotiator in this affair of marriage; & Jack Hills came to the house on a very queer footing. He must have come the night my mother died. For I remember the doctors had gone; it was desperate but not hopeless; it was after dinner; & Aunt Mary poured out coffee. (Stella being in the bedroom.)"

We were in the back drawing room, and there was the tea tray, for we had a curious habit of drinking tea about nine o'clock. The silver hot water jug which I still possess – but it has a hole in it – had a handle that grew hot. Aunt Mary, summoned from Brighton, picked it up and put it down quickly.* "Only Mrs Stephen and Stella can manage that", said Jack Hills with the queer sad little smile that went with the little joke. And I remember that he said 'Stella'. And since he was there, that last night, the affair must have been in being – sufficiently so to make it possible for him to be with us in intimacy. That was the 4th May, 1895.

The next thing I remember is the night at Hindhead (August 22nd 1896) – the black and silver night of mysterious voices, the night when father packed us off to bed early; and we heard voices in the garden; and saw Stella and Jack passing; and disappearing; and the tramp came; and Thoby countered him; and Nessa and I sat up in our bedroom waiting; and Stella never came; and at last in the early morning she came and told us that she was engaged; and I whispered, "Did mother know?" and she murmured, "Yes".

And next morning at breakfast there was excitement and emotion and gloom. Adrian cried; and Jack kissed him; and father said gently but seriously: "We must all be happy, because Stella is happy" – a command which, poor man, he could not himself obey.

But Jack Hills? He had been at Eton with George. He stands in my mind's picture gallery for a type – and a desirable type; the English country gentleman type, I might call it, by way of running a line round it; and I add, it is a type I have seldom been intimate with; perhaps no one is ever intimate with the country gentleman type; yet for nine years I was intimate with Jack Hills; a reason perhaps why we became so completely separate later; it was impossible to begin again formally after that intimacy. And the country gentleman came to the surface and separated us.

Can I quickly fill in that outline? To begin then, he was the son of a commonplace little round man – Judge Hills – 'Buzzy' he was called in the family – and like a bluebottle, buzzing, I still remember him; short, jocular, in knickerbockers, giving us Russian toffee up at Corby. Buzzy had once written a sonnet that had been taken for Shakespeare's, and liked to make little facetious jokes with young ladies – I remember Susan Lushington "didn't know which way to look", she said, when he chaffed her about a husband – "I seemed to be sitting on a tripod and looking into the future", Buzzy said, having archly used the word husband when it should have been father – Buzzy lived chiefly in Egypt, and Mrs Hills – Anna her name was – lived mostly alone at Corby. She was a hard, worldly woman, tightly dressed

---

* Aunt Mary (née Jackson), Julia's elder sister who married Herbert Fisher and had seven sons and four daughters.

in black satin in London; up at Corby, a county lady, collecting Chelsea enamel snuff boxes, with ambitions to be the friend of intellectual men. She detested women; she got on very well with Andrew Lang. He stayed there often; and she described a party when the local dentist came in a frock coat – "all the other men looking so picturesque in knickerbockers." And she said: "I was in mourning for nine people at Easter"; also, looking at horses in the paddock, "That makes the <u>second</u> pair"; also she stressed "<u>under</u> housemaid" to impress us that she had several; and dwelt on the noble descent of the Curwens, to whom they were related; and went weekly to Naworth with a wreath to lay on Christopher Howard's grave. It was handed in at the carriage; like a picnic basket – the weekly wreath. And I still see her in shiny black satin and feathered Victorian hat bending over the grave in Naworth burial ground; and Susan whispering in agitation "Suppose Lady Carlisle or one of them should come out and catch us!" These recollections spring from that dreary and terrifying week at Corby after Stella's death in the autumn of 1897. They leased Corby from the Howards; the lion stood with his tail perfectly straight on top of the roof. The river dashed through the grounds; and there I saw Jack catch a salmon; for the first time after those desperate months he looked triumphant; and worn as he [had] come to look, I was struck by his sudden exultation as the line tautened and he held the fish there in the river. We saw it afterwards in the game larder; and Mrs Hills asked: "Has he those little creatures on him?" It was a proof of freshness, I think, if you found lice on a salmon. Tuddenham, the keeper, who stood by us on the bank, said: "He's hooked him."

To return to Anna Hills. She hated women. But I doubt that she was sexually ambitious. I think all she wanted was to rule a little court of well brushed, mildly well-known males; in the decorous, snobbish Victorian manner. She was thankful, I remember she told us, that she had no daughters; and it was plain she detested having us two rather gawky girls to stay. "Your hair's parted awry", she said, fixing me with her little black eyes. Fortunately she had three sons; and they were sent to Eton and Oxford. She liked the soft sweet voiced Eustace with his drawl, and his pleasant manners, and his gentle ways, far the best. Jack and she were on very distant terms. Thus it was natural that when he was living alone in Ebury Street, very hard up, very hard worked, stammering, and lonely, that he came to my mother for sympathy. They were very intimate. Indeed Kitty Maxse said, discussing my mother and her masterful ways once: "For instance, how could Mrs Hills have liked it – Jack treating your mother as if she were his?" He was, roughly speaking, affectionate, honest, domestic, and a perfect gentleman. He was a real [countryman] too; not a fake; a passionate countryman. He rode very well; he fished very well; and there was too a vein of poetry in him. Once when we met years later he told me he read every book of new poetry that

came out; and thought the young poets (then Siegfried Sassoon; Robert
Graves; and de la Mare) every bit as good as the old. He read philosophy too;
Nettleship, the Oxford philosopher, had been a kind of god to him. "He was
like Christ", I remember his saying, in his emphatic sententious way, as he
tried very laboriously to explain Nettleship's philosophy; he lent us the book;
it was at Warboys that I remember him explaining Plato to me and Nessa and
Marny Vaughan.* Gerald, who sat beneath the window, sneered later: "Well,
how did the Sunday prayer meeting go off?" But he was not, compared with
my own friends, anything but a simple, primitive-minded man. Unlike them,
however – was it for this I liked him, yet could never be altogether at my ease
with him? – he was an all-round man; without any gift that dominated, he did
a great many different things. He was a Gunner. "I have heard of him
standing on one foot, driving three horses", Ethel Dilke wrote when the
engagement was public, "and I've no doubt he does other things as well." He
was a good solicitor. Doggedly he worked his way high up into the firm of
Roper and Whateley; of Whateley he used to tell many stories: "a disgusting
man, but in some ways the ablest man I have ever known. He was a great
fisherman – so they say. And I like his fishing books." Politics came later. He
was also very deft with his hands. But as I heard my mother tell my father
once, he was 'nothing out of the way' intellectually. His appearance was in
keeping with this rough sketch. He had beautiful brown eyes, a nose with an
obstinate knob at the end of it; curious wrinkles, like a dachshund's, round
his retreating chin. (He was of course very fond of dogs.) He stammered, and
his stammer made his very positive statements – "A duck must have water"
– all the more positive when at last he got them out. We laughed at him and
could imitate him as time went on. He was scrupulously clean; he washed all
over ever so many times a day, and was scrupulously well dressed, as a
Victorian city solicitor; also as a countryman. The word 'scrupulous'
suggests itself when I think of Jack Hills. He was scrupulously honest,
honourable, in the Eton and Balliol sense, but there was more to his
scrupulosity than that. He it was who first spoke to me openly and
deliberately about sex – in Fitzroy Square, with the green carpet and the red
Chinese curtains.† He opened my eyes on purpose, as I think, to the part
played by sex in the life of the ordinary man. He shocked me a little,
wholesomely. He told me that young men talked incessantly of women; and
'had' them incessantly. "But are they—" I hesitated for a word and then
ventured "honourable?" He laughed, "of course – of course", he assured me.

* Margaret, one of the Vaughan cousins whom the young Stephens saw
frequently.
† 29 Fitzroy Square, Bloomsbury, where Virginia and Adrian moved after
Vanessa's marriage to Clive Bell in 1907.

Sexual relations had nothing to do with honour. Having women was a mere trifle in a man's life, he explained, and made not a jot of difference to their honourableness – to their reputation with other men. I was incredibly, but only partially, innocent. I knew nothing about ordinary men's lives, and thought all men, like my father, loved one woman only, and were 'dishonourable' if unchaste, as much as women; yet, at the same time I had known since I was sixteen or so, all about sodomy, through reading Plato. That was Jack's honesty; and it differed from George's or Gerald's. Neither of them would have spoken to any girl as cleanly, humorously, openly, about sex. That quality penetrated to us as children, and he brought too, country life into our distinguished literary, book-loving world. He taught us to sugar trees; he gave us his copy of Morris's *Butterflies and Moths*,* over which I spent many hours, hunting up our catches among all those pictures of hearts and darts and setaceous Hebrew characters.† For I had the post of name finder in our Entomological Society; and was scolded severely by Thoby, I remember, for slackness. At dinner one night Gerald disclosed, with his teasing and treacherous laughter, how we had a store of dying insects in old tooth-powder jars at the bottom of the well. Greatly to our relief instead of scolding and forbidding, mother and, I think, father recognised our mania; and put it on a legal basis, bought us nets and setting boards; and indeed she went with Walter Headlam‡ down to the St Ives public house and bought us rum. How strange a scene – my mother buying rum. She would go round the sugar after we were in bed.

But to return to Jack – when Stella accepted him, we approved, in our republic, which, though rapidly losing shape, was still in being after mother's death. The marriage would have been, I think, a very happy marriage. It should have borne many children. And still she might have been alive. Certainly he was passionately in love; she at first passively. And it was through that engagement that I had my first vision – so intense, so exciting, so rapturous was it that the word vision applies – my first vision then of love between man and woman. It was to me like a ruby; the love I detected that winter of their engagement, glowing, red, clear, intense. It gave me a

---

* Francis Orpen Morris (1810–93) wrote popular books on natural history. He published *A History of British Butterflies* (London, 1853) and *A History of British Moths* in four volumes (1859–70) but no book with the title *Butterflies and Moths*.

† These are the vernacular names of common British moths. VW's ts has 'harts and darts and sequacious Hebrew characters'.

‡ Walter Headlam, Fellow of King's College, Cambridge, distinguished Hellenist and minor poet, was an old friend of the Stephen family with whom Virginia carried on a flirtation after the marriage of Vanessa. He died in 1908.

conception of love; a standard of love; a sense that nothing in the whole world is so lyrical, so musical, as a young man and a young woman in their first love for each other. I connect it with respectable engagements; unofficial love never gives me the same feeling. "My Love's like a red, red rose, that's newly sprung in June" – that was the feeling they gave; the feeling that has always come back, when I hear of 'an engagement'; not when I hear of 'an affair'. It derives from Stella and Jack. It springs from the ecstasy I felt, in my covert, behind the folding doors of the Hyde Park Gate drawing room. I sat there, shielded, being half insane with shyness and nervousness; reading Fanny Burney's diary; and feeling come over me intermittent waves of very strong emotion – rage sometimes; how often I was enraged by father then! – love, or the reflection of love, too. It was bodiless; a light; an ecstasy. But also extraordinarily enduring. Once I came on a letter from him which she had slipped between the blotting paper – a sign of the lack of privacy in which we lived – and read it. "There is nothing sweeter in the whole world than our love", he wrote. I put the page down, not so much guiltily, at having pried; but in a quiver of ecstasy at the revelation. Still I cannot read words that give me that quiver twice over. If I get a letter that pleases me intensely, I never read it again. Why I wonder? For fear lest it shall dwindle? This colour, this incandescence, was in Stella's whole body. Her pallor became lit up, her eyes bluer. She had something of moonlight about her that winter, as she went about the house. "There's never been anything like it in the world", I said – or something like it – when she found me awake one night. And she laughed, tenderly, very gently, and kissed me and said, "Oh lots of people are in love as we are. You and Nessa will be one day", she said. Once she told me, "You must expect people to look at you both".

"Nessa", she said, "is much more beautiful than I ever was" – at twenty-six she spoke of her beauty as a thing of the past. She told Aunt Mary – I think I read this too, nefariously, in some letter in a blotting book, she could only be neat and tidy now; she was to float us on the life of love; to launch us out on the ordinary woman's life that promised such treasures. At some party, perhaps Nessa's first party, a party where she wore white and amethysts perhaps, a party where Desmond* remarked her 'like a Greek slave', she was certain that George Booth† had fallen in love, and feared, tenderly foreboding, yet proudly, and gladly, how the Booths would mind if Nessa rejected him. Had Stella lived, the recollection makes me reflect, how

* Desmond MacCarthy, who belonged to the inner circle of Bloomsbury from its earliest days.

† George Booth was the son of Charles Booth, author of *Life and Labour of the People in London*. The Booths were 'Hyde Park Gaters', as Adrian was later to call them.

different 'coming out' and those Greek slave years and all their drudgery and tyranny and rebellion would have been!

For some reason Stella and Jack's engagement lasted all the months from July till April. It was a clumsy, cruel, unnecessary trial for them both. Looking back, it seems everything was done without care or consideration, clumsily, wantonly. I conceive that as the months of that long waiting time passed she slowly roused herself out of the numb, frozen state in which mother's death had left her. At first she found in Jack rest and support; a refuge from all the worries and responsibilities of 'the family', relief too from those glooms which father never controlled, and spent on her. Slowly she became more positive, less passive; and asserted Jack's rights; her desire too for her own house; her own husband; a life, a home of their own. At last the promise, apparently exacted by father, and tacitly accepted, that they were to live on with us after their marriage, an arrangement now incredible but then accepted, became intolerable; and she went up to father one night in his study; and told him so; and there was 'an explosion'.

As the engagement went on, father became indeed increasingly tyrannical. He didn't like the name 'Jack', I remember his saying; it sounded like the smack of a whip. He was jealous clearly. But in those days nothing was clear. He had his traditional pose; he was the lonely; the deserted; the old unhappy man. In fact he was possessive; hurt; a man jealous of the young man. There was every excuse, he would have said, had he been asked, for his explosions. And as by this time he had entrenched himself away from all truth, in a world which it is almost impossible to describe, for I know no one now who could inhabit such a world – the engagement was incredibly involved, frustrated, and impeded. At last in April 1897 the marriage took place – conventionally, ceremoniously, with bells ringing, and company collected, and silver engraved wedding invitations, at St Mary Abbots. Nessa and I handed flowers to the guests; father marched up the aisle with Stella on his arm.

"He took it for granted that he was to give her away", George and Gerald grumbled. He ignored the fact that they had any claim. No one would have dared to take that privilege from him. It was somehow typical – his assumption; and his enjoyment of the attitude. They went to Italy; we to Brighton. One fortnight was the length of their honeymoon. And directly she came back she was taken ill. It was appendicitis; she was going to have a baby. And that was mismanaged too; and so, after three months of intermittent illness, she died – at 24 Hyde Park Gate, on July 27th, 1897.*

---

* The A.5a typescript ends here. The text now follows the BL 61973 typescript. See Editor's Note, p. 177.

*

The present. June 19th 1940. As we sat down to lunch two days ago, Monday 17th, John* came in, looked white about the gills, his pale eyes paler than usual, and said the French have stopped fighting. Today the dictators dictate their terms to France. Meanwhile, on this very hot morning, with a blue bottle buzzing and a toothless organ grinding and the men calling strawberries in the Square, I sit in my room at 37 M[ecklenburgh] S[square]† and turn to my father.

My father now falls to be described, because it was during the seven years between Stella's death in 1897 and his death in 1904 that Nessa and I were fully exposed without protection to the full blast of that strange character. Nessa, when Stella died, was just eighteen; I fifteen and a half. In order to explain why I say "exposed", and why, though the word is not the right one – but I cannot find one that is – I call him a strange character, I should have to be able to inhabit again the outworn shell of my own childish mind and body. I am much nearer his age now than my own then. But do I therefore 'understand' him better than I did? Or have I only queered the angle of that immensely important relationship, so that I shall fail to describe it, either from his point of view or my own? I see him now from round the corner; not directly in front of me. Further, just as I rubbed out a good deal of the force of my mother's memory by writing about her in *To the Lighthouse*, so I rubbed out much of his memory there too. Yet he too obsessed me for years. Until I wrote it out, I would find my lips moving; I would be arguing with him; raging against him; saying to myself all that I never said to him. How deep they drove themselves into me, the things it was impossible to say aloud. They are still some of them sayable; when Nessa for instance revives the memory of Wednesday and its weekly books, I still feel come over me that old frustrated fury.

But in me, though not in her, rage alternated with love. It was only the other day when I read Freud‡ for the first time, that I discovered that this violently disturbing conflict of love and hate is a common feeling; and is called ambivalence. But before I analyse our relation as father and daughter, I will try to sketch him as I think he must have been, not to me, but to the world at large.

He was a little early Victorian boy, brought up in the intense narrow, evangelical yet political, highly intellectual yet completely unaesthetic,

* John Lehmann, who eventually became a partner of The Hogarth Press.

† The Woolfs' London residence from July 1939.

‡ Diary entry for 2 December 1939, "Began reading Freud last night; to enlarge the circumference, to give my brain wider scope, to make it objective; to get outside. Thus defeat the shrinkage of age." *Diary of Virginia Woolf*, V, p. 248.

Stephen family, that had one foot in Clapham, the other in Downing Street. Such is the obvious first sentence of his biography. And as it goes on, it is all so obvious that I cannot bring myself to follow it – how he went to Eton and was unhappy; went to Cambridge and was in his element; was not elected an Apostle, was muscular; coached his boat; and Christian; but shed his Christianity – with such anguish, Fred Maitland* once hinted to me, that he thought of suicide, and how then, like Pendennis or any other of the Victorian young men of intellect – he was typical of them – took to writing for the papers, went to America; and was, so far as I can see, the very type, or mould, of so many Cambridge intellectuals – like George Trevelyan, like Charlie Sanger, like Goldie Dickinson – whom I knew later. It bores me to write of him, to try to describe him, partly because it is all so familiar; partly because it is a type that for me lacks picturesqueness, oddity, romance. That type is like a steel engraving, without colour, or warmth or body; but with an infinity of precise clear lines. There are no crannies or corners to catch my imagination; nothing dangles a spray at me. It is all contained and complete and already summed up. Of course, I say to myself, I admire them. I go on: I respect them, I say; I admire their honesty, their integrity, their intellect. I have so clear an impression of them on my surface that if I am in the same room with them I feel I know exactly where I am; indeed, if I am in the same room with other types, like Harold Nicolson or Hugh Walpole, I have my Cambridge intellectual yard measure handy; and say silently: How terribly you fall short. How you miss the mark, here and here and here. But at the same time I am seduced; and feel that my measure has been proved faulty. The Harold Nicolsons and the Hugh Walpoles give me colour and warmth; they amuse and stimulate me. But still I do not respect them as I respect George Moore.

But I can add something to my father's steel engraving – a violent temper. Even as a child Aunt Anny† told me, he would work himself into such violent rages that – I forget how she finished the sentence, but I think it had something to do with smashing a flower pot in a greenhouse; and nobody – nobody – could control him, she said. This temper that he could not control, and that, considering his worship of reason, his hatred of gush, of exaggeration, of all superlatives, seems inconsistent. It was due, I suppose, to the fact that he was spoilt as a child; because of his nervous delicacy; and that delicacy excused his extreme irritability. But it was also, I guess, the convention, supported by the great men of the time, Carlyle, Tennyson, that

---

* Frederick William Maitland wrote the authorized 'Life' of Leslie Stephen. He married Florence Fisher, one of Aunt Mary's daughters.

† Anne Ritchie (née Thackeray).

men of genius were naturally uncontrolled. And genius when my father was a young man was in full flower. A man of genius meant a man who had fits of positive inspiration; "Ah but," I can remember my father saying of Stevenson, "he was a man of genius." Those who had genius in the Victorian sense were like the prophets; different, another breed. They dressed differently; wore long hair, great black hats, capes and cloaks. They were invariably "ill to live with". But it never struck my father, I believe, that there was any harm in being ill to live with. I think he said unconsciously as he worked himself up into one of those violent outbursts: "This is a sign of my genius," and he called in Carlyle to confirm him, and let himself fly. It was part of the convention that after these outbursts, the man of genius became "touchingly apologetic"; but he took it for granted that his wife or sister would accept his apology, that he was exempt, because of his genius, from the laws of good society. But was he a man of genius? No; that was not alas quite the case. "Only a good second class mind," he once told me, as we walked around the croquet lawn at Fritham. And he said he might have done well to be a scientist.

This frustrated desire to be a man of genius, and the knowledge that he was in truth not in the first flight – a knowledge which led to a great deal of despondency, and to that self-centredness which in later life at least made him so childishly greedy for compliments, made him brood so disproportionately over his failure and the extent of it and the reasons for it – these are qualities that break up the fine steel engraving of the typical Cambridge intellectual. He had considerably more idiosyncrasy, more character as a man – for I am trying to see him as a man not as a father – than the stock Cambridge type. For men like Lowell and Fred Maitland and Herbert Fisher not only admired him; but felt a protecting humorous love for him; so I judge from his power to breed stories; to create a legend. Fred Maitland for instance told how they marched over the Cornish moors all day and Leslie was silent; "but I felt we had become friends"; and Lytton told me of some Strachey cousin who had watched my father as he sat by the fire swinging his foot, and every time his foot swung it knocked against a fire dog; and every time my father said "Damn"; but not another word. And the Strachey cousin was attracted. Mrs Cornish too, speaking of his great attractiveness to Fred Benson, said: "He did by instinct all the little things that women like."

He had clearly that – something – which is not this quality or that quality, but all sorts of qualities summed up into what one calls "character"; personality; a way of impressing silence; a way of impressing the word "damn"; so that if one points to his obvious qualities – his honesty, his unworldliness, his lovableness, his perfect sincerity – one is singling out from a whole single qualities which were part of that whole; and the whole was different from the qualities of which it was made. At any rate, I gather from stories, from memories, that Leslie Stephen apart from his books was a figure; a man who if he came into the room changed what was said and felt; and lived a very real life in the minds of men like Walter Headlam or Herbert Fisher; to whom he was a representative man; a man with a standard they often referred to. If a man like Leslie Stephen likes *Tristram Shandy*, Walter Headlam wrote to someone, then it must be all right. That gives what I mean.

And thus as I dribble on, purposely letting my mind flow, I am introducing a picturesque element into the steel engraving; something that one cannot analyse. Was I not conscious of this as a child? Was it not the origin of the love half of my ambivalent feeling? I too felt his attractiveness. It arose – to name some elements at random – from his simplicity, his integrity, his eccentricity – by which I mean he would say exactly what he thought, however inconvenient; and do what he liked. He had clear, direct feelings. He had certain ruling passions. Off he would stride with his sandwiches for some tremendous walk. Out he would come with some fact, or opinion, no matter who was there. And he had very strong opinions; and he was extremely well informed. What he said was thus most respectfully listened to. He had a godlike, yet childlike, standing in the family. He had an extraordinarily privileged position. I twisted my hair, imitating him. "Father does it," I told my mother when she objected. "Ah but you can't do everything father does," she said, conveying to me that he was licensed, for he was somehow not bound by the laws of ordinary people.

He was a curious figure thus sitting often dead silent at the head of the family dinner table. Sometimes he was caustic; sometimes to Thoby especially instructive. He would ask what was the cube root of such and such a number; for he always worked out mathematical problems on railway tickets; or told us how to find the "dominical number" – when Easter falls was it? And mother would protest; no mathematics, she would say, at meals. Sometimes with an old friend he would laugh, at a college story I suspect, till the veins swelled on his forehead. Yes, certainly I felt his presence; and had many a shock of acute pleasure when he fixed his very small, very blue eyes upon me and somehow made me feel that we two were in league together. There was something we had in common. "What have you got hold of?" he would say, looking over my shoulder at the book I was reading; and how proud, priggishly, I was, if he gave his little amused surprised snort, when he found me reading some book that no child of my age could understand. I was a snob no doubt, and read partly to make him think me a very clever little brat. And I remember his pleasure, how he stopped writing and got up and was very gentle and pleased, when I came into the study with a book I had done; and asked him for another. Indeed I was often on his side, even when he was exploding. He had come back, I remember, from a Sunday tramp, smelling airy and muddy in his rough suit, and there on the hearthrug was the stout imperturbable Dermod O'Brien,* in love with Stella, and asked, out of kindness, to stay to dinner. Again my father strode up and down the drawing room, groaning, swearing. He could say much more than anyone could believe without caring if the victim – stout Dermod – overheard. The genius mood was on him; and must be accepted. Did he mind if it wasn't? For some reason that night while noting my mother's half laughing deprecation – she was guilty of impulsive hospitality – I shared his mood not hers. You are right, you are right, I kept repeating, surveying the scene from my station on the raised step. I affirmed my sympathy, felt my likeness. And to top it all, though I never saw him with anything like the clarity that I saw my mother, he was, intermittently, especially when his hair was curled in a thick bob behind his ears, a very striking, indeed a magnificent figure; well dressed in his Hill Brothers' clothes; a swallow tail coat; very lean and tall and bent, with his beard flowing so that his little scraggy tie scarcely showed. His chin I think retreated; perhaps his mouth, which I never saw, was a little looselipped; but his forehead rose and swelled; his skull was magnificent, with a little dent over the arch of the brain, that he made me feel once; and though his eyes were very small, with hairy eyebrows hanging over them, they were pure bright forget-me-not blue. His hands were beautifully shaped; and he wore a signet ring with his double eagle crest engraved on a pale blue stone. As a trifling sign of his indifference to appearances, he went on wearing the ring when the stone was lost. He must have put on his clothes automatically, to the sound of poetry, I expect; the waistcoat was often unbuttoned; sometimes the fly buttons; and the coat was often grey with tobacco ash. He smoked pipes incessantly as he wrote, but never in the drawing room. There he sat in his own chair, with a little table beside him on which was a lamp and two or three books, and my mother sat behind him at her writing table built into a very dark angle of the room;† with Lowell's snuffers to snuff her candles; and as my father read he kicked his foot up and down, and twisted and untwisted the lock behind his ear. He was always absorbed; often seemed completely unconscious of his surroundings; and lived by rote – that is always at a certain moment would be up and off – upstairs to work, out to walk; every Saturday to visit James Payn‡; or off to some meeting. And out of doors he strode along, often shaking his head

* Dermod O'Brien (1865–1945), a well-known amateur painter who was later active in Irish affairs.

† VW has written in the margin, "built in is accurate – at least of some of the cabinets; when we left H.P.G. part of the wall had to be cut down before this Italian cabinet was extricated."

‡ James Payn, novelist and editor of the *Cornhill Magazine*.

emphatically as he recited poetry, and giving his stick a flourish. He wore a billycock hat always, which sat rather oddly upon that great head with the thick bush of hair flowing out on either side. And I remember him too in very respectable evening dress dining out with my mother; and his black waistcoat had a cord round the edge, and he wore elastic sided boots. "I shall be glad when all this dining out is over, Jinny," he said to me, standing waiting by the lamp; and I was flattered by his confidence; yet felt that he enjoyed it.

They dined out quite often in those days, and gave dinner parties too. Indeed for all his unconventionality, he accepted the social conventions so much more completely than we do that I wonder how it is that I feel that he was remote from all that.* It came quite naturally to him to drive off in a hansom in evening dress; he made no bones about dinner parties of eight or ten; and a hired parlour-maid, and a dinner which had ever so many courses and different wines. I can see him taking a lady downstairs on his arm; and laughing. He cannot have been as severe and melancholy and morose as I make him out. He must have made conversation and told anecdotes, and he had, now I come to think of it, a little card case and went calling, like other Victorian gentlemen of a Sunday afternoon. Undoubtedly I colour my picture too dark, and the Leslie Stephen whom the world saw in the eighties, and in the nineties until my mother died, must have been not merely a Cambridge steel engraving intellectual. He must have been† an attractive man at fifty; a man who had four small children, and a beautiful wife; a man who came into the drawing room in evening dress and marched off down to dinner with Mrs Gosse, or Lady Romer, or Mrs Booth, or Lady Lyttleton, just as he presided over London Library meetings and went to the Ad Eundem dinner at Oxford or at Cambridge. There was a Leslie Stephen who played his part normally, without any oddity or outburst, in drawing rooms and dining rooms and committees. Still, I cannot conceive my father in evening dress. I cannot conceive him hearing everything that was said, and making jokes and being, of course, an intellectual man, but still a man of that well to do sociable late Victorian world. I remember my amazement, my envy, when the Booths said their father took them to dances. How astonished I felt when Charles Booth said something humorous about "shepherding my flock" and I realised that Charles Booth took Meg and Imogen to parties. When he and my mother drive off in their hansom which Amy has whistled off the rank, standing out in the street in her cap and apron and giving two shrill blasts till the hansom comes trotting – sometimes two hansoms raced each other and disputed which had come first – when they descend the many

---

* VW has drawn a line through, "It is I suppose that I see only a fragment of him".
† VW has drawn a line through, "a man of distinction".

steps from the front door to the street, he passes beyond my horizon. I have never met anyone who knew my father in evening dress; I have never met him thus dressed in memoirs even. Yet he had great charm for women, and was often attracted, as I could tell from something gallant and tender in his manner, by the young and lovely. The name of an American, Mrs Grey, comes back to me, and my mother somehow conveying to me that I might tease him, as I extricated crumbs from his beard, about "flirting with pretty ladies". Those were the words I used; and he looked at me not angry, for I was only acting a parrot; still I remember the sudden shock, then he controlled what might have been a snort; and said something emphatic, as if to show me he would stand no jokes about that. There succeeds to that shock a memory of the immense emphasis with which once, when we were disputing were mother's eyes large or small: "Your mother's eyes are the most beautiful in the world." All the same I like to remember, for it gives humanity to his austere figure, that he was so struck, so normally and masculinely affected by Mrs Langtry's beauty, that he actually went to the play to see her. Otherwise he never went to a play; never went to picture galleries; had no ear whatsoever for music – when Joachim played at Little Holland House, he asked, when is it going to begin? – the Beethoven or the Mozart being to his ears only "tuning up". In all his life he never troubled to visit Italy or France. Going abroad meant to him solely going to Switzerland to climb mountains; or going to Switzerland to look at mountains.

Mecklenburgh Square again on a hot summer day, July 1940. Invasion still impends. My book* is out; and jaded and distracted I return to this free page.

The sociable father then I never knew. Father as a writer I can get of course in his books; the father who is related to the man's Leslie Stephen, I suppose. The Leslie whom so many writers and scholars admired, though many thought him cold and sneering; just as many thought him formidable and wild and inapproachable. He is to be found here and there in memoirs. He never spoke a word when Stevenson and Gosse lunched with him, and sat silent with his long cold hands and his fan shaped beard flowing over his breast. When I read his books I get a critical grasp on him; I always read *Hours in a Library* by way of filling out my ideas, say of Coleridge, if I'm reading Coleridge; and always find something to fill out; to correct; to stiffen my fluid vision. I find not a subtle mind; not an imaginative mind; not a suggestive mind. But a strong mind; a healthy out of door, moor striding mind; an impatient, limited mind; a conventional mind entirely accepting his own standard of what is honest, what is moral, without a shadow of doubt accepting this is a good man; that is a good woman; I get a sense of Leslie

* *Roger Fry: A Biography* was published on 25 July.

Stephen, the muscular agnostic; cheery, hearty; always cracking up sense and manliness; and crying down sentiment and vagueness, yet putting in a dab of sentiment in the right place – "I will say no more . . . exquisite sensibility . . . thoroughly masculine . . . feminine delicacy . . .". That shows a very simply constructed view of the world; and the world was, I suppose, more simple then. It was a black and white world compared with ours; obvious things to be destroyed – headed humbug, obvious things to be preserved – headed domestic virtues. I admire (laughingly) that Leslie Stephen; and sometimes lately have envied him. Yet he is not a writer for whom I have a natural taste. Yet just as a dog takes a bite of grass, I take a bite of him medicinally, and there often steals in, not a filial, but a reader's affection for him; for his courage, his simplicity, for his strength and nonchalance, and neglect of appearances.

Through his books I can get at the writer father still; but when Nessa and I inherited the rule of the house, I knew nothing of the social father, and the writer father was much more exacting and pressing than he is now that I find him only in books; and it was the tyrant father – the exacting, the violent, the histrionic, the demonstrative, the self-centred, the self pitying, the deaf, the appealing, the alternately loved and hated father – that dominated me then. It was like being shut up in the same cage with a wild beast. Suppose I, at fifteen, was a nervous, gibbering, little monkey, always spitting or cracking a nut and shying the shells out, and mopping and mowing, and leaping into dark corners and then swinging in rapture across the cage, he was the pacing, dangerous, morose lion; a lion who was sulky and angry and injured; and suddenly ferocious, and then very humble, and then majestic; and then lying dusty and fly pestered in a corner of the cage.

Now I shall try to describe the cage – 22 Hyde Park Gate – as it was in July 1897. Two nights ago I lay awake in Mecklenburgh Square going over each of the rooms. I began at the basement; in the servants' sitting room. It was at the back; very low and very dark; there was an ottoman covered in shiny black American cloth along one wall; and a vast cracked picture of Mr and Mrs Pattle covered the wall above it. I remember a very tall young man with tight trousers strapped over the instep, and white socks. It was relegated to the room because it was so big, so cracked, so bad – compared with the Watts portraits upstairs. One could hardly see it – who was the woman? I cannot see her – or anything else; for the creepers hung down in front of the window, in summer strung with hand-shaped semi-transparent leaves. There was an iron trellis to support them, and outside the little, dust-smelling, patchy square of wall-circled back garden. I remember the wood cupboard in the passage; piled with bundles of fire-wood tied with tarry string; once when I rummaged there for a stick to whittle, two eyes glowed in a corner, and Sophie warned me that a wild cat lived there. Wild cats might have lived there. The basement was a dark insanitary place for seven maids to live in. "It's like hell," one of them burst out to my mother as we sat at lessons in the dining room. My mother at once assumed the frozen dignity of the Victorian matron; and said (perhaps): "Leave the room"; and she (unfortunate girl) vanished behind the red plush curtain which, hooped round a semi-circular wire, and anchored by a great gold knob, hid the door that led from the dining room to the pantry.

It was in the dining room, at the long baize covered table, that we did our lessons. My mother's finger with the opal ring I loved pointed its way across French and Latin Grammars. The dining room had two little windows filled with bottle glass at one end. Built into the alcove was a heavily carved sideboard; on which stood a blue china dumb-waiter; and a biscuit tin shaped like a barrel. The room smelt slightly of wine, cigars, food. It was lit also by a skylight, one pane of which lifted in a wind and made me shiver, lest it should crash on our heads. Round the walls hung Sir Joshua engravings; in the corner on a pedestal of mottled yellow marble stood the bust of the first Sir James* – an eyeless, white man who still presides in the hall of Adrian's house in Regents Park. It was a very Victorian dining room; with a complete set of chairs carved in oak; high-backed; with red plush panels. At dinner time with all its silver candles, silver dishes, knives and forks and napkins, the dinner table looked very festive. A twisting staircase led to the hall. In the hall lay a dog, beside him a bowl of water with a chunk of yellow sulphur in it. In the hall facing the front door stood a cabinet with blue china; and on it a gold faced clock. In the hall was a three-cornered chair; and a chest in which rugs were kept; and on this chest was a silver salver deep in visiting cards; and a plush glove for smoothing the silk of George's and Gerald's top hats; and I also remember nailed over the fire place a long strip of chocolate coloured cardboard on which was written: "What is to be a gentleman? It is to be tender to women, chivalrous to servants . . ." – and what else I cannot remember; though I used to know it by heart. What innocence, what incredible simplicity of mind it showed – to keep this cardboard quotation – from Thackeray I think – perpetually displayed, as if it were a frontispiece to a book – nailed to the wall in the hall of the house.

The two drawing rooms opened out of the hall; the front and the back drawing room. The front, facing the street, was comparatively light; the Watts portrait of father faced the door, a flattered, an idealised picture, up to which father would lead admiring ladies; and pause and contemplate it, with some complacency. But "Lowell said it makes me look like a weasel," he once said. There was the grand piano upon which Christmas presents were

* Sir James Stephen.

stood; and Stella's writing table in the window; and the round table in the middle, which, when supplemented by a small folding table which has followed me, unwelcomed, even to Monks House, made the tea table. The tea table, the very hearth and centre of family life, the tea table round which sat innumerable parties; on which, when Sunday came – the tea table's festival day – pink shell plates were placed, full of brown Sunday buns, full of very thin slices of white and brown bread and butter.

The tea table rather than the dinner table was the centre of Victorian family life – in our family at least. Savages I suppose have some tree, or fire place, round which they congregate; the round table marked that focal, that sacred spot in our house. It was the centre, the heart of the family. It was the centre to which the sons returned from their work in the evening; the hearth whose fire was tended by the mother, pouring out tea. In the same way, the bedroom – the double bedded bedroom on the first floor was the sexual centre; the birth centre, the death centre of the house. It was not a large room; but its walls must be soaked, if walls take pictures and board up what is done and said with all that was most intense, of all that makes the most private being, of family life. In that bed four children were begotten; there they were born; there first mother died; then father died, with a picture of mother hanging in front of him. The house mounted in three roomed storeys above that bedroom. Above father's and mother's bedroom floor were the three bedrooms of George, Gerald, and Stella; above their bedrooms our night and day nurseries; above that the great study with its high ceiling of yellow stained wood; and the servants' bedrooms. There were different smells on different landings of that tall dark house. One landing smelt perpetually of candle grease; for on a high cupboard stood all the bedroom candles. On another half landing was the water closet; with all the brass hot water cans standing by a sink. On another half landing was the solitary family bath. (My father all his life washed in a yellow tin bath with flat ears on which the soap stood.) Further up, was a brown filter from which once the drinking water presumably was supplied: in our day it only dripped a little. At that height – it was on the study half landing – carpets and pictures had given out, and the top landing of all was a little pinched and bare. Once when a pipe burst and some young man visitor – Peter Studd? – volunteered help and rushed upstairs with a bucket, he penetrated to the servants' bedrooms, and my mother, I noted, seemed a little 'provoked', a little perhaps ashamed, that he had seen what must have been their rather shabby rooms. My father's great study – that study had been built on, when the family grew – was a fine big room, very high, three windowed, and entirely booklined. His old rocking chair covered in American cloth was the centre of the room which was the brain of the house. He had written all his books lying sunk in that deep rocking chair; which swung up and down; for it was so deep that his feet were off the ground. Across it lay his writing board; with the sheets of foolscap always folded down the middle, so that he could make corrections in the margin. And there was his fine steel pen and the curious china inkpot, with a well, lidded, out at the side. All his books were dipped out of that well on the point of Joseph Gillott's long shanked steel pens. And I remember the little flat shield that his pen had rubbed smooth and hard on the joint of his forefinger. Minny's* portrait by Watts – a charming shy face – nestling away, not noble, not heroic, but shy and sweet, hung over the fireplace; and in the corner by the window stood a stack of rusty alpenstocks. From the three long windows one looked out over the roofs of Kensington, to the presiding Church of St Mary Abbots, the church where our conventional marriages were celebrated – and one day standing there father saw an eagle. It was, I thought, like him that he knew it for an eagle at once; and at once verified the fact, from the paper, that it was an eagle that had escaped from the Zoo. He would not make up stories about wild eagles flying over London. The room smelt perpetually of tobacco smoke.

The street below was a cul-de-sac. Our house was near the blank brick wall at the end. Hyde Park Gate, which led nowhere, but made a little sealed loop out of the great high road running from Hammersmith to Piccadilly, was something like a village street. One heard foot steps tapping along the pavement. Most of the people passing bowed to each other as they met. One recognised them approaching. That was Mrs Muir-MacKenzie; handsome, distinguished. That was the pale Miss Redgrave; or that was the red-nosed Miss Redgrave; or that was the ancient Mrs Redgrave, veiled, in widow's weeds; going out in her bath chair with a Miss Redgrave in attendance – if it was wet she had a glass pane let down so that she looked like a museum specimen preserved under glass. There was also, in a house with a queer flight of angular steps, 'Her Grace' as the nurses called her – an old Duchess of Grafton. There was the house of the famous – somehow infamous – Mrs Biddulph Martin, the rich American, whose garden wall bulged out. "Why don't you make a good job of it?" said George to the workmen who were pointing the wall. They said they could only carry out orders; the wall continued to bulge. Mrs Biddulph Martin was tarnished perhaps by some connection with women's rights. So too certainly was Mrs Ashton Dilke, our next door neighbour. Indeed a man threw a stone at her at some meeting; and my mother, who had signed an anti-suffrage manifesto, holding that women had enough to do in their own homes without a vote, made kind enquiries through us, of the Dilke's governess. But Mrs Dilke, save for that

* Harriet Marian Thackeray, the first Mrs Leslie Stephen.

eccentricity, was the pink of fashion; a very pretty woman, and so well dressed, that we used to notice her new dress, and to say "Mrs Dilke has far more new clothes than you have" to mother, who never had new clothes, and dressed always, I think, in a very simple sewing woman made black dress. And further up the street was Aunt Minna's* house, where she lived solitary with her perennial parrot and her perennial Italian manservant. He changed; but his name was always Angelo; and he was always small and greasy; and played bagatelle with us in his shirtsleeves in the basement. The house with the locked gate and the many steps in the middle of the street was famous for the 'big dog'. People called Maude lived there; impecunious, shifty, disreputable people; who could not pay their bills; and thus kept their gate locked and the big dog behind it to frighten duns. As one passed he sprang down the steps barking; and one day knocked me over and bit or bruised my arm. Then the villagers got together and brought a police court case: and Mr Plowden the magistrate was so impressed by my evidence – or rather my state of mind – that he ordered the dog to be destroyed. "But we don't want him destroyed," Mrs MacKenzie insisted, "only restrained." For it was agreed that it wasn't the poor Maude girls' fault – the handsome dark girls who lived behind the locked gate, scaring duns, were to be pitied for their disreputable parents' discreditable imprisoned lives.

Everybody knew everybody, and everything about everybody, in Hyde Park Gate. It was a trial, if you disliked the gradual approach of a familiar face as I did, to see the MacKenzies or the Redgraves coming nearer and nearer until you had to stop or at least smile. The houses were all individual houses; some towering high, like ours; others, like the Redgraves', long low houses almost country houses; some had strips of garden; others were flush with the street. But they became stereotyped, pillared, and pompous up at the top fronting the main road. Incredible as it now seems, I can remember that one of these pompous houses had a carriage and pair with a coachman and footman who wore powdered wigs, and yellow plush knee breeches and silk stockings. Yet the owners were of no particular importance; and yet nobody thought such magnificence was strange. Perhaps one house out of every six in Hyde Park Gate kept a carriage, or hired one from Hobbs whose livery stable opened its great yard in the middle. For there was only the red bus to take people "into Town," as father called it, or, if you could afford it, a hansom or four wheeler from the rank. The underground, a sulphur smelling steam clouded tunnel with trams running, I suppose, rather seldom, was far away – at Kensington High Street, or Gloucester Road. My father and mother always took the red bus, to them a hansom by day was an

* Sarah Emily Duckworth, the sister-in-law of Julia Stephen.

unknown luxury. My mother did all her immense rounds – shopping, calling, visiting hospitals and work houses – in omnibuses. She was an omnibus expert. She would nip from the red to the blue, from the blue to the yellow, and make them somehow connect and convey her all over London. Sometimes she would come home very tired, owning that she had missed her bus or the bus had been full up, or she had got beyond the radius of her favourite buses. But more often she would have some story to tell of her bus adventures – a talk she had had with the conductor, or how a fellow passenger had said this or that. "She sat weeping," I remember she said, "and I could only lend her my scent bottle." My father always climbed on top and smoked his pipe; she I think never did that, but, if she could, chose the corner seat and talked to the conductor. He would tell her his troubles; as the two stubby horses ploughed their way along the streets, those old omnibus horses who lived, it was said, only a year or two, for the pulling up to take in passengers destroyed their constitutions. Once a year about Christmas we saw a brace of pheasants swinging from the driver's seat – the gift of the Rothschilds.

The streets were full of horses. The streets were littered with little brown piles of steaming horse dung which boys, darting out among the wheels, removed in shovels. The horses kicked and reared and neighed. Often they ran away. Carriages crashed together I remember in High Street; horses went sprawling; they shied; they reared; wheels came off. The street rocked with horses and smelt of horses. The horses were often gleaming, spick and span horses, with rosettes in their ears; the footmen wore cockades in their hats; foam flecked the bright silver harness; coronets and coats of arms were painted on panels and among the sounds of the street – the tap of hoofs, the rush of wheels – one heard a jingling and metallic noise as the harness shook and rattled. But only solitary hansoms, or little high butchers' carts, or private broughams came clopping down our quiet Hyde Park cul-de-sac – our "backwater," as father called it.

My room in that very tall house was at the back. When Stella married, Vanessa and I were promoted to separate bed sitting rooms; that marked the fact that we had become, she at eighteen, I at fifteen, young ladies. My room, the old night nursery, was a long narrow room, with two windows; the fireside half was the living half; the washstand half was the sleeping half. It had been 'done up' at George's cost, I rather think; all traces of the night nursery were abolished. In the living half was my wicker chair, and Stella's writing table made after her design with crossed legs, and stained green and decorated by her with a pattern of brown leaves (at that time staining and enamelling and amateur furniture decorating were much the rage). On it stood open my Greek lexicon; some Greek play or other; many little bottles of ink, pens innumerable; and probably hidden under blotting paper, sheets of foolscap covered with private writing in a hand so small and twisted as to be a family joke.

The sleeping side was dominated by the long Chippendale (imitation) looking glass, given me by George in the hope that I should look into it and learn to do my hair and take general care for my appearance. Between it and the washstand, under the window, was my bed. On summer nights, I would lie with the window open, looking up at the sky, thinking, for I recall a story I wrote then, about the stars and how in Egypt some savage was looking at them; and also listening. Very far off there was a hum of traffic. In the mews one heard the stamp of horses; a clatter of the wheels and buckets. In a bedroom window, one of the Queen's Gate back windows opposite, I could see Sir Alfred Lyall dressing and undressing. One of the windows was broken; the servants said there lay the wedding feast still untouched; for a bridegroom had failed, or a bride had died. Certainly there was a dusty broken window. Of a summer night I sometimes heard dance music and saw the dancers sitting out on the leads; saw them passing and repassing the window on the stairs. One night I lay awake horrified hearing, as I imagined, an obscene old man gasping and croaking and muttering senile indecencies – it was a cat, I was told afterwards; a cat's anguished love making. George, on the floor below, kept a store of old electric light bulbs which he shied at cats – pop-pop they would explode against the wall. Often I would lie awake till two or three, waiting for Nessa to come and see me after her party. I would read by the light of a candle, and blow it out as I heard her and Gerald approaching. But Gerald pinched the top of the candle, found the wax soft, and so detected me.

Which should I describe first – the living half of the room, or the sleeping half? They must be described separately; yet they were always running together. How they fought each other; that is, how often I was in a rage in that room; and in despair; and in ecstasy; how I read myself into a trance of perfect bliss; then in came – Adrian, George, Gerald, Jack, my father; how it was there I retreated to when father enraged me; and paced up and down scarlet; and there Madge* came one evening; and I could scarcely talk for happiness; and there I droned out those long solitary mornings reading Greek . . . And it was from that room Gerald fetched me when father died. There I first heard those horrible voices. . . .

If that room, which is now I think cut into cubicles for the hotel guests – after we left it it became a Guest house – could bring out its ghosts, the business man from Birmingham, the lady from Cheltenham up to see the Royal Academy, would be amused; also pitiful; and perhaps one of them would say what an odd, what an unwholesome life for a girl of fifteen; I

* Margaret Vaughan (née Symonds).

suppose they would add: "Such a life is quite impossible nowadays." And I suppose that, if one of them had read *To the Lighthouse*, or *A Room of One's Own*, or *The Common Reader*, he or she might say: "This room explains a great deal."

But of course I was not thinking when I lived in my back room at H[yde] P[ark] G[ate] of Birmingham business men or ladies from Cheltenham. But I was thinking; feeling; living; those two lives that the two halves symbolized with the intensity, the muffled intensity, which a butterfly or moth feels when with its sticky tremulous legs and antennae it pushes out of the chrysalis and emerges and sits quivering beside the broken case for a moment; its wings still creased; its eyes dazzled, incapable of flight.

Anyone, whether fifteen or not, whether sensitive or not, must have felt something very acute, merely from what had happened. My mother's death had been a latent sorrow – at thirteen one could not master it, envisage it, deal with it. But Stella's death two years later fell on a different substance; a mind stuff and being stuff that was extraordinarily unprotected, unformed, unshielded, apprehensive, receptive, anticipatory. That must always hold good of minds and bodies at fifteen. But beneath the surface of this particular mind and body lay sunk the other death. Even if I were not fully conscious of what my mother's death meant, I had been for two years unconsciously absorbing it through Stella's silent grief; through my father's demonstrative grief; again through all the things that changed and stopped; the ending of society; of gaiety; the giving up of St Ives; the black clothes; the suppressions; the locked door of her bedroom. All this had toned my mind and made it apprehensive; made it I suppose unnaturally responsive to Stella's happiness, and the promise it held for her and for us of escape from that gloom; when once more unbelievably – incredibly – as if one had been violently cheated of some promise; more than that, brutally told not to be such a fool as to hope for things; I remember saying to myself after she died: "But this is impossible; things aren't, can't be, like this" – the blow, the second blow of death, struck on me; tremulous, filmy eyed as I was, with my wings still creased, sitting there on the edge of my broken chrysalis.

Yesterday (18th August 1940) five German raiders passed so close over Monks House that they brushed the tree at the gate. But being alive today, and having a waste hour on my hands – for I am writing fiction; and cannot write after twelve – I will go on with this loose story.*

By the time I had that room, when I was fifteen that is, "us four" as we

---

* The material that follows is a revision of the manuscript MH/A. 5d which was transcribed on pp. 107–37 in the original edition of *Moments of Being*. See Editor's Note, p. 177.

called ourselves had become separate. That was symbolized by our separate rooms. Yet we were not so separate as boys and girls, brothers and sisters, often become when the boys go to public schools and the sisters stay at home. Mother's and Stella's deaths, I suppose, united us. We never spoke of them. I can remember how awkwardly Thoby avoided saying "Stella" when a ship called *Stella* was wrecked. (When Thoby died, Adrian and I agreed that we would go on talking about him, "for there are so many dead people now.") This silence, we felt, covered something; something that most families had not. But without that bond, mine was from my earliest childhood so close with both Nessa and Thoby that if I describe myself I must describe them.

When Stella died Thoby was seventeen – two years older than I. But long after that I was acutely conscious of him. Even as a little boy he was dominant among us. He could impose himself. He was not clever; he was not a funny talkative child; he was a clumsy awkward little boy, very fat, bursting through his Norfolk jacket. He dominated and led in our world. But even to the grown ups he was rather formidable. Father had to be sent for once or twice: I remember Thoby struggling like a tiger with Gerald. He was large and clumsy. He grew very quickly out of nursery ways. I cannot remember him childish, as Adrian was. But then mother was not so much at her ease with him as with Adrian. Nor he with her. He was not clever; but gifted. And his gifts were natural to him, naturally it came to him to look distinguished; to be silent, to draw. He would take a sheet of paper, hold it at an odd angle and begin easily, naturally, drawing a bird, not where I expected, but at some queer place, so that I could not guess how the bird would become a bird. He was not precocious; but won prizes now and then, yet failed to win a scholarship at Eton. His Latin and Greek were very rough, I think the masters said. But his essays showed great intelligence. Yet it was through him that I first heard about the Greeks. The day after he came back from Evelyns, the first time, he was very shy; and odd; and we went walking up and down the stairs together; and he told me the story of Hector and of Troy. I felt he was too shy to tell it sitting down; and so we kept walking up stairs and then down; and he told me the story rather fitfully, but excitedly. Also he told me stories about the boys at Evelyns. Those stories went on all through Evelyns, through Clifton, and through Cambridge. I knew all his friends through those stories. He had a great power for liking people, for admiring them. And they amused him; I think I felt that he enjoyed Evelyns; and Clifton, because he liked being on his own, and held his own; and was admired, but was also dominant there too. He held his own, he put up with disagreeables; he was far more philosophic, because more in his element at school than Adrian was. And he exacted his rights. The Pup had to apologise when he put another boy over him as head of the house; he was not going to be passed over. He was not easy to put upon. And yet he had no reason to assert himself; he did not expect to win things; he admired the boys who were good at football; good at Latin; but unenviously. I felt he had taken stock of his own powers; would come into possession of them all in good time; and enjoyed slowly and deliberately without being worried or upset whatever came his way at Clifton. He was tolerant; not critical; not precocious; biding his time, and serenely taking his place. And beneath this reserve, when he was with us, I felt, though he could not say a word ever about his feelings, a dumb affectionateness, a pride in us, and something melancholy too – perhaps the deaths of mother and Stella made him older than his age. And father's extraordinary demonstrative love for him.

I continue (22nd September 1940) on this wet day – we think of weather now as it affects invasions, as it affects raids, not as weather that we like or dislike privately – I continue, for I am at a twist in my novel,* to fill in another page. I was writing about Thoby when I left off. And last night, trying to soothe myself to sleep (for I was in a pucker, as Clive calls it, about the Anreps† coming here) I thought about St Ives. I will write about St Ives, and so fittingly, though indirectly, lead up to Thoby again. St Ives will fill him in.

Father on one of his walking tours, it must have been in 1881, I think – discovered St Ives. He must have stayed there, and seen Talland House to let. He must have seen the town almost as it had been in the sixteenth century, without hotels, or villas; and the Bay as it had been since time began. It was the first year, I think, that the line was made from St Erth to St Ives – before that, St Ives was eight miles from a railway station. Munching his sandwiches up at Tregenna perhaps, he must have been impressed, in his silent way, by the beauty of the Bay; and thought: this might do for our summer holiday, and worked out with his usual caution ways and means. I was to be born in the following January; and, though they wished to limit their family, and did what they could to prevent me, he must have known that they were not successful in the steps they took; Adrian was born a year after me (1883) – again, in spite of precautions. It proves the ease and amplitude of those days that a man to whom money was an obsession thought it feasible to take a house on the very toenail, as he called it, of England, so that every summer he would be faced with the expense of moving children, nurses, servants from one end of England to the other. Yet he did it. They rented the house

---

* She was now at work on *Between the Acts* which at this period is referred to as 'PH' in *A Writer's Diary*, for 'Poyntzet Hall' or 'Poyntz Hall'.

† VW was upset because she feared – mistakenly as it turned out – that Helen Anrep, the companion of Roger Fry until his death, was planning to move permanently to Rodmell with her son and daughter.

from the Great Western Railway Company. The distance did prove in one way a drawback; for we could only go there in the summer. Our country thus was canalised into two or at most into three months of the year. The other months were spent entirely in London. Yet in retrospect nothing that we had as children made as much difference, was quite so important to us, as our summer in Cornwall. The country was intensified, after the months in London to go away to Cornwall; to have our own house; our own garden; to have the Bay; the sea; the moors; Clodgy; Halestown Bog; Carbis Bay; Lelant; Trevail; Zennor; the Gurnard's Head; to hear the waves breaking that first night behind the yellow blind; to dig in the sand; to go sailing in a fishing boat; to scrabble over the rocks and see the red and yellow anemones flourishing their antennae; or stuck like blobs of jelly to the rock; to find a small fish flapping in a pool; to pick up cowries; to look over the grammar in the dining room and see the lights changing on the bay; the leaves of the escallonia grey or bright green; to go down to the town and buy a penny box of tintacks or a pocket knife; to prowl about Lanhams – Mrs Lanham wore false curls shaking round her head; the servants said Mr Lanham had married her 'through an advertisement'; to smell all the fishy smells in the steep little streets; and see the innumerable cats with their fishbones in their mouths; and the women on the raised steps outside their houses pouring pails of dirty water down the gutters; every day to have a great dish of Cornish cream skinned with a yellow skin; and plenty of brown sugar to eat with black-berries . . . I could fill pages remember one thing after another. All together made the summer at St Ives the best beginning to life conceivable. When they took Talland House father and mother gave us – me at any rate -- what has been perennial, invaluable. Suppose I had only Surrey, or Sussex, or the Isle of Wight to think about when I think of my childhood.

The town was then much as it must have been in the sixteenth century, unknown, unvisited, a scramble of granite houses crusting the slope in the hollow under the Island. It must have been built for shelter; for a few fishermen, when Cornwall was more remote from England than Spain or Africa is now. It was a steep little town. Many houses had a flight of steps, with a railing leading to the door. The walls were thick blocks of granite built to stand the sea storms. They were splashed with a wash the colour of Cornish cream; and their roughness was like the clot of cream. There was nothing mellow about them; no red brick; no soft thatch. The eighteenth century had left no mark upon St Ives, as it has so definitely upon every southern village. It might have been built yesterday; or in the time of the Conqueror. It had no architecture; no arrangement. The market place was a jagged cobbled open place; the Church was on one side; built of granite, ageless, like the houses; the fish market stood beside it. There was no grass in front of it. It stood flush to the market place. There were no carved doors, large windows, no lintels; no moss; no comely professional houses. It was a windy, noisy, fishy, vociferous, narrow-streeted town; the colour of a mussel or a limpet; like a bunch of rough shell fish clustered on a grey wall together.

Our house, Talland House, was just beyond the town, on the hill. For whom the Great Western Railway had built it, I do not know. It must have been in the forties, or fifties; a square house, like a child's drawing of a house; remarkable only for its flat roof, and the crisscrossed railing that ran round the roof; again, like something a child draws. It stood in a garden that ran downhill; and had formed itself into separate gardens, surrounded by thick escallonia hedges, whose leaves, pressed, gave out a very sweet smell. It had so many angles cut off, and lawns surrounded, that each had a name; there was the coffee garden; the Fountain – a basin with a funnel that dripped, hedged in with damp evergreens; the cricket lawn; the Love Corner, under the greenhouse, where the purple jackmanii grew – where Leo Maxse proposed to Kitty Lushington (I thought I heard Paddy talking to his son, Thoby said, overhearing the proposal). Then there was the kitchen garden; the strawberry beds; the pond where Willy Fisher sailed the little steamers he made with a paddle worked by an elastic band; and the big tree. All these different, cut off places were contained in that one garden of not more than two or three acres. One entered by a large wooden gate, the sound of whose latch clicking was one of the familiar sounds; up the carriage drive one went, under the steep wall of rock, sprinkled with the fleshy leaves of the mesembryanthemums; and then came to the Lookout place, between the clumps of pampas grass. The Lookout place was a grassy mound, that jutted out over the high garden wall. There we were often sent to stand to look out for the fall of the signal. When the signal fell it was time to start for the station to meet the train. It was the train that brought Mr Lowell, Mr Gibbs, the Stillmans, the Lushingtons, the Symondses. But it was a grown-up affair – receiving friends. We never had friends to stay with us. Nor did we want them. "Us four" were completely self-sufficient. Once when a child called Elsie was brought by Mrs Westlake to play with us I "broomed her round the garden". I remember scuffling her like a drift of dead leaves in front of me.

From the Lookout place one had then, a perfectly open view across the Bay. (Mr Symonds said that the Bay reminded him of the Bay of Naples.) It was a large Bay, many curved, edged with a slip of sand, with green sand hills behind; and the curves flowed in and out to the two black rocks at one end of which stood the black and white tower of the Lighthouse; and at the other end, Hayle river made a blue vein across the sand, and stakes, on which always a gull sat, marked the channel into Hayle Harbour. This great flowing basin of water was always changing in colour; it was deep blue; emerald green; purple and then stormy grey and white crested. There was a great coming and going of ships across the bay. Most usually, it was a Haines steamer, with a red or white band round the funnel, going to Cardiff for coal. In rough weather, sometimes one would wake to find the whole bay full of ships, that had come in overnight for shelter – little tramp steamers mostly, with a dip in the middle. But sometimes a big ship would be anchored there; once a battle ship; once a great sailing ship; once a famous white yacht. Then every morning the clumsy luggers went out, deep sea fishing; and in the evening there was the mackerel fleet, its lights dancing up and down; and the fleet returning, rounding the headland and suddenly dropping their sails. We would stand with mother on the Lookout place watching them.

Every year, about the first week in September, we would cry "The pilchard boats are out!" There they were being hauled down the beach, where they lay one behind another all the rest of the year. Horses were struggling to draw them over the beach. They were anchored near the shore, and looked like long black shoes, for each had a hood for the watchman at one end, and a great coil of net – seines they were called – at the other. The tarring of the pilchard boats was a regular occupation; and made the beach always smell slightly of tar. There they lay week after week, and were still lying when we left in October, waiting for the Huer who sat at his telescope up in the white shelter of Carbis Bay point to sight a shoal.* He sat there looking for a purple stain of pilchards to come into the bay and beside him was a great horn of some kind. Year after year the boats lay in the bay. The seines were never shot. The fishermen grumbled that the steam trawlers at Newlyn (perhaps) had disturbed the pilchards; and driven them out to sea. Once, though, as we sat at lessons we heard the Huer's cry – a long high clear hoot of sound. Then fishermen rowed out to the boats. We stopped lessons. The seines were shot. A dotted circle of corks floated here and there over the dark net beneath. But the pilchards passed out of the bay that time; and the seines were drawn in again. (It was in 1905, when we four took a lodging at Carbis Bay that the pilchards came. We rowed out early in the morning. The sea spurted and spat and bubbled with silver. A stranger in the next boat shovelled armfuls of that bubbling mass into our boat. "Like some fresh fish for breakfast?" he said – everyone was excited and jubilant; and boat after boat was weighed down to the water line with fish. And we went down to the harbour and saw them packed. I wrote a description of it, and sent it to some paper; which rejected it. But Thoby told Nessa, who told me, that he thought I might be a bit of a genius.) All the years we were at St Ives the pilchards never came into the bay; and the pilchard boats lay there, anchored, waiting; and we used to swim out and hang on to the edge, and see the old man lying in his brown tarpaulin tent, keeping watch. The waiting pilchard boats

* "We would often stop and talk to him" is lightly pencilled through.

was [sic] a sight that made father pish and pshaw at table. He had a curious sympathy for the poverty of the fisher people: a respect for fishermen, like his respect for Alpine guides. And mother, of course, got to know them in their houses; and went about, "doing good" as Stella wished to have it said on her tombstone; she visited, helped, and started her nursing society. After her death it became the Julia Prinsep Stephen Nursing Association; Meredith* and the Symondses and Stillmans contributed to it; and Ka Arnold-Forster† told me not so long ago that it still exists.

Every year, in August, the Regatta took place in the bay. We watched the Judges' boat take its station, with lines of little flags hung from mast to mast. The St Ives notables went on board. A band played. Wafts of music came across the water. All the little boats came out of the harbour. Then a gun was fired, and the races began. Off went the boats – the luggers, the pleasure boats, the rowing boats; racing round the different courses that were marked by flags round the bay. And while they raced, the swimmers got ready in a line on the Regatta boat for their races. The gun fired; they plunged and we could see the little heads bobbing and the arms flashing and heard the people shouting as one swimmer gained on another. One year our charming curly headed postman (I remember the brown linen bag in which he carried letters) should have won; but he explained to Amy later "I let the other chap win, because it was his last chance."

It was a very gay sight, with the flags flying, the guns firing, the boats sailing, and the swimmers plunging or being hauled back on board. A crowd of St Ives people gathered to watch in the Malakoff, that octagonal space at the end of the Terrace which had been built, presumably, in the Crimean War and was the only attempt that the town made at ornament. St Ives had no pleasure pier, no parade, only this angular gravelly patch of ground, set with a few stone seats upon which retired fishermen in their blue jerseys smoked and gossiped. The Regatta day remains in my mind, with its distant music, its little strings of flags, the boats sailing, and the people dotted on the sand, like a French picture.

In those days St Ives, save for ourselves and casual wandering painters, had no summer visitors. Its customs were its own customs; its festivals its own too. There was the August Regatta. Then once in every twelve years or so,‡ old men and women over seventy danced round Knills Monument – a granite steeple in a clearing – and the couple who danced longest were given

---

* George Meredith, the novelist and poet.

† Ka Arnold-Forster, née Katherine Cox, a 'Neo-Pagan', Fabian and Newnhamite, who lived in Zennor, near St Ives.

‡ This ceremony takes place every five, not every twelve, years.

a shilling? half a crown? – by the Mayor – Dr Nicholls, on that occasion, who wore a long fur trimmed cloak. St Ives had a relic, but a relic in use, of the past – Charlie Pearce, the town crier. Now and again he shuffled along the front swinging a muffin bell and crying "Oyez, Oyez, Oyez." What he went on to say, I do not know, save that on one occasion, when a visitor at Talland House lost a brooch, she had it cried by Charlie Pearce. He was blind, or nearly; with a long wasted face, grey eyes, like the eyes of a fish that has been boiled, and he wore a battered top hat, a frock coat tightly buttoned round his angular body, and he shuffled oddly from side to side as he went swinging his bell, and crying "Oyez, Oyez, Oyez." We knew him, as we knew so many of the town characters, through the servants, in particular through Sophie, who had many friends among them. We knew all the tradespeople, who came up the drive to the kitchen door, carrying their parcels – Alice Curnow, with the washing in a great basket; Mrs Adams the fisherwoman, who brought fish in another basket – the lobsters still alive, still blue, hobbling about in the basket. The lobster would be set on the kitchen table, and the great claw would open and shut and pinch one. Can I be remembering a fact when I think I remember a long thick fish wriggling on a hook in the larder, and that Gerald beat it to death with a broom handle?

The kitchen, Sophie's kitchen, for she was dominant over all the other "denizens of the kitchen", as we called them in the *Hyde Park Gate News*, was directly beneath our night nursery. At dinner time we would let down a basket on a string, and dangle it over the kitchen window. If she were in a good temper, the basket would be drawn in, laden with something from the grown-ups' dinner and pushed swaying out again. If she was "in one of her tempers," the basket was sharply jerked, the string cut, and we [were] left holding the dangling string. I can remember the sensation of the heavy basket, and of the light string.

Every afternoon we "went for a walk". Later these walks became a penance. Father must have one of us to go out with him, Mother insisted. Too much obsessed with his health, with his pleasures, she was too willing, as I think now, to sacrifice us to him. It was thus that she left us the legacy of his dependence, which after her death became so harsh an imposition. It would have [been] better for our relationship if she had left him to fend for himself. But for many years she made a fetish of his health; and so – leaving the effect upon us out of the reckoning – she wore herself out and died at forty-nine; while he lived on, and found it very difficult, so healthy was he, to die of cancer at the age of seventy-two. But, though I slip in, still venting an old grievance, that parenthesis, St Ives gave us all the same that "pure delight" which is before my eyes at this very moment. The lemon-coloured leaves on the elm tree; the apples in the orchard; the murmur and rustle of the leaves makes me pause here, and think how many other than human forces are always at work on us. While I write this the light glows; an apple becomes a vivid green; I respond all through me; but how? Then a little owl [chatters]* under my window. Again, I respond. Figuratively I could snapshot what I mean by some image; I am a porous vessel afloat on sensation; a sensitive plate exposed to invisible rays; and so on. Or I fumble with some vague idea about a third voice; I speak to Leonard; Leonard speaks to me; we both hear a third voice. Instead of labouring all the morning to analyse what I mean, to discover whether I mean anything real, whether I make up or tell the truth when I see myself taking the breath of these voices in my sails and tacking this way and that through daily life as I yield to them, I note only the existence of this influence; suspect it to be of great importance; cannot find how to check its power on other people – does Louie feel it? Does Percy? Which of the people watching the incendiary bomb extinguished on the hill last night would understand what I mean if they read this? – I erect a finger post here, to mark a vein I will some time try to work out; and return to the surface; that is St Ives.

The regular Sunday walk was to Trick Robin or, as father liked to call it, Tren Crom. From the top, one could see the two seas; St Michael's Mount on one side; the Lighthouse on the other. Like all Cornish hills, it was scattered with blocks of granite; said some of them to be old tombs and altars; in some, holes were driven, as if for gate posts. Others were piled up rocks. The Loggan rock was on top of Tren Crom; we would set it rocking; and be told that perhaps the hollow in the rough lichened surface was for the victim's blood. But father, with his severe love of truth, disbelieved it; he said, in his opinion, this was no genuine Loggan rock; but the natural disposition of ordinary rocks. Little paths led up to the hill, between heather and ling; and our knees were pricked by the gorse – the blazing yellow gorse with its sweet nutty smell. Another walk, a short children's walk, was to Fairyland, as we called that solitary wood, with a broad wall circling it. We walked on the wall, and looked down into a forest of oak trees, and great ferns, higher than our heads. It smelt of oak apples; it was dark, damp, silent, mysterious. A longer, an adventurous walk was to Halestown Bog. Again father corrected us; Helston Bog we called it; the real name was Halestown. In that bog we sprang from hag to hag; and the hags squelched and we plunged up to the knee in the brown bog water. There the Osmunda grew; and the rare maiden-hair fern. Better than these walks, a treat announced perhaps once a fortnight, was an afternoon sailing. We would hire a lugger; the fisherman went with us. But once Thoby was allowed to steer us home. "Show them you can bring her in, my boy," father said, with his usual trust and pride in

* A line has been drawn through 'chatters' and an indecipherable word has been pencilled in.

Thoby. And Thoby took the fisherman's place; and steered; flushed and with his blue eyes very blue, and his mouth set, he sat there, bringing us round the point, into harbour, without letting the sail flag. One day the sea was full of pale jelly fish, like lamps, with streaming hair; but they stung you if you touched them. Sometimes lines would be handed us; baited by gobbets cut from fish; and the line thrilled in one's fingers as the boat tossed and shot through the water; and then – how can I convey the excitement? – there was a little leaping tug; then another; up one hauled; up through the water at length came the white twisting fish; and was slapped on the floor. There it lay flapping this way and that in an inch or two of water.

Once, after we had hung about, tacking, and hauling in gurnard after gurnard, dab after dab, father said to me: "Next time if you are going to fish I shan't come; I don't like to see fish caught but you can go if you like." It was a perfect lesson. It was not a rebuke; not a forbidding; simply a statement of his own feeling, about which I could think and decide for myself. Though my passion for the thrill and the tug had been perhaps the most acute I then knew, his words slowly extinguished it; leaving no grudge, I ceased to wish to catch fish. But from the memory of my own passion I am still able to construct an idea of the sporting passion. It is one of those invaluable seeds, from which, since it is impossible to have every experience fully, one can grow something that represents other people's experiences. Often one has to make do with seeds; the germs of what might have been, had one's life been different. I pigeonhole 'fishing' thus with other momentary glimpses; like those rapid glances, for example, that I cast into basements when I walk in London streets.

Oak apples, ferns with clusters of seeds on their backs, the regatta, Charlie Pearce, the click of the garden gate, the ants swarming on the hot front door step; buying tintacks; sailing; the smell of Halestown Bog; splits with Cornish cream for tea in the farm house at Trevail; the floor of the sea changing colour at lessons; old Mr Wolstenholme in his beehive chair; the spotted elm leaves on the lawn; the rooks cawing as they passed over the house in the early morning; the escallonia leaves showing their grey undersides: the arc in the air, like the pip of an orange, when the powder magazine at Hayle blew up; the boom of the buoy – these for some reason come uppermost at the moment in my mind thinking of St Ives – an incongruous miscellaneous catalogue, little corks that mark a sunken net.

And to pull that net, leaving its contents unsorted, to shore, by way of making an end where there is no such thing, I add: for two or three years before mother's death (1892–3–4, that is) ominous hints reached the nursery that the grown ups talked of leaving St Ives. The distance had become a drawback; by that time George and Gerald had work in London. Expense, Thoby's school, Adrian's school, became more urgent. And then just opposite the Lookout place a great square oatmeal coloured hotel appeared when we came down in July. My mother said, with her dramatic gestures, that the view was spoilt; that St Ives would be ruined. For all these reasons, then, a house agent's board appeared one October in our garden; and as it needed repainting, I was allowed to fill in some of the letters – This House to Let – from a pot of paint. The joy of painting mingled with the dread of leaving. But for a summer or two no tenant came. The danger, we hoped, was averted. And then in the spring of 1895 mother died. Father instantly decided that he wished never to see St Ives again. And perhaps a month later Gerald went down alone; settled the sale of our lease to some people called Millie Dow, and St Ives vanished for ever.

I recover then today (October 11th 1940) a mild Autumn day (London battered last night) from these rapid notes only one actual picture of Thoby; steering us round the point without letting the sail flap. I recover the picture of a schoolboy whose jacket was rather tight; whose arms shot out of their sleeves. He looked sulky; grim; his eyes became bluer when he was thus on his mettle; his face flushed a little. He was feeling earlier than most boys, the weight laid on him by father's pride in him; the burden, the responsibility of being treated as a man.

Why do I shirk the task, not so very hard to a professional – have I not conveyed Roger from one end of life to the other? – like myself, of wafting this boy from the boat to my bed sitting room at Hyde Park Gate? It is because I want to go on thinking about St Ives. I have the excuse that I could, if I went on thinking, recall many other pictures; bring him in again and again. And it is not only an excuse; for always round him, like the dew that collects in beads on a rough coat, there hangs the country; butterflies; birds; muddy roads; muddy boots; horses.

But it is true, I do not want to go into my room at Hyde Park Gate. I shrink from the years 1897–1904, the seven unhappy years. Not many lives were tortured and fretted and made numb with non-being as ours were then. That, in shorthand, was the legacy of those two great unnecessary blunders; those two lashes of the random unheeding, unthinking flail that brutally and pointlessly killed the two people who should have made those years normal and natural, if not 'happy'.

I am not thinking of mother and of Stella; I am thinking of the damage that their deaths inflicted. I will describe it more carefully later, I will illustrate with a scene or two. That is why I do not wish to bring Thoby out of the boat into my room.

Without those deaths, to hark back to an earlier thought, it is true that he would not have been so genuinely, though dumbly, bound to us. If there is any good (I doubt it) in these mutilations, it is that it sensitises. If to be aware of the insecurity of life, to remember something gone, to feel now and then, overwhelmingly, as I felt for father when he made no claim to it, a passionate fumbling fellowship – if it is a good thing to be aware of all this at fifteen, sixteen, seventeen, by fits and starts – if, if, if—. But was it good? Would it not have been better (if there is any sense in saying good and better when there is no possible judge, no standard) to go on feeling, as at St Ives, the rush and tumble of family life? To be family surrounded; to go on exploring and adventuring privately while all the while the family as a whole continued its prosaic, rumbling progress; would this not have been better than to have had that protection removed; to have been tumbled out of the family shelter; to have had it cracked and gashed; to have become critical and sceptical of the family—? Perhaps to have remained in the family, believing in it, accepting it, as we should, without those two deaths, would have given us greater scope, greater variety, and certainly greater confidence. On the other hand, I can put another question: Did those deaths give us an experience that even if it was numbing, mutilating, yet meant that the Gods (as I used to phrase it) were taking us seriously, and giving us a job which they would not have thought it worthwhile to give – say, the Booths or the Milmans? I had my usual visual way of putting it. I would see (after Thoby's death) two great grindstones (as I walked round Gordon Square)* and myself between them. I would stage a conflict between myself and 'them'. I would reason that if life were thus made to rear and kick, it was a thing to be ridden; nobody could say 'they' had fobbed me off with a weak little feeble slip of the precious matter. So I came to think of life as something of extra reality. And this of course increased my sense of my own importance. Not in relation to human beings; in relation to the force which had respected me sufficiently to make me feel myself ground between grindstones.

It seems to me therefore that our relation (Thoby's and mine) was more serious than it would have been without those deaths. The unspoken thought – I have roughly visualised it – was there, in him; in me; when he came into my room at Hyde Park Gate. It was behind our arguments. We were, of course, naturally attracted to each other. Besides his brother's feeling (and he was protective) he had I think an amused, surprised, questioning attitude to me as an individual. I was a year and a half younger; and a girl. A shell-less little creature, I think he thought me; so sheltered, in my room, compared with him; an ingenuous, eager listener to his school stories; without any experience of my own with which to cap his; but not passive; on the contrary, bubbling, inquisitive, restless, contradicting. We had branched off, after that rambling up and down stairs, to read on our own. He had consumed

* When Leslie Stephen died in 1904 the four Stephens moved from 22 Hyde Park Gate to 46 Gordon Square, Bloomsbury.

Shakespeare, somehow or other, by himself. He had possessed himself of it, in his large clumsy way, and our first arguments, since I listened passively to the story of the Greeks on the stairs outside the water closet, outside the candle grease smelling landing, were about Shakespeare. He would sweep down upon me, with his assertion that everything was in Shakespeare. He let the whole mass that he held in his grasp descend in an avalanche on me. I revolted. But how could I oppose all that? Rather feebly; getting red and agitated. Still it was then my genuine feeling that a play was antipathetic to me. How did they begin? With some dull speech a hundred miles from anything interesting. To prove it I opened [*Twelfth Night*]* and read "If music be the food of love, play on . . ." I was downed that time. And he was ruthless; exasperating; downing me, overwhelming me; with enough passion to make us both heated. So that my opposition cannot have been quite ineffectual. He made me feel his pride, it was like his pride in his friends, in Shakespeare – shuffling off Falstaff, he pointed out, without a sign of sympathy. That large natural inhumanity in Shakespeare delighted him. It was a tree's way of shedding its leaves. On the other hand, when Desdemona wakes again, he thought possibly Shakespeare was 'sentimental'. These are the only particular criticisms that I remember, for he was not, as I am, a breaker off of single words, or sentences, not a note taker. He was more casual, rough and ready and comprehensive. And so I did not get from him any minute comments; but felt rather that Shakespeare was to him his other world; the place where he got the measure of the daily world. He took his bearings there; and sized us up from that standard. I felt once that he was half thinking of Falstaff and Hal and Mother Quickly and the rest, in a third class smoker in the underground, when there was some squabble between drunken men; and he sat in the corner, with his pipe in his mouth, looking over the edge of a newspaper; surveying them; unperturbed; equipped; as if placing it all. I felt (not only then) that he knew his own place; and relished his inheritance. I felt he scented the battle; was already, in anticipation, a law maker; proud of his station as a man; ready to play his part among men. Had he been put on, he would have proved most royally. The words Walter Lamb used of him were very fitting.†

So we argued; about Shakespeare; about many many things; and often lost our tempers; but were attracted by some common admiration. The spot in Grays' Inn where, walking home one night, he said to me: "I always wonder

* The typescript leaves a blank space for the title.

† From the final speech of Fortinbras in *Hamlet*, "Let four captains / Bear Hamlet like a soldier to the stage, / For he was likely, had he been put on, / To have proved most royal. . . ." Walter Lamb, elder brother of the painter Henry Lamb and close friend of Thoby, was at Trinity College, Cambridge.

what the man in green is thinking" – (where does that come from?) by which I was elated, knowing him to mean that he wanted me to talk – [wanted] my opinion – that flag stone in the dark is still one of my unsubmerged islands. But how reserved we were! Brothers and sisters today talk quite freely together about – oh everything. Sex, sodomy, periods, and so on. We never talked much about ourselves even; I can recall no confidences, no compliments; no kisses; no self analysis between me and him. As for sex, he passed from childhood to boyhood, from boyhood to manhood under our eyes, in our presence, without saying a single word that could have been taken for a sign of what he was feeling. Did other boys fall in love with him? Not he with them, for a certainty. From Clive I learnt later (when talk was about everything) that Lytton's sodomy was to him one of the stock jokes; one of the Strache's preposterous, laughable absurdities. Yet beneath that silence – it may be kept cool and sweet, it may be given a depth and seriousness, an emotional power and quality that speech destroys – dwelt as I felt great susceptibility; great sensibility; great pride in us whose photographs were always on his fireplace at Cambridge; and all those desires which would have made him a lover; a husband; a father. His loves were already distinctly sketched though so submerged; was there some dancing mistress, at Cambridge, brought to light by Gerald who found her photograph? And then of course Elena; and then Irene. But again how ceremonious, how formal, his approach to loving women was. How very silent in words; yet how apparent in its tremble and quiver without words. That would have been his private life. Publicly, he would have been, had he been put on, a judge certainly. Mr Justice Stephen he would be today; with several books to his credit; one or two on law; some essays exposing humbugs; perhaps a book on birds, with drawings by himself. By this time, aged sixty, he would have been a distinguished figure; but not prominent; for he was too melancholy, too independent, unconforming, to take any ready made mould. He would have been more of a character than a success, I suppose; had he been put on.

The knell of those words affects my memory of a time when in fact they were not heard at all. We had no kind of foreboding that he was to die when he was twenty-six and I was twenty-four. That is one of the falsifications – that knell I always find myself hearing and transmitting – that one cannot guard against, save by noting it. Then I never saw him as I see him now, with all his promise ended. Then I thought only of the moment; him there in the room; just back from Clifton; or from Cambridge; dropping in to argue with me. It was, whatever date I give it, an exciting moment; in which we both pushed out from the mists of childhood; and each saw the other emerging; and each felt new qualities, he in himself, me in myself; both in each other. They were days of discovery. Exciting days, whether one called them happy or unhappy; or agitating. Externally I remember the discovery that he looked astonishingly handsome, in his new J. Hills suit of blue serge. That was in October 1899 when he first went to Cambridge. The summer at Warboys I discovered that he smoked a pipe. He never had it out of his mouth. Then term after term I discovered Bell, the Strache, and Sydney-Turner.* But I am rushing too far ahead of myself in Hyde Park Gate. I go back then to the year that Stella died – 1897.

I could sum it all up in one scene. I always see when I think of the months that followed her death a leafless bush, a skeleton bush, in the dark of a summer's night. This rather finely drawn many twigged tree stands outside a garden house. Inside I am sitting with Jack Hills. He grips my hand in his. He wrings my hand. He groans: "It tears one asunder . . ." He gripped my hand to make his agony endurable; as women in childbirth grip a sheet. "But you can't understand", he broke off. "Yes I can", I murmured. Subconsciously, I knew that he meant his sexual desires tore him asunder; I knew that he felt that at the same time as his agony at Stella's death. Both tortured him. And the tree outside in the August summer half light was giving me, as he groaned, a symbol of his agony; of our sterile agony; was summing it all up. Still the leafless tree is to me the emblem, the symbol, of those summer months.

He came every weekend to the house we had at Painswick. Every night either Vanessa or I wandered off with him alone after dinner. Every day he wrote to one or the other. We bore the brunt of his anguish. He was in agony. "Poor boy, he looks very bad", Father once muttered audibly. And Jack, overhearing, stammered some awkward sentence to cover up, to prevent him from saying more. He looked anguished; yet dogged; all in coal black. George, Gerald, Jack were all in black from head to toe. The leafless tree and Jack's hand gripping my wrist; they come back together when I think of that summer.

The leafless tree was behind our ostensible lives for many months. But trees do not remain leafless. They begin to grow little red chill buds. By that image I would convey the misery, the quarrels, the irritations, half covered, then spurting out, the insinuations, which as soon as family life started again began to prove that Stella's death had not left us more united; as father said; but had left us all ill adjusted; growing painfully into relations that her death had distorted.

Another garden scene – this time at Fritham – comes back to me. George had taken my arm in his. Indoors father was playing his nightly whist with

* Clive Bell, Lytton Strachey and Saxon Sydney-Turner, Thoby's Trinity College friends who were to form part of the nucleus of 'old Bloomsbury'.

the others. George singled me out, and walked me off round the lawn. I cannot remember any phrase exactly. A sound of mumbling comes back; his pressure on my hand; and then I gathered that very emotionally and ambiguously, with many such words as "Darling old Goat", "old party", and so on, he was telling me that people were saying that Vanessa was in love with Jack; it was illegal; their marriage he meant; could I not speak to her; persuade her – It was a blurred night talk; with the usual resonance of emotional chords; and I was flattered; perhaps felt important; and must have promised I would say whatever it was he wanted me to say. What? I do not remember what I said; only her answer, and its bitterness: "So you take their side too."

Then I realised that she had her side; if that were so, of course I was on her side. Confusedly, I wobbled at once from George's side to her side. But my vagueness and confusion show that I knew very little of the exact state of things; I had not been called in until George had tried other measures – for one thing as Nessa told me later, he had spoken to father; and he, with that backbone of intellect which would have made him, had we lived to be at ease with him, so dependable in serious relations, had said simply; she must do as she liked; he was not going to interfere. That was what I admire in him; his dignity and sanity in the larger affairs; so often covered up by his irritations and vanities and egotisms.

These scenes, by the way, are not altogether a literary device – a means of summing up and making a knot out of innumerable little threads. Innumerable threads were there; still, if I stopped to disentangle, I could collect a number. But whatever the reason may be, I find that scene making is my natural way of marking the past. A scene always comes to the top; arranged; representative. This confirms me in my instinctive notion – it is irrational; it will not stand argument – that we are sealed vessels afloat upon what it is convenient to call reality; at some moments, without a reason, without an effort, the sealing matter cracks; in floods reality; that is a scene – for they would not survive entire so many ruinous years unless they were made of something permanent; that is a proof of their "reality". Is this liability of mine to scene receiving the origin of my writing impulse? These are questions about reality, about scenes and their connection with writing to which I have no answer; nor time to put the question carefully. Perhaps if I should revise and rewrite as I intend, I will make the question more exact; and worry out something by way of answer. Obviously I have developed the faculty, because in all the writing I have done (novels, criticism, biography) I almost always have to find a scene; either when I am writing about a person, I must find a representative scene in their lives; or when I am writing about a book, I must find the scene in their poems or novels. Or is this not quite the same faculty?

So that was one of the little red buds or thorns, on the skeleton tree; Vanessa was in love with Jack; Jack was absorbing her selfishly; people were talking; and George and Gerald (to a lesser degree) were getting their hackles up. That is one of the aspects of death that is left out when people talk – as father talked – of the message or teaching of sorrow. They never mention its unbecoming side; its legacy of bitterness, bad temper; ill adjustment; and what is to me the worst of all – boredom.

(15th November 1940) We never spoke, during those unhappy years, of those scenes. (Scenes, I note, seldom illustrate my relation with Vanessa; it has been too deep for 'scenes'.) Thoby, I imagine, never guessed at their existence. He may have had a vague conception that something, as he would have put it, was 'up' between Jack and Vanessa. But his general attitude was aloof – was he not a man? Did not men ignore domestic trifles? – and judicial. From his remote station, as schoolboy, as undergraduate, he felt generally speaking that we should accept our lot; if George wanted us to go to parties, why not? If father – who was not, he once told me, a normal specimen of manhood – wished us to walk, we should. Once at Salisbury, when the Fishers were neighbours, Vanessa, detesting them, and in particular Aunt Mary, who had viciously interfered, writing surreptitious letters addressed to Cope's studio, criticising her behaviour towards George and Jack – when Vanessa refused to visit them, and cut them in the street, Thoby pronounced one of his rare impressive judgements. He said gruffly it was not right to treat Aunt Mary like that.

It thus came about that Nessa and I formed together a close conspiracy. In that world of many men, coming and going, in that big house of innumerable rooms, we formed our private nucleus. I visualise it as a little sensitive centre of acute life; of instantaneous sympathy, in the great echoing shell of Hyde Park Gate. The shell was empty all day. In the evening back they would all come; Adrian from Westminster; Jack from Lincoln's Inn Fields; Gerald from Dents; George from the Post office or the Treasury, back to the focus, the tea table, where Nessa and I presided. The staple day would be spent (after the morning's work) together. Together we shaped our own angle, and from it looked out at a world that seemed to both of us much the same. Very soon after Stella's death we realised that we must make some standing place for ourselves in this baffling, frustrating whirlpool. Every day we did battle for that which was always being snatched from us, or distorted. The most imminent obstacle, the most oppressive stone laid upon our vitality and its struggle to live was of course father. I suppose hardly a day of the week passed without our planning together: was he by any chance to be out, when Kitty Maxse or

Katie Thynne* came? Must I spend the afternoon walking round
Kensington Gardens? Was old Mr Bryce coming to tea? Could we possibly
take our friends up to the studio – that is, the day nursery? Could we avoid
Brighton at Easter? And so on – day after day we tried to remove the
pressure of his tremendous obstacle. And over the whole week brooded the
horror, the recurring terror of Wednesday. On that day the weekly books
were given him. Early that morning we knew whether they were under or
over the danger mark – eleven pounds if I remember right.† On a bad
Wednesday we ate our lunch in the anticipation of torture. The books were
presented directly after lunch. He put on his glasses. Then he read the
figures. Then down came his fist on the account book. His veins filled; his
face flushed. Then there was an inarticulate roar. Then he shouted . . . "I
am ruined." Then he beat his breast. Then he went through an
extraordinary dramatisation of self pity, horror, anger. Vanessa stood by
his side silent. He belaboured her with reproaches, abuses. "Have you no
pity for me? There you stand like a block of stone . . ." and so on. She stood
absolutely silent. He flung at her all the phrases about shooting Niagara,
about his misery, her extravagance, that came handy. She still remained
static. Then another attitude was adopted. With a deep groan he picked up
his pen and with ostentatiously trembling hands he wrote out the cheque.
Slowly with many groans the pen and the account book were put away.
Then he sank into his chair; and sat spectacularly with his head on his
breast. And then, tired of this, he would take up a book; read for a time; and
then say half plaintively, appealingly (for he did not like me to witness
these outbursts): "What are you doing this afternoon, Jinny?" I was
speechless. Never have I felt such rage and such frustration. For not a word
of what I felt – that unbounded contempt for him and of pity for Nessa –
could be expressed.

That, as far as I can describe it, is an unexaggerated account of a bad
Wednesday. And bad Wednesdays always hung over us. Even now I can
find nothing to say of his behaviour save that it was brutal. If instead of
words he had used a whip, the brutality could have been no greater. How
can one explain it? His life explains something. He had been indulged, ever
since he broke the flower pot and threw it at his mother (whatever the truth
of that story, it ran something like that). Delicacy was the excuse then. Later
there was the 'genius' legend to which I have referred. And first his sister,
Carry,‡ then Minny, then my mother, each accepting the legend, and

* Lady Katherine Thynne who married Lord Cromer.

† A passage of eight sentences is crossed through and reworked, with minor
changes, in the lines that follow.

‡ Caroline Emilia Stephen.

bowing to it, increased the load for the other. But there are additions and qualifications to be made. To begin with, it is notable that these scenes were never indulged in before men. Fred Maitland thus resolutely refused to believe, though tactfully instructed by Carry, that Leslie's tempers were more than what he called (in his biography) coloured showers of sparks. If Thoby had given him the weekly books, or George, the explosion would have been minimised. Why then had he no shame in thus indulging his rage before women? Partly of course because woman was then (though gilt with an angelic surface) the slave. But that does not explain the histrionic element in these displays; the breast beating, the groaning, the self-dramatisation. His dependence on women helps to explain that. He needed always some woman to act before; to sympathise with him, to console him ("He is one of those men who cannot live without us," Aunt Mary whispered to me once. "And it is very nice for us that it should be so." Coming downstairs arm in arm with her, I laid that remark aside for further inspection.) Why did he need them? Because he was conscious of his failure as a philosopher. That failure gnawed at him. But his creed, the attitude, that is to say, adopted by him in his public relations, made him hide the need he had for praise; thus to Fred Maitland and to Herbert Fisher he appeared entirely self deprecating, modest, and ridiculously humble in his opinion of himself. To us he was exacting, greedy, unabashed* in his demand for praise. If then, these suppressions and needs are combined, it seems possible that the reason for this brutality to Vanessa was that he had an illicit† need for sympathy, released by the woman, stimulated; and her refusal to accept her role, part slave, part angel, exacerbated him; checked the flow that had become necessary of self pity, and stirred in him instincts of which he was unconscious. Yet also ashamed. "You must think me," he said to me after one of these rages – I think the word he used was "foolish". I was silent. I did not think him foolish. I thought him brutal.

If someone had said to him simply and straightforwardly: "You are a brute to treat a girl like that . . ." what would he have said? I cannot imagine that the words would have meant anything to him. The reason for that complete unconsciousness of his own behaviour is to be found in the disparity, so obvious in his books, between the critical and the imaginative power. Give him a thought to analyse, the thought say of Mill or Bentham or Hobbes, and he is (so Maynard‡ told me) a model of acuteness, clarity, and impartiality.

* Doubtful reading.

† 'violent' is crossed through and 'illicit' is added above, followed by a comma and an illegible word.

‡ John Maynard Keynes.

Give him a character to explain, and he is (to me) so crude, so elementary, so conventional that a child with a box of chalks could make a more subtle portrait. To explain this one would have to discuss the crippling effect of Cambridge and its one sided education. One would have to follow that by a discussion of the writer's profession in the nineteenth century and the mutilations of intensive brain work. He never used his hands.* And one would have to show how both these influences told upon a nature that was congenitally unaware of music, of art, and puritanically brought up.† All this would have to be considered and its effect in intensifying certain sensibilities and reducing others to atrophy.

The fact remains that at the age of sixty-five he was a man in prison, isolated. He had so ignored, or disguised his own feelings that he had no idea of what he was; and no idea of what other people were. Hence the horror and the terror of those violent displays of rage. There was something blind, animal, savage in them. Roger Fry said that civilisation means awareness; he was uncivilised in his extreme unawareness. He did not realise what he did. No one could enlighten him. Yet he suffered. Through the walls of his prison he had moments of realisation.

From it all I gathered one obstinate and enduring conception; that nothing is so much to be dreaded as egotism. Nothing so cruelly hurts the person himself; nothing so wounds those who are forced into contact with it.

But from my present distance of time I see too what we could not then see – the gulf between us that was cut by our difference in age. Two different ages confronted each other in the drawing room at Hyde Park Gate. The Victorian age and the Edwardian age. We were not his children; we were his grandchildren. There should have been a generation between us to cushion the contact. Thus it was that we perceived so keenly, while he raged, that he was somehow ridiculous. We looked at him with eyes that were looking into the future. What we saw was something that is so obvious now to any boy or girl of sixteen or eighteen that it is hardly to be described. But while we looked into the future, we were completely under the power of the past. Explorers and revolutionists, as we both were by nature, we lived under the sway of a society that was about fifty years too old for us. It was this curious fact that made our struggle so bitter and so violent. For the society in which we lived was still the Victorian society. Father himself was a typical Victorian. George and Gerald were consenting and approving Victorians. So that we had two quarrels to wage; two fights to fight; one with them individually; and

* "He never used his hands" is a marginal note, the rest of which is illegible because of the deterioration of the paper.

† "a self-centred narrow nature" is crossed through.

one with them socially. We were living say in 1910; they were living in 1860.

Hyde Park Gate in 1900 was a complete model of Victorian society. If I had the power to lift out of the past a single day as we lived it about 1900, it would give a section of upper middle class Victorian life, like one of those sections with glass covers in which ants and bees are shown going about their tasks. Our day would begin with family breakfast at 8.30. Adrian bolted his, and whichever of us, Vanessa or myself, was down would see him off. Standing at the front door, we would wave a hand till he had disappeared behind the bulging wall of the Martins' house. This hand waving was a relic left us by Stella – a flutter of the dead hand which lay beneath the surface of family life. Father would eat his breakfast sighing and snorting. If there were no letters, "Everyone has forgotten me", he would exclaim. A long envelope from Barkers would mean of course a sudden roar. George and Gerald would come later. Vanessa disappeared behind the curtain with its golden anchor. Dinner ordered, she would dash for the red bus to take her to the Academy. If Gerald coincided, he would give her a lift in his daily hansom, the same generally; in summer the cabby wore a red carnation. George, having breakfasted more deliberately, would persuade me sometimes to sit on in the three-cornered chair and would tell me scraps of gossip about last night's party. Then he would kiss me, button up his frock coat, give his top hat a promise with the velvet glove and trot off, handsome, debonair, in his ribbed socks and very small well polished shoes to the Treasury.

Left alone in the great house, father shut in his study at the top, Lizzie polishing brass stair rods, another maid doing bedrooms, Shag asleep on his mat, while Sophie, I suppose, stood at the back door taking in joints, milk, vegetables from tradespeople in their little carts, I mounted to my room; spread my Liddell and Scott upon the table, and settled down to read Plato, or to make out some scene in Euripides or Sophocles for Clara Pater, or Janet Case.*

From ten to one Victorian society did not exert any special pressure upon us. Vanessa, under the eye of Val Prinsep,† or Mr Ouless, R.A.‡ or occasionally of the great Sargent himself, made those minute pencil drawings of Greek statues which she brought home and fixed with a spray of odd smelling mixture; or painted a histrionic male model rather like Sir Henry

---

* Clara Pater, the sister of Walter Pater, who taught Virginia Greek and Latin before Miss Case. Janet Case, in addition to being a severe and thorough teacher, became a lifelong friend of Virginia's.

† Julia Stephen's cousin, son of Sarah and Thoby Prinsep.

‡ Walter William Ouless R.A. (1848–1933).

Irving in oils. I read and wrote. For three hours we lived in the world which we still inhabit. For at this moment (November 1940) she is painting at Charleston; and I am writing here in the garden room at Monks House. Nor would our clothes be very different; the skirts a little shorter perhaps. My hair not much tidier then than now; and Vanessa in a blue cotton smock; as no doubt she is at this moment.

Victorian society began to exert its pressure at about half past four. In the first place, we must be in; one certainly, preferably both. For at five father must be given his tea. And we must be tidied and in our places, she at the tea table, I on the sofa, for Mrs Green was coming; or Mrs Humphrey Ward; if no one came, it was still necessary to be there; for father could not give himself his tea in the society of those days.

The pressure of society made itself apparent as soon as the bell rang and Lizzie, also dressed in her afternoon black with a white apron, announced the visitor. For then instantaneously we became young ladies possessed of a certain manner. We both still possess that manner. We learnt it partly from remembering mother's manner; Stella's manner, and it was partly imposed upon us by the visitor who came in. For the manner in which a young man – say Ronny Norman* – addressed young ladies was a marked manner. The visitors upon that day were, let us suppose, Ronny Norman, Eveline Godley, Elsa Bell and Florence Bishop. We should have first to make conversation. It was not argument, it was not gossip. It was a concoction, a confection; light; ceremonious; and of course unbroken. Silence was a breach of convention. At the right moment, one of us would take father's trumpet and convey some suitable portion to him. And then, if we could contrive it, the trumpet would be skilfully transferred to Florence Bishop. And our concoction would begin again with Ronny Norman. He would say something about an awfully jolly play; or an awfully jolly picture perhaps. Light remarks about friends were allowed. Elsa Bell, to recall an exact sentence, said in her society way: "My brothers always take off their hats if they meet me in the street." Light discussion of brothers and their manners followed. At this point father, groaning, would intervene.†

[. . . father would be irritated: Florence Bishop would too and [would] withdraw her unlucky remark – that he looked well; Ronny Norman would ask him if he remembered Mill; he would unbend – for he liked Ronny

---

* Ronald Norman, distant relative of the Camerons; later Chairman of the B.B.C.

† The next page of the BL typescript is missing. As mentioned in the Editor's Note, p. 177, the relevant passage from the earlier version, MH/A. 5a, has been inserted within brackets.

Norman – and say how he had met Mill with his father in Chelsea.* "Oh dear, these old stories . . ." he would say. Well, the talk had its little steeps and waterfalls – its dangers: but it went something like that: and the whole was enclosed in the Victorian manner. It may have been natural for Ronny Norman, for Eveline Godley, for Miss Bishop. It was not natural for Vanessa or myself. We learned it. We learned it partly from memory: and mother had that manner: it was imposed on us partly by the other side – if Ronny Norman said that, one had to reply in the same style. Nobody ever broke the convention. If you listened, as I did, it was like watching a game. One had to know the rules.]

We both learnt the rules of the game of Victorian society so thoroughly that we have never forgotten them. We still play the game. It is useful. It has also its beauty, for it is founded upon restraint, sympathy, unselfishness – all civilized qualities. It is helpful in making something seemly out of raw odds and ends. Major Gardner, Mrs Chavasse, and Mr Dutton need some solving to make it into a sociable party. But the Victorian manner is perhaps – I am not sure – a disadvantage in writing. When I read my old *Literary Supplement* articles, I lay the blame for their suavity, their politeness, their sidelong approach, to my tea-table training. I see myself, not reviewing a book, but handing plates of buns to shy young men and asking them: do they take cream and sugar? On the other hand, the surface manner allows one, as I have found, to slip in things that would be inaudible if one marched straight up and spoke out loud.

Society – upper middle class Victorian society – came into being when the lights went up. About seven thirty the pressure of the machine became emphatic. At seven thirty we went upstairs to dress. However cold or foggy, we slipped off our day clothes and stood shivering in front of washing basins. Each basin had its can of hot water. Neck and arms had to be scrubbed, for we had to enter the drawing room at eight with bare arms, low neck, in evening dress. At seven thirty dress and hair overcame paint and Greek grammar. I would stand in front of George's Chippendale mirror trying to make myself not only tidy, but presentable. On an allowance of fifty pounds it was difficult, even for the skilful, and I had no skill, to be well dressed of an

---

* In the ms, VW refers to the guests around the tea-table by their initials, but not consistently which would suggest that convenience rather than a stylistic effect was her motive. Thus, the full names have been restored in the text. P. 49 of the ms booklet which does not appear to belong to the version of the text used here provides a fuller context for Miss Bishop's remark. The first half-dozen lines read: "Florence Bishop had said that she thought him looking remarkably well. This was an insult – a breach of the code: it was essential that he should receive sympathy. And so we must brush up our talk with that."

evening. A home dress, made by Jane Bride, could be had for a pound or two; but a party dress, made by Mrs Young, cost fifteen guineas. The home dress therefore might be, as on one night that comes back to mind, made cheaply but eccentrically, of a green fabric, bought at Story's, the furniture shop. It was not velvet; nor plush; something betwixt and between; and for chairs, presumably, not dresses. Down I came one winter's evening about 1900 in my green dress; apprehensive, yet, for a new dress excites even the unskilled, elated. All the lights were turned up in the drawing room; and by the blazing fire George sat, in dinner jacket and black tie, cuddling the dachshund, Schuster, on his knee. He at once fixed on me that extraordinarily observant scrutiny with which he always inspected our clothes. He looked me up and down for a moment as if I were a horse brought into the show ring. Then the sullen look came into his eyes; the look which expressed not simply aesthetic disapproval; but something that went deeper. It was the look of moral, of social, disapproval, as if he scented some kind of insurrection, of defiance of his accepted standards. I knew myself condemned from more points of view than I could then analyse. As I stood there I was conscious of fear; of shame; of something like anguish – a feeling, like so many, out of all proportion to its surface cause. He said at last: "Go and tear it up." He spoke in a curiously tart, rasping, peevish voice; the voice of the enraged male; the voice which expressed his serious displeasure at this infringement of a code that meant more to him than he could admit.

George accepted Victorian society so implicitly that to an archaeologist he would be a fascinating object. Like a fossil he had taken every crease and wrinkle of the conventions of upper middle class society between 1870 and 1900. He was made presumably of precisely the right material. He flowed into the mould without a doubt to mar the pattern. If father had graved on him certain large marks of the age – his belief that women must be pure and men manly; his hatred of strong language – "Damn!" Gerald said once, and up flew his hands in protest; when Rezia Corsini* smoked a cigarette after tea, "I won't have my drawing room turned into a bar parlour!" he exclaimed – still he smoothed out the petty details of the Victorian code with his admirable intellect, with his respect for reason – no one was less snobbish than he, no one cared less for rank or luxury. But if father had the larger lines of the age stamped on him, George filled them in with a crisscross, with a crowquill etching of the most minute details. No more perfect fossil of the Victorian age could exist. And so, while father preserved the framework of 1860, George filled in the framework with all kinds of minutely-teethed saws; and the machine into which our rebellious bodies were inserted in 1900

* Lucrezia Rasponi who had married Filippo Corsini in 1901.

not only held us tight in its framework, but bit into us with innumerable sharp teeth.

But what material was George made of so that he took the pattern so completely? In the first place, he was almost brainless; in the second he had an abundance of feeling. His physical passions were strong. This mixture was poured into a perfectly adapted physical vessel. He was in a conventional way as handsome as a man could be. He was precisely six foot in height; well proportioned; and, as the old ladies said, well set up in every respect. His eyes were too small and too stupid to light up this great framework. He had over a thousand a year of unearned income. He could supply frock coats, hats, shoes, ties, horses, guns, bicycles, as the occasion required. Thus furnished and equipped society opened its arms wide to him and embraced him. He can never have met with any opposition at Eton, at Cambridge, or in London. He offered none. He had no instinct, no ability to make him stray beyond the circle of the upper middle class world in the evening drawing room. He was never rebuffed or criticised because he never went an inch out of his orbit. Any defiance therefore was unfamiliar to him; and my green dress set ringing in him a thousand alarm bells. It was extreme; it was artistic; it was not what nice people thought nice. Was that the formula, he said to himself, as he saw me come into the room? Did he too feel that it threatened something in himself? Was I somehow casting a shadow in his world; pointing a finger of scorn at him? I do not know. Gerald, I remember, spoke up for me good naturedly. "I don't agree," he said. "I like you in that dress." To my discredit, I never wore it again in George's presence. I knuckled under to his authority.*

It is true that George was thirty-six when I was twenty. And he had [a] thousand pounds [a] year whereas I had fifty. These were good reasons why it was difficult not to submit to whatever he decreed. But there was another element in our relationship. Besides feeling his age and his power, I felt too what I have come to call the outsider's feeling. I felt as a gipsy or a child feels who stands at the flap of the tent and sees the circus going on inside. I stood in the drawing room at Hyde Park Gate and saw society in full swing. I saw George as an acrobat jumping through hoops. I saw him, perhaps with fear, perhaps with admiration. The patriarchal society of the Victorian age was in full swing in our drawing room. It had of course many different parts. Vanessa and I were not called upon to take part in some of those acts. We were only asked to admire and applaud when our male relations went

---

* The following lines are crossed through and reworked in the next paragraph, "In my defence I must say that he was fifteen years older; and he made it difficult not to comply because whereas I had £50 a year he had a thousand a year. And he gave us presents.

through the different figures of the intellectual game. They played it with great skill. Most of our male relations were adept at that game. They knew the rules, and attached extraordinary importance to those who won the game. Father for example laid immense stress upon school reports; upon scholarships; triposes and fellowships. The male Fishers went through those hoops to perfection. They won all the prizes, all the honours. What, I asked myself, when I read Herbert Fisher's autobiography the other day, would Herbert have been without Winchester, New College and the Cabinet? What would have been his shape had he not been stamped and moulded by that great patriarchal machine? Every one of our male relations was shot into that machine at the age of ten and emerged at sixty a Head Master, an Admiral, a Cabinet Minister, or the Warden of a college. It is as impossible to think of them as natural human beings as it is to think of a carthorse galloping wild maned and unshod over the pampas.

George had not been able to enter the intellectual machine. He tried again and again to enter the diplomatic service, but failed. There was however the other machine – the social machine. That he entered; and he learnt the rules of the game so well and played it so assiduously that he emerged at the age of sixty with a Lady Margaret for wife, with a knighthood, with a sinecure of some sort, three sons, and a country house. In ways so indefinite that I cannot name them, I felt, at twenty, that George no less than Herbert Fisher was going through the hoops; doing the required acts. In a thousand ways he made me feel that he believed in society. A belief which is so commonly accepted, as his was by all his friends, had depth, swiftness, inevitability. It impresses even the outsider by the sweep of its current. Sometimes when I hear God Save the King I too feel a current belief but almost directly I consider my own splits asunder and one side of me criticises the other. George never questioned his belief in the old tune that society played. He rose and took his hat off and stood. Not only did he never question his behaviour; he applauded it, enforced it.

These perceptions, however slight and transient they were then, gave my attitude to George a queer twist. I must obey because he had force – age, wealth, tradition – behind him. But even while I obeyed, I marvelled – how could anyone believe what George believed? There was a spectator in me who, even while I squirmed and obeyed, remained observant, note taking for some future revision. The spectacle of George, laying down laws in his leather arm chair so instinctively, so unhesitatingly, fascinated me. Upstairs alone in my room I wrote a sketch of his probable career; which his actual career followed almost to the letter.*

---

* There follows a deleted paragraph which is reworked, with minor changes in the passage that follows.

But unfortunately, though we could and indeed must, sit passive and applaud the Victorian males when they went through the intellectual hoops, George's hoops – his social triumphs – needed our help. Here, of course, his motives were – as indeed they always were – mixed. Naturally, at eighteen or so, we had to be brought out. And he naturally, as we had no mother, took her place. What proved unnatural, however, was his insistence that we should go where he wished us to go, and do as he wished us to do. Here the other motive came in; his desire to make us share his views, approve of his beliefs. I cannot even now understand why it was that he attached so much emotion to this desire. No, I puzzle; but I cannot find the true reason. Some crude wish to dominate there was; some jealousy, of Jack no doubt; some desire to carry off the prize; and, as became obvious later, some sexual urge. At any rate this matter of taking us out became an obsession with him. And thus, when the London season began, several times a week we would go upstairs after dinner – after the post had come, the tea had been drunk, and father had gone up to his study – and change into long satin dresses, for which Sally Young would charge fifteen guineas, pull on long white gloves, slip on satin shoes, and snap a row of pearls, of amethysts, round our necks. The cab would be called; and off we would drive along the silver plated streets, for the wood pavements were beaten to silver on a dry summer's night, to the house where there was an awning, bright windowed, and perhaps a strip of red carpet, and a little cluster of gaping passers by.

Society exerted its full pressure about eleven o'clock on a June night in 1900. I remember the dazed, elated, frozen feeling as the lights beat on me, going upstairs with George following behind. He held his opera hat always under his arm. He would introduce me with his little bow: "And this is my sister, Virginia." Can I remember anything further – any words, any human emotions? There, at the Savoy, was Mrs Joseph Chamberlain, the very image of womanly charm. We were going to the opera, *The Ring*; it was broad daylight, and George, with a lack of tact with which he reproached himself afterwards – he would tot up the night's successes and failures – had placed her opposite the window; and she was then not quite at her prime. Eddie Marsh sat next me, as I now suppose. That night I called him Richard Marsh; and vaguely connected him with fiction. After a pause, he did his duty by me; "What is your father writing now?" A blank occurs. But I visualise my own efforts to keep up the conversation as the wild flounderings and scrapings of a skater who cannot skate. At the Chamberlains' I sat next to a chubby spruce boy, perhaps a private secretary. We discussed public speaking. "Our host", he reminded me, for I had been denouncing the death of oratory, "is generally supposed to be a good speaker." And then on I plunged, and told him – the words come back – that snobbishness, that money making, deserved imprisonment as well as theft and murder. But I had plunged too deep; the glue stuck to my quivering feet. On the steps of a ball room I can see the romantic figure of Geoffrey Young; blue eyed; bland, immaculate. "But how very good of you to have come", he replied superciliously; for had I not told him that I hated dancing? Then he left me. At Lady Sligo's I remember pressing some spruce boy to tell me how life was lived in the peerage; whether Garters were taken seriously. Again silence. At the Lyulph Stanleys' I stood unclaimed against a door. Up came Elena Rathbone* and nailed the coffin of my failure by introducing me to a girl, also partnerless. And soon she discovered, as all my partners discovered, that I could not dance. The humiliation of standing unpartnered returns to me. But at the same time I recall that the good friend who is with me still, upheld me; that sense of the spectacle; the dispassionate separate sense that I am seeing what will be useful later; I could even find the words for the scene as I stood there. At the same time, there was the thrill; and the oddity. For the first time one was in touch with a young man in white waistcoat and gloves; and I too was in white and gloves. If it was unreal, there was a thrill in that unreality. For when at last I came back to my bedroom, it looked small, untidy; and I would ride the waves of these fragmentary feelings – repeat these scraps of talk – say it all over to myself – what I said – what he said – and next morning would still be going over it as I read my Sophocles for Miss Case.

None of this is strange; nor if this had been all would there have been much in these parties to come back to mind. They would have slid off one's back like so much sparkling water. But there was George. And he made us feel that every party was a test; if a success, then the prize was ours; we had satisfied Lady Sligo; looked lovely; so and so had said I have never seen a lovelier girl and so on. But if it was a failure, then doom was before us; we would fall into the depths of dowdiness; of eccentricity. The importance of the party either way was enormous. But why? This question could not be asked. If, plucking up courage, one of us, opening one of those stiff envelopes with an engraved card on it, should say: "But if I hate going to parties, why should I accept this one?" He would instantly wrinkle his cheek lines; and announce tartly: "You're too young to pick and choose . . ." There would be silence. Then changing his mood, opening his arms, he would cry: "Besides, I want you to come. I hate going alone . . . beloved. Say you will come?" Duty and emotion muddied the stream. And over that turbulent whirlpool the ghosts of mother and Stella presided. How could we do battle with all of them?

By degrees then these parties, these tests, for which one had to prepare so carefully, became ordeals. "Only three weeks till the end of July I would

---

* Elena Rathbone who later married Bruce Richmond, editor of the *Times Literary Supplement*.

say," as the cards arrived. But before the three weeks were over there would be coaxing and hinting; and when the night came, a battle, and Vanessa would stalk off, if beaten, to dress herself in the famous black velvet dress, and George, left in the drawing room, would pace up and down; and protest that he could not take her if she looked like that. And yet other girls would give their eyes to be asked – wherever it was. Did he feel, I return to the puzzle, that we criticised his conception? Was it again the sexual jealousy that fermented in his depths? At any rate, he would run through an astonishing range of emotions about these parties. He would upbraid us with selfishness, with narrowness. Caustic phrases would hint at his displeasure. He complained to his circle of dowagers. He invoked their help.* And he succeeded, of course, in impressing the outsiders. How could we resist his wishes? Was not George Duckworth wonderful? And anyhow what else did we want? Society in those days was a perfectly competent, perfectly complacent, ruthless machine. A girl had no chance against its fangs. No other desires – say to paint, or to write – could be taken seriously. Even Beatrice Thynne,† when I told her I meant to be a writer, said at once: "I'll ask Alice to invite you to meet Andrew Lang",‡ and when I boggled, thought me excessively foolish.

The division in our lives was curious. Downstairs there was pure convention; upstairs pure intellect. But there was no connection between them. This was partly, of course, due to father's deafness, which had cut off his intercourse with the younger generation of writers. Young writers, young painters never came to Hyde Park Gate. When Will Rothenstein§ somehow drifted into father's study, he was terror struck. Leslie Stephen opened book after book and pointed silently, trying, apparently, to show him Thackeray drawings. Yet he kept his own intellectual attitude – the old Cambridge attitude – perfectly pure. Nobody respected intellect more. Thus I would go from the drawing room, where George was telling one of his little triumphs – "Mrs Willie Grenfell asked me to come for a weekend. And I said on the whole I thought I wouldn't . . . She was taken by surprise . . ." – up to father's study to fetch a book. I would find him swinging in his rocking chair,

---

* A line is drawn through: "He paid for clothes; he bought enamel brooches; to the public he represented the good brother; doing his duty by motherless girls".

† Lady Beatrice Thynne, daughter of the Marchioness of Bath and sister of Katherine and Alice.

‡ Andrew Lang (1844–1912) was a journalist and a man of letters who wrote on an immense variety of subjects.

§ Sir William Rothenstein describes this alarming incident in his autobiography, *Men and Memoirs: 1872–1938* (abridged ed., Chatto & Windus, London, 1978), p. 61.

pipe in mouth. Slowly he would unwrinkle his forehead and come to ground and realise with a very sweet smile that I stood there. Rising he would go to the shelves, put the book back, and ask me gently, kindly: "What did you make of it?" Perhaps I was reading Boswell; without a doubt, I would be gnawing my way through the eighteenth century. Then, feeling proud and stimulated, and full of love for this unworldly, very distinguished and lonely man, whom I had pleased by coming, I would go back to the drawing room and hear George's patter. There was no connection. There were deep divisions.

Great figures stood in the background. Meredith, Henry James, Watts, Burne-Jones, Sidgwick, Haldane, Morley. But with them again we had no close connection. My memories of them are strong; but only of figures looming large in the distance. I can still see Symonds, as I saw him from the landing at Talland House. I looked down on his crinkled yellow face; and noted his tie — a yellow cord to which two balls of yellow plush were attached. I remember the roll and rear of Meredith's voice; pointing to a flower and saying "that damsel in the purple petticoat." I remember still more clearly the ceremony of our visits to great men. For father and mother were equally respectful of greatness. And the honour and the privilege of our position impressed themselves on us. I remember Meredith dropping slices of lemon into his tea. I remember that Watts had great bowls of whipped cream; and a plate of minced meat. "I kissed him", said mother, "before he dipped his moustache in the cream." He wore ruffles at his wrists, and a long grey dressing gown. And we went to Little Holland House always on a Sunday morning. I remember that Lowell had a long knitted purse, constrained by two rings; and that a sixpence always slipped out of the slit. I remember Meredith's growl; and I remember the hesitations and adumbrations with which Henry James made the drawing room seem rich and dusky. Greatness still seems to me a positive possession; booming; eccentric; set apart; something to which I am led up dutifully by my parents. It is a bodily presence; it has nothing to do with anything said. It exists in certain people. But it never exists now. I cannot remember ever to have felt greatness since I was a child.*

[There they were, on the verge of the drawing room, these great men: while, round the tea table, George and Gerald and Jack talked of the Post Office, the publishing office, and the Law Courts. And I, sitting by the table, was quite unable to make any connection. There were so many different

* The British Library typescript ends here, omitting the last paragraph of MH/A. 5d. This has been included within brackets as it is unusual for VW to omit entire paragraphs from the manuscript version in the typescript. See Editor's Note, p. 177.

worlds: but they were distant from me. I could not make them cohere; nor feel myself in touch with them. And I spent many hours of my youth restlessly comparing them. No doubt the distraction and the differences were of use; as a means of education; as a way of showing one the contraries. For no sooner had I settled down to my Greek than I would be called off to hear George's case; then from that I would be told to come up to the study to read German; and then the gay world of Kitty Maxse would impinge.]

Appendix A

The following alterations have been made to the text with the aim of correcting what appear to be oversights on Virginia Woolf's part.

Page	Line	Ts or Ms (VW)	Reading Adopted
3	28	tonight	that night
15	38	and sharpness (after 'silence')	deleted
18	21	depended doubtless	doubtless depended
20	3	atmosphere merely	merely as the atmosphere
21	14	on	at
21	32	Once your uncle	Your uncle
27	8	they	it
31	17	sobbed	cried
36	16	hostesses	peers
50	13	Turner	him
50	15	who	he
54	21	We true	True, we
55	7	because	that
74	7	and	who
96	21–2	of the painting	of painting
96	24	I	one
97	5	of course	omitted
98	17	had	and
99	13	are	is
110	27	intimacy formally	to begin again formally

Appendix B

Preface to the Second Edition

THE second edition incorporates a seventy-seven-page typescript version of "Sketch of the Past" acquired by the British Library in the early 1980s. Written in 1940, this hitherto unknown material provides the missing link between the typescript and the manuscript which were brought together as "Sketch of the Past", the most substantial and significant of the autobiographical writings in *Moments of Being*.

The British Library typescript contains twenty-seven pages of entirely new material in which Virginia Woolf describes her father, Leslie Stephen, and the ambivalence of her relationship to him which her recent readings of Freud had caused her to reassess. Her mature, analytic account illuminates one of the most important influences on her development both as an individual and as a writer, and provides a valuable corrective to the earlier version which, because it is partial, is also misleading.

The typescript, a reworked and more polished version of the manuscript transcribed in the first edition, gives this new version greater stylistic coherence than the earlier one. Furthermore, a number of passages of particular interest, such as Virginia Woolf's reflections on her methods of writing and on the nature of consciousness, are expanded and clarified.

Editor's Note

THIS collection of autobiographical writings by Virginia Woolf brings together unpublished material selected from the Woolf archives at the British Library and the University of Sussex Library. The latter archive, known as the 'Monks House Papers', belonged to Leonard Woolf. When he persuaded Quentin Bell to write the authorized biography of Virginia Woolf he placed the papers at the disposal of Professor Bell who quoted brief passages from them in the biography. After the death of Leonard Woolf the papers passed, through the generosity of the executrix of the estate, Mrs Trekkie Parsons, to the University of Sussex.

The decision to publish material which would have been extensively revised by Virginia Woolf and most of which – unlike the essays published posthumously by Leonard Woolf – was never intended for publication, was not taken without the most careful consideration. The undeniable interest and value of these memoirs, however, left those involved in the decision with no doubts. Publication which would make readily available to a wide audience material that so richly illuminates the vision and sensibility of a writer whose contribution to the history of English literature was so profoundly individual could not but be worthwhile. These memoirs have a unique place in the documentation of her life and art.

It was Virginia Woolf's practice to write out one or more rough drafts of a work and then to type out complete revisions, sometimes as many as eight or nine. The material in this collection is in various stages of revision but with the exception of the first memoir the scripts bear signs of 'work in progress', notwithstanding that the Memoir Club Contributions were in fact read by Virginia Woolf to the audiences for whom they were intended. Corrections, additions, deletions, sometimes hastily made and incomplete, are scattered throughout the work and in some cases whole passages are revised within the text. No attempt has been made in this edition to present a record of these textual revisions and variations. To have done so would have greatly impaired the enjoyment of most readers. For anyone seriously interested in studying this aspect of Virginia Woolf's memoirs, the material is available at the University of Sussex Library and the British Library. However, the desire to present a readable text has at no point been allowed to take precedence over what must be the commitment of primary importance, that of following faithfully Virginia Woolf's last intentions regarding the material as far as they are known or can be reasonably surmised, or to state the reason for not doing so and to indicate doubt where it exists. It is hoped that the 'editorial machinery' will not be unpleasantly obtrusive to the general reader – and Editor's Notes to the individual texts have been provided to minimize this danger – but that it is in evidence has at least the advantage of keeping before the reader the fact that these texts were not prepared for publication by Virginia Woolf, and hence they should not be judged by the same criteria as would be applied to texts published during her lifetime.

Because the memoirs are in different stages of revision it has occasionally been necessary to adapt editorial practice to deal with specific problems. When this has been done, mention has been made in the appropriate note. With that exception, the following editorial principles have been applied to the texts uniformly.

Deletions made by Virginia Woolf have not been included unless they are necessary for the sense of the passage and no substitute has been provided. In such cases the deleted words have been enclosed in square brackets. Partial deletions, which are not uncommon, have been silently completed. In those few cases where Virginia Woolf added a word or a phrase but failed to make the deletion necessary to accommodate the addition, the oversight has been silently corrected. For example, in "Old Bloomsbury", the first version of one passage reads: "True, we still had Thursday evenings as before. But they were always strained and ended generally in dismal failure." Virginia Woolf then added 'often' before 'ended' but failed to delete 'generally'. Where an addition has made it necessary to alter the grammatical form of a word, the change has been listed in Appendix A. Deletions which are of interest have been noted.

Just as some of Virginia Woolf's deletions were incomplete, so were some of her additions and corrections. When it was impossible to incorporate them into the text without serious disruption to the thought they have been omitted and noted. In those instances where a word or phrase was added by Virginia Woolf in such a way as to make it clear that it was merely being considered as an alternative, the later version has been used except where the first is clearly preferable. In very few instances indeed is any point of significance involved; however, alternative readings have been noted if they are of interest or if there is doubt as to the choice Virginia Woolf would have made.

In early drafts, Virginia Woolf's practice regarding punctuation, spelling and capitalization was highly erratic and she often used abbreviations which never appeared in her published work. On occasion, obvious oversights coupled with typing mistakes and incomplete or hastily made corrections have resulted in a profusion of errors; at others, the careful attention to these matters which characterizes her published works is evident. It was Virginia Woolf's practice to submit her work to her husband, Leonard, for revision of these details and he, in publishing her posthumous works, did not hesitate, as he writes in the editorial preface to *The Death of the Moth*,* 'to punctuate' the essays and correct 'obvious verbal mistakes'. Although the liberties that Leonard Woolf would have been justified in taking could not be similarly justified by anyone else, his practice has at least served as a general guideline for the kinds of corrections which have been made in the present text; for it is equally clear that in the case of these memoirs – unlike that of the Diary or the Letters – Virginia Woolf would most certainly have made the spelling, punctuation and capitalization conform to standard usage, except where a nuance was involved, had she decided to publish them.

Hence punctuation has been altered to conform to Virginia Woolf's own practice in her published works. Hyphens, italics, question marks, full stops, double quotes for dialogue, apostrophes for possessives and contractions have been added where appropriate; 'and' has been substituted for the ampersand; abbreviations and numbers have been written out where it was her practice to do so. Apart from these uncontroversial examples, punctuation has been altered only to avoid ambiguity, to correct obvious oversights, or to conform to a pattern established in a sentence or passage which was momentarily overlooked. No attempt has been made to make Virginia Woolf's idiosyncratic and highly expressive punctuation conform in other respects to conventional usage. When, for example, an exclamation point occurs in the middle of a sentence, it is retained if it is appropriate to the sense of the passage. All typing errors have been corrected. Spelling and capitalization have been regularized to conform to common usage unless a nuance is involved.

The sense or the grammar of a sentence has occasionally necessitated the addition of a word which has been enclosed in brackets. However, more than one word in brackets without a note indicates words deleted by Virginia Woolf as explained above. All doubtful readings and illegible words have been noted except in those few cases where a legible and acceptable alternative is available.

The individual Editor's Notes contain a brief description of the subject matter of the memoir in order to avoid cumbersome annotations of the text; the date and circumstances of writing; and a description of the typescript or manuscript on which the edited text is based as well as any unusual problems.

For the sake of brevity, the initials 'VW' and 'LW', for Virginia and Leonard Woolf respectively, have been used in the footnotes. The

---

* The Hogarth Press; London, 1942.

manuscripts and typescripts (ms and ts) are referred to by their Library reference numbers, for example, 'MH/A.5a', except that after the initial mention, the 'MH' (Monks House) has been omitted because all the papers come from that collection. The two-volume biography by Quentin Bell* is referred to simply as 'QB' followed by the appropriate volume and page numbers. The letters, edited by Nigel Nicolson, assisted by Joanne Trautmann, are referred to as '*Letters*', followed by the appropriate volume number. No attempt has been made to be exhaustive in the identification of persons mentioned in the memoirs. In those cases where the individual was of minor or passing significance to Virginia Woolf, or significant because of being representative of a type, as the context makes clear, identification has not generally been made. Quentin Bell's biography is available for those interested in such details; also the six volumes of *Letters*, as mentioned above, and the five-volume *Diary of Virginia Woolf*, edited by Olivier Bell, assisted by Andrew McNeillie. The period in general and 'Bloomsbury' in particular are amply documented.

Jeanne Schulkind
1976

* The Hogarth Press; London, 1972.

Reminiscences

THESE reminiscences of Julia Stephen, Stella Duckworth and Vanessa Bell, the three figures who stood successively at the heart of the Stephen/Duckworth ménage at 22 Hyde Park Gate, were addressed to the first child of Vanessa and Clive Bell. Julian, however, can only be held responsible in a very remote sense for inspiring this memoir; for, according to Quentin Bell, it was begun before Julian's birth (February 1908) when Virginia was spending the summer holidays of 1907 in Playden, just north of Rye, where the Bells were staying.* The memoir is mentioned in two letters after Julian's birth: one, from Virginia to Clive, written on 15 April 1908, and another from Vanessa to Virginia from Cleeve House, of 20 April 1908.† In the letter to Clive it is clear that Virginia's feeling for Vanessa was a major source of inspiration: "I have been writing Nessa's life; and I am going to send you 2 chapters in a day or two. It might have been so good! As it is, I am too near, and too far and it seems to be blurred, and I ask myself why write it at all? seeing I never shall recapture what you have, by your side this minute."‡

At the age of twenty-five, Virginia Woolf was very conscious of being an apprentice at her chosen craft. She had been reviewing since the end of 1904, but her own first 'work of imagination' as she called 'Melymbrosia' (published in 1915 as *The Voyage Out*) was only just begun. Of the exercises which she conscientiously assigned herself, descriptions of places visited and the lives of close friends or relations formed an important part.§ She showed these experiments only to a few intimates and on various occasions she declared her intention of rewriting them at

---

* QB, I, p. 122.

† In the Berg Collection, the New York Public Library.

‡ *Letters*, I, No. 406.

§ At this period of her life she wrote, for example, 'lives' of her intimate friend Violet Dickinson, her Quaker Aunt Caroline Emelia Stephen and her Aunt Mary Fisher. The 'Life' of Violet is in the Berg Collection ('Friendship's Gallery') but the comic lives of the two aunts have not come to light. See *Letters*, I, No. 199.

set intervals. It is in such a provisional light that the "Reminiscences" should be read.

Yet, in addressing the memoir to the next generation and in broadening her subject to include the Stephen family so that no meaningful distinction can be made here between biography (of Vanessa) and autobiography, Virginia Woolf continued a practice which might almost be said to have attained the status of a family tradition. For her grandfather, James Stephen, had written his memoirs for the use of his children* and her father, Leslie, had followed suit in writing the 'Mausoleum Book', addressed to his children and step-children.†

Virginia Woolf begins the memoir with her childish impressions of Vanessa, who was three years her senior, recreating as she goes a vivid impression of the vitality, affection and security which distinguished life in the Stephen family. This family life was brutally transformed by the deaths of Julia, her mother, and then Stella, those traumatic events which seemed to bear the message that life had begun in earnest for the Stephen children.

Julia Jackson, daughter of Maria, one of the beautiful Pattle sisters, and Dr Jackson, was born in 1846. In 1867, when she was twenty-one, she married Herbert Duckworth, a barrister, who died three years later on 19 September 1870. The three children of the marriage were George (b. 1868); Stella (b. 1869); and Gerald, born after the death of his father in 1870. Eight years of widowhood ended in 1878 when Julia married Leslie Stephen whose first wife Minny, daughter of Thackeray, had died in 1875 leaving one child, Laura, whose mental deficiency was becoming increasingly apparent. There were four children born to Julia and Leslie Stephen: Vanessa (b. 1879); Thoby (b. 1880); Virginia (b. 1882) and Adrian (b. 1883). When Julia died in 1895 Stella assumed her responsibilities in the house at Hyde Park Gate. She married John Waller (Jack) Hills in 1897; she died three months later. It was now Vanessa's turn to be her father's 'angel in the house', a role which ill suited her. Jack is just emerging from the black grief into which Stella's death had plunged him when the memoir ends somewhat abruptly – perhaps because of the difficulty, as Quentin Bell has suggested, of describing Vanessa's affair with Jack.

The text (Library reference number MH/A. 6) is based on fifty-six pages typed by Virginia Woolf, with corrections by her in soft black and blue lead pencil and black ink.‡ The corrections are minor, confined for the most part

---

* *The Memoirs of James Stephen. Written by Himself for the Use of His Children*, ed. M. M. Bevington (The Hogarth Press; London, 1954).

† See note, p. 8.

‡ The finer, hard lead pencil marks were made by Clive Bell in 1908.

to single words or phrases which involve matters of style rather than changes of thought. The typing, for Virginia Woolf, is unusually careful. There are a number of infelicitous phrases, inelegant repetitions, grammatical confusions and obscurities of thought such as are rarely found in her later work and which she would surely have resolved had she prepared the text for publication.

The Memoir Club Contributions

THESE three memoirs were written by Virginia Woolf to be read aloud to the Memoir Club which had been formed in March 1920. It represented a re-grouping of 'Old Bloomsbury' which had dispersed during the war. According to Leonard Woolf, the thirteen original members of the Memoir Club corresponded exactly to the group of friends known to each other as 'Old Bloomsbury' and to the outside world, more simply, as 'Bloomsbury'.* He includes the following: Vanessa and Clive Bell, Virginia and himself, Desmond and Molly MacCarthy, Adrian Stephen, John Maynard Keynes, E. M. Forster, Roger Fry, Duncan Grant, Saxon Sydney-Turner and Lytton Strachey. Quentin Bell, in his book on Bloomsbury, does not mention Adrian Stephen and Saxon Sydney-Turner in the list of original members of the Memoir Club but adds that had it been formed in 1913 it would probably have included not only these two but 'Gerald Shove perhaps and H. T. J. Norton'.† Such a discrepancy calls attention to an important fact, perhaps one of the few indisputable facts about Bloomsbury, and that is that the vagueness which characterizes its outer limits extends, although to a lesser degree, to its innermost circle.

The group met periodically to dine, to read memoirs and enjoy each other's company. They agreed at the start upon 'absolute frankness' and this comes through in the memoirs that follow but, as Leonard Woolf warns, 'absolute frankness, even among the most intimate, tends to be relative frankness', and there is a hint of that too.‡ In each of the selections there is an author playing to her audience: familiar but not exactly intimate, reminiscent but never sentimental, clever and often facetious, gambolling over surface oddities rather than probing – thoughtfully, hesitantly – the nature of memory and consciousness, of self and reality, as in "Sketch of the Past".

* *Beginning Again: An Autobiography of the Years 1911 to 1918* (The Hogarth Press; London, 1964), p. 22.

† *Bloomsbury* (Weidenfeld & Nicolson; London, 1968), pp. 14–15.

‡ *Downhill All the Way: An Autobiography of the Years 1919 to 1939* (The Hogarth Press; London, 1967), p. 114.

22 *Hyde Park Gate*

Editor's Note

"22 Hyde Park Gate", although written almost twenty years before "Sketch of the Past", takes up the narrative of the Stephens not much beyond the point where the latter ends, that is, after Stella's death but before the death of Leslie Stephen in 1904 and the move of the remaining Stephens to Bloomsbury. In his role as elder brother, George Duckworth undertook, on his own initiative, to chaperone first Vanessa's, and then Virginia's, launching into 'Society'. Needless to say, it was not, in either case, a successful launch.

In the entry for 26 May 1921 in *A Writer's Diary*, Virginia Woolf refers to a conversation she had had on the 25th with Maynard Keynes. "The best thing you ever did, he said, was your Memoir on George. You should pretend to write about real people and make it all up. I was dashed of course (and Oh dear what nonsense – for if George is my climax I'm a mere scribbler)."* The memoir must have been presented to the Memoir Club some time between its formation in March 1920 and 25 May 1921, the date of the conversation with Keynes.†

The text brings together two typescripts: MH/A.14 and MH/A.15. A.14 consists of twenty-one pages typed by Virginia Woolf with a great many corrections in pen and pencil. The pages have been erratically numbered, suggesting that the typescript may have passed through several stages of revision. A.15 consists of fifteen pages typed by Virginia Woolf, with more than her customary care;‡ yet, on the last page, the line of type slopes off the page, in mid-sentence. There are no written corrections. A.15 is without

---

* (The Hogarth Press; London, 1959), p. 35.

† Anne Olivier Bell suggests 17 November 1920 as the date on which VW read "22 Hyde Park Gate" to the Memoir Club (*Diary of Virginia Woolf*, II, p. 77n). No minutes of the meetings of the Memoir Club are known to have survived.

‡ VW wrote to Ethel Smyth on 2 February 1932: "I'll copy out an old memoir that tumbled out of a box when I was looking for something else, that I wrote ten years ago about our doings with George Duckworth when we were so to speak virgins. It might amuse you: but it needs copying such a mess it's in." (*The Letters of Virginia Woolf*, ed. N. Nicolson & J. Trautmann, The Hogarth Press, Vol. V, p. 13.)

doubt a revision of pages 1–11 of A.14 for it incorporates the pen and pencil corrections on these pages. The text below follows the A.15 typescript as far as it goes and then continues with the A.14 typescript where it joins A.15 in mid-sentence (p. 11, l. 19). Although A.15 is clearly more finished stylistically than A.14, the difference between the two texts is not substantial. The copious written corrections of A.14 indicate considerable reworking, although there is little doubt that many further changes would have been made had Virginia Woolf completed the A.15 version.

Old Bloomsbury

"Old Bloomsbury" followed "22 Hyde Park Gate" as Virginia Woolf's contribution to the Memoir Club and was probably delivered within a year of the latter, that is, near the end of 1921 or in 1922.[*] It takes up where "22 Hyde Park Gate" ends, at "the height of the season of 1903", but it passes quickly over the move from Hyde Park Gate after Leslie Stephen's death to the establishment of the Stephens at 46 Gordon Square, Bloomsbury.

In viewing the origins of "Old Bloomsbury" from the angle of Hyde Park Gate, Virginia Woolf is giving an account which would, in some respects at least, differ from that given by one who had passed through Cambridge on the way to Bloomsbury; just as the accounts of those who belonged to the Cambridge 'Apostles' do not in every respect accord with that of Clive Bell, for example, who did not belong.[†] The many versions of where it all started and when – at Cambridge with the 'Midnight Society' or the 'Apostles' in 1899, with 'Thursday evenings' at Gordon Square in 1905, or in the district of Bloomsbury about 1912, as Leonard Woolf suggests[‡] – merely underline once again the vagueness of the limits of Bloomsbury.

The throwing open of windows which flooded with fresh air and light the dark, cramped, heavily upholstered upper middle class Victorian world in which many of the 'Bloomsberries' had spent their youth, did not happen all at once, as this memoir makes clear. Virginia Woolf conveys – albeit with the emphasis other than where it might have been placed by one of the painters of the group, say Vanessa Bell or Roger Fry – the drama and the humour of certain critical events in the development of pre-war Bloomsbury.

The text (Library reference number MH/A.16) is based on thirty-seven pages typed by Virginia Woolf with corrections in pen and pencil. The

---

[*] Quentin Bell writes "that it was read to the Memoir Club (in about 1922)." (QB, I, pp. 124–5n; and Lee, pp. 18, 155.)

[†] *Old Friends* (Chatto & Windus; London, 1956), p. 129.

[‡] *Beginning Again*, pp. 21–22.

beginning of the last paragraph, however, comes from a one-page mutilated and corrected typescript which was separated from A.16 and is now in the Berg Collection. The curator has generously given permission for this fragment to be included here. The typescript is erratically paginated in overlapping groups; the quality of the typing is poor; and the corrections are sometimes lengthy and often difficult to decipher.

Am I a Snob?

EDITOR'S NOTE

Virginia Woolf wrote "Am I a Snob?" when she was at the height of her fame and near the end of the career that was being so painstakingly prepared when the first memoir in this collection was written. It was read to the Memoir Club on 1 December 1936.*

In "Sketch of the Past", Virginia Woolf noted the curious division in her life at Hyde Park Gate: "Downstairs there was pure convention; upstairs pure intellect." After the first years in Bloomsbury the world of 'convention' – the world of George Duckworth, of Kitty Maxse – had clearly given way to the world of intellect. Humiliation, frustration and sheer boredom had marked many of her early encounters with the '*beau monde*' and yet some aspects of 'society' never ceased to fascinate her: the bright lights, the people talking, the strip of red carpet rolled out on the pavement.

The text is based on thirty-two variously sized leaves dry-welded to form a booklet. The Library reference number is MH/A.17. The typing is by Virginia Woolf, with corrections in pen and pencil. The letters from Margot Oxford and Sibyl Colefax which are incorporated into the present text appear in the booklet on separate sheets preceding the pages for which they were intended. The typing is, however, clearly Virginia Woolf's and it is unlikely that the letters included are other than rather freely interpreted recollections of the originals.

The quality of the typing is poor even by Virginia Woolf's none too stringent standards; punctuation and spelling errors abound. Yet the thought flows smoothly and there are few corrections or additions involving more than a sentence; there are some pages with no corrections at all.

It is probable that this typescript was the text read to the Memoir Club although, according to Quentin Bell, it is unlikely that Virginia Woolf would have kept very closely to the text.

---

* *Diary of Virginia Woolf*, V, p. 26n. The entry for 30 October 1936 describes VW's visit to Argyll House which is used as the basis for the concluding pages of "Am I a Snob?"

Sketch of the Past

EDITOR'S NOTE

"Sketch of the Past" covers some of the same ground as "Reminiscences" but from such a different angle of vision that there is not, in a significant sense, any repetition. Virginia Woolf is near sixty when she begins this memoir. The present moment – 1939–40 – is the platform on which she stands to explore the meaning behind certain indelibly printed experiences of her childhood and the figures who dominated that world. The first memories lead her, through the central figure of her mother, to St Ives, Cornwall, and Talland House where the Stephens spent their summer holidays from 1882 to 1894. This idyllic 'country' world is countered by descriptions of life in London, of the young Stephens growing up at 22 Hyde Park Gate enmeshed in a large network of relations and friends at the very nub of which is always Julia Stephen. Once again the shattering effect of her death is described and the reordering of family life around the eldest daughter, Stella, begins. Virginia's first mental illness occurs at this time but it is mentioned only in an earlier, rejected version, MH/A.5c. The new arrangement of family life is first disturbed by Stella's marriage to Jack Hills and then destroyed by her death a bare three months later. The tensions within the household which hardly seemed to exist in Julia's lifetime and which were glossed over during Stella's reign become more pronounced: the serious, open-minded Stephen girls are forced to submit to George Duckworth's plans for their advancement, to enter 'Society' with its glitter, emptiness and rigid conventions; the young Stephens are silently antagonistic to the ageing Leslie Stephen who is increasingly deaf, increasingly isolated from reality and, at times, rudely tyrannical to his daughters. The outside world begins to exert a greater influence on the lives of the Stephens and the memoir closes on a typical day, around 1900, in this Victorian upper middle class family.

"Sketch of the Past" was begun by Virginia Woolf on 18 April 1939, as relief from the exacting labours imposed by the writing of the biography of Roger Fry. The last entry is dated 17 November 1940, some four months before her death. The text that follows is based on two separate typescripts, one in the University of Sussex Library (MH/A.5d) and the other in the

British Library (BL 61973). They were clearly intended to run consecutively. Had this memoir been completed, it would undoubtedly have been considerably revised and extended.

A.5a consists of seventy pages typed by Virginia Woolf with corrections by her in black ink and soft lead pencil and by Leonard Woolf in blue ink. Leonard Woolf's corrections involve punctuation, spelling, clarification of Virginia's manuscript additions and the sorting out of the more obscure typing errors. These corrections have been retained when they conform to the principles set forth in the 'Editor's Note'.

BL 61973 is a seventy-seven-page typscript contained in a multi-grip folder (from which it has been removed) labelled by Virginia Woolf "Sketch of the Past I" and numbered 70–147. Page 132 is missing. It is corrected in both pen and pencil by Virginia Woolf and further emended and elucidated by Leonard Woolf in pen and pencil. The first ten pages which are dated 'June 19th 1940' are typed on a different machine to the main body of the work. The Woolfs, who lived during the war at Monks House, were, according to Olivier Bell, in London at Mecklenburgh Square for three days, 17–20 June 1940. The British Library typescript is a much reworked and improved revision of MH/A.5d manuscript which was transcribed in the original edition of *Moments of Being* (on pages 107–37). The first twenty-seven pages (numbered 70–96), however, represent entirely new material for which there is no known manuscript version, apart from an eight-page manuscript fragment in the Berg Collection, "The tea table was the centre of Victorian life . . .". Two of the entries have dates prior to those of the related manuscript entries yet there is no doubt that the typescript is the later version as it incorporates many marginal notes in the manuscript and is far more polished in every respect. In most cases, Virginia Woolf did not trouble to delete material which she proceeded directly to rework. Such passages have been omitted in the present edition except when they clarify her thought or are themselves of interest. In such cases the reworked material has been included in a footnote. The relevant section of MH/A.5d has been inserted within brackets for the missing page in BL 61973, as has the last paragraph from MH/A.5d which contains material not reworked in the typescript.

Apart from A.5d, other items in the Monks House Papers are connected with the present text: A.5b; A.5c; A.5e; and A.13a. Their value lies chiefly in the insight they afford into Virginia Woolf's working methods. The most interesting of them is A.5c, a twenty-one-page manuscript, a part of which is an earlier version of a section of A.5a. On occasion it has proved useful in resolving obscurities in the latter. The remainder of the material of A.5c consists of lists of names, events and ideas to be developed later or brief sketches of other figures related to the Stephens which were not included in the 'a' revision. These items taken together with the more carefully revised 'a' typescript, the less revised 'd' manuscript, and the British Library typescript, represent a cross-section of various stages through which a work of Virginia Woolf's might characteristically pass – from the rough notes and first tentative sketches to a draft approaching the final stage of preparation – with, of course, the important exception of the complete typed revisions of which there might be many.

Index